Across *the* Water

Across *the* Water

Irishness
in modern Scottish writing

edited by
James McGonigal
Donny O'Rourke
& Hamish Whyte

Argyll
publishing

© the contributors 2000

First Published 2000
Argyll Publishing
Glendaruel
Argyll PA22 3AE
Scotland

The authors and editors have asserted their moral rights.

**British Library Cataloguing-in-Publication Data.
A catalogue record for this book is available from
the British Library.**

ISBN 1 902831 15 2

Subsidised by the Scottish Arts Council

Cover illustration
Permission Scottish National Gallery
Detail from William McTaggart *The Coming of St Columba*

Typeset & Origination
Cordfall Ltd, Glasgow

Printing
Omnia Books Ltd, Glasgow

To forefathers and foremothers

'Och, feyther,' Kathleen said. His anger was becoming ridiculously disproportionate. 'Ye've said yerself ma Grandpa goes oan aboot Ireland at an awfu' rate.'

'Whit if Ah have? An' you're another yin. Lady Muck. Ah've heard ye complainin' aboot the mess o' the fire-end wi' him. This is a hoose. No' a hotel. An' if Ah fa' oot wi' him aboot Ireland, well, that's a private argument.' He looked round them all. 'An' jist all of ye remember. He's where ye come fae. An' whaurever ye go, ye'll have tae take 'im wi' ye.'

William McIlvanney
Docherty (1975)

ACKNOWLEDGEMENTS

The editors are grateful to all the copyright owners, publishers and authors who granted permission to print or reprint work. For help and encouragement they would especially like to thank Freddy Anderson, Janette McGinn and Amina Shah.

Contents

ACROSS THE WATER

The first people who called themselves Scots were immigrants
. . . a set of Irish invaders.

(Alasdair Gray *Why Scots Should Rule Scotland* 1992)

THIS BOOK maps for the first time a hidden country and the verbal arts of the people who crossed the Irish Sea to live there. It explores the place of 'the Irish' or 'Irishness' in modern Scottish writing, through the words of poets, singers, storytellers and playwrights who speak out of an experience of immigration and uneasy assimilation that has been in progress for the past 150 years and more. Even a decade ago this map could hardly have been sketched, and yet a glance at the contents will reveal the range and significance of the writers listed. The place of such writers at the start of the millennium seems assured, yet in many cases their own sense of Scottish identity is far more ambiguous. Hence the tentative quotation marks round 'the Irish' in Scotland, who otherwise have seemed to be all too visible and vocal in their political, economic, religious and cultural impact. Just why this anthology's time has so suddenly and decidedly come is one of the many questions we should attempt to answer.

For 'Irish' many would read 'Catholic', but this is also in warning quotation marks, since our writers include many, possibly most, who would no longer define themselves in that way, and some others who come from a contrary Ulster presbyterian background or tradition. The to and fro of emigration and settlement between the North of Ireland and the West of Scotland has been recorded in history since the monks of Columba and the tribes of Dalriadic Scots first gave Scotland a mission and a name. Serenity and violence, it seems, have been at war in our hearts ever since.

In 1993 the Irish writer Colm Tóibín arrived in Scotland to research a travel book, published as *The Sign of the Cross: Travels in Catholic Europe* (1994). He found Glasgow hard to handle:

> In one of my early encounters in Glasgow I asked an innocent question. There is a new movement in Scottish writing, full of social engagement and formal energy. I could list ten or twelve Scottish writers, most of them uncompromising figures, distant from southern English gentility. I casually asked a journalist in Glasgow who among the writers was Catholic and who was not. I presumed that maybe half the writers were Catholic. He stopped and thought for a while. He shook his head. He said that he had never been asked the question before, or thought about it. There must be one, he replied, but he couldn't think of a name.
>
> Unless I wanted to include Muriel Spark. She was a convert, I said, that was different. Do you mean, I asked, that all of the writers, with their street credibility and their working class heroes, are Protestants? Yes, he said. And do you mean, I went on, that no one has ever raised this matter? Correct, he said. And do you mean that most people do not think it is a significant fact? Correct, once more.

The editors of this anthology are now raising the matter, and registering its significance, by firstly putting the record straight. The forty five writers here are a selection to be going on with. Yet it is true that a generation ago an anthology like this one would have been impossible to put together. With a very few exceptions, writers from immigrant Irish backgrounds had not only failed to make their mark on Scottish literature, they had failed to write at all. As exceptions go, James Macfarlan and William McGonagall in the nineteenth century and Patrick MacGill, Edward Gaitens, Matt McGinn and George Friel in the twentieth, were genuinely exceptional. For the most part, 'Irish Scots' were written about rather than writing themselves; and they were described in alarmed and unflattering terms, as a set of social problems. For instance, the numerous 'Paddy' songs in the Poet's Box collection in Glasgow's Mitchell Library illustrate graphically popular attitudes to the Irish from the 1850s on.

That these immigrants were dirty and ill-educated, and drank to dull the sharpness of their deprivation, had some basis in fact. The industrial folklore that they depressed wages, broke strikes and stole jobs tends to ignore the role of Scottish industrialists in manipulating the situation to their own advantage. It is also to downplay the crucial role of such a raw pool of labour in building and then sustaining an industrial revolution dependent on manpower for the interlocking heavy industries of iron and steel working, coal mining and shipyard and railway construction. Scotland's wealth in exports to England and the Empire benefited hugely; the health of the Irish workers less so, although at least they were no longer, or not literally, famished.

Perhaps it was their religion which really rankled. As late as the 1930s some prominent members of the Church of Scotland were calling for the forced repatriation of the Irish. The historian Tom Devine reminds us that the industrial Depression of the 1920s, combined with cultural anxieties about the sheer amount of Scottish blood lost in the Great War, were reflected in that crusade. Yet it is shocking to contemplate, nevertheless. Because these newcomers *were* poor and disadvantaged, their educational impoverishment took decades to overcome, particularly in the Victorian age when Protestant evangelisation of inner cities and imperial outposts was in expansionary mood, and school boards and syllabuses sustained a presbyterian culture absolutely at odds with Catholic practice and belief. It was in this context that separate schools were established, funded by parishes and sometimes staffed by religious sisters or brothers from teaching orders set up to cope with the social crises of the newly industrialised cities.

Whatever we may now think of separate schools (which remain a traditionally vexatious issue in the new Scotland) it was these schools, later incorporated into the state system under the 1918 Education Act, which ensured that in the industrial areas of Scotland children of Irish descent got the chance to learn and to better themselves. From these schools in due course came further lay teachers who would encourage later generations of pupils to enter the more prestigious professions of medicine, the law and university teaching. Entry was not always ungrudgingly given. As men (and then women) with Irish surnames began to seize these opportunities, they gradually acquired the cultural confidence not just to 'make it' but to make out, so that in the fullest sense they could say *we have made something of ourselves.* Writers need that confidence too.

For those educated in Catholic schools (as two of the editors were) it was possible to remain in relative ignorance of the actual roots of the ambivalence and bigotry which their religion aroused, even well into the second half of the twentieth century. A protestant and radical religious system, which was generally considered to have shaped an egalitarian culture in Scotland, based upon 'the democratic intellect' and progress through merit not birth, clearly found it difficult to cope with some deeper residue of fear and guilt in the post-Reformation years. Within a short period of time in the sixteenth century one religious system had been speedily erased and a reformed kirk set in its place. Although Catholic and Episcopalian worship continued in a few of the straths and glens of the north, for most of Scotland a remarkable revolution had taken place, which was soon sustained through wars and sanctified by its own martyrs in the Covenanting times. We learned little of that bitter history, though we lived daily with its consequences.

The depth of feeling and sense of antipathy on both sides of the religious divide remains powerfully present and unresolved. Fears of the Irish immigrants taking a lead from either republican Dublin or illiberal Rome or both have been slow to die. Yet Scottish Catholicism was, and is, far from monolithic. There were early power struggles between native Scots priests and Irish clergy brought in to develop pastoral work in the expanding urban parishes; there were quarrels between priests and parishioners over involvement in the Liberal politics of Home Rule and the Labour politics of socialist action; in time there were tensions between the immigrants' growing material or intellectual confidence and loss of some of the spiritual life or deference which had kept them or their (great-grand) parents going through early hardships. Tensions within or about the Catholic Church in Scotland continue in the present day.

All of that cultural background is becoming increasingly available to the Scottish public through the books of such historians as Tom Devine and Michael Lynch. The oral culture of story and song which carried the identity, expressed the wit or shared the sensibilities of the under-educated is less obviously open to research, although it had its influence, no doubt, on the comic style and pace of speech in the West of Scotland. Billy Connolly could be said to have a decidedly and hilariously 'Irish' cast of mind; not gags but stories; language as a pleasure in and of itself. It has had its influence on the writers gathered here.

These, it must be said, are mainly based in the West. We must not forget that other areas have their stories to tell, such as Dundee (with its Lochee enclave) and Edinburgh (especially the Cowgate). In respect of Edinburgh, at least, Seán Damer redresses the balance a little.

What, then, can these writers who have come from that background tell us about ourselves? When Andrew O'Hagan was shortlisted for the Booker Prize, he bemoaned in print the lack of role models or of any writers whatsoever from backgrounds like his: Scottish Irish Catholic working class. It suited the media, and possibly his own publishers, to portray this outstanding young writer as one lonesome wee shamrock in a presbyterian desert. One could cavil and mention again MacGill, Gaitens and Friel, as well as the oddly Oedipal (O'edipal?) omission of his Ayrshire neighbour and predecessor, William McIlvanney (also included here). And yet O'Hagan was right in highlighting the newness of this wave of younger writers, emerging fast out of the obscurity in which their ancestors worked and died. Writers are now appearing with a confidence born out of an educational system which had either recognised their ability, or had given time for it to develop, or at worst provided a structure of customs or beliefs against which they could push, and argue for a different vision.

What is genuinely different about this anthology, and proof

of how far and fast things have changed, is its presentation of new and published work together with a reflection from each living writer on the impact of Ireland. It records any influence of ancestral 'Irishness' on his or her life and art. It notes the almost tidal movements of writers from Ireland to Scotland and back again. In so doing it moves with the current of the times we live in, as both countries strive to deal with the complexities of their political and cultural heritage, in relation to England, of course, and to each other, within a new European and devolved political perspective.

The editors are aware of the dangers involved in this enterprise: they could not just light the green touchpaper and stand well clear. Irish questions are tricky. It was important to us that we could recognise our stances on different sides of various fences, and yet work the same soil productively together. Each of us has ninetenth century Northern Irish ancestry, from Donegal, Antrim and County Down. Two are Catholic, one increasingly lapsed, one intuitively devout, or seeming so. The third is a lapsed presbyterian, bemused by the oddness of his fellow editors (and teased by them as 'the gentle Prod'). All of us have noted, through various anthologies separately edited over the last ten years, that the emergent issue of Ireland and writing in Scotland deserved its own treatment. We tried to be inclusive and canvassed as many writers with Irish surnames or an Irish connection as we could. Unfortunately not all felt able to respond.

The book is arranged chronologically by writers' dates of birth. As it approaches the present a growing number of women writers make their presence felt, we are happy to note, as they overcome what might be seen as their double disadvantage within an immigrant community. Their work is often (though not always) accessible and familial; they may be bearers in the contemporary world of an ancient and inclusive oral tradition, but sharpened by feminist awarenesses.

What emerges then, from our selection of writers and material? Firstly, and perhaps most importantly, is the honesty of the contributors: if they want to be identified as Irish or not, if they exhibit contradictions, if they are angry, sad or whatever, they are not afraid to say so. Secondly, there is a chronological sweep, which we have limited to the twentieth century, recording the movement from navvy culture and slum living into the complex and oddly uneasy experience of living still slightly on the margins of contemporary Scottish life (or at an angle to it) while also contributing to its development. The cultural impasse of early immigrant life changes slowly into aspirations and a sense of freedom, as the Irish make their lives on this side of the water, and become another mossy weave in Scotland's tartan.

Like the pipes in the song 'Danny Boy', their call has echoed 'from glen to glen': from the glens of Antrim to Glenboig and Rutherglen. There is a sense of the nomadic, a displaced quality, running from Patrick MacGill and Seán Rafferty to Gerald Mangan and Christopher Whyte. We can see a late twentieth century replay of this subtle movement in the differing stories from one of our most distinguished prose writers, Bernard MacLaverty, and from his daughter, Ciara MacLaverty, or caught in the ambiguities of a single tale from Brian McCabe. A fidelity to the subtlety of weather and the spirit of the natural world (found everywhere in early Irish poetry) can also be noted in the imagery of several of the writers: Gerry Loose, James McGonigal, John Burnside and Gerry Cambridge. Yet the younger of these are also members of an urban or even postmodern peasantry, exploiting the contradictions of contemporary life rather than being exploited by them.

They realise that intelligence is not education. Communication isn't only writing. There was no linguistic famine, no shortage of wonderful words among the migrant Gaels. In their ancient tribal society, culture was transmitted orally. The talent for talk was a common trait in the mines, smelters, shipyards, factories and pubs of industrial Scotland, where the heirs of the bards improvised a literature out of inspired garrulity and Irish blah, that almost cocky Celtic brio. One of the editors has described Des Dillon as an 'urban sennachie'. As his memoir in the anthology makes clear, this writer is no shrinking shamrock! And Dillon himself cites the importance of the story, the tall tale, the joke, the family reminiscence, that sustained and entertained gifted but underschooled immigrants living poor hard lives.

Much potential prose and poetry was never transcribed. We are not suggesting Scotland lament a lost Hibernian Homer, but a lot of excellent work was just not written down. That John Byrne, Tom McGrath, Anne Downie, Stephen Mulrine, Susie Maguire, the Dannys Boyle and McCahon have been drawn to stage and screen rather than the book is not coincidental. Patter and patterning, a streetwise rococo, long lyric speeches, with a come all ye swagger and an elegiac sombreness to contrast with that, this seems recognisably Irish, much more Sean O'Casey than James Bridie. When a people has its language taken from it, the oppressors' tongue is first resisted then subverted. Ireland's revenge on the invaders was to use English better, or at least with more pizzaz and pyrotechnics, than the English themselves.

However, some writers are sensitised even to the point of refusing to be 'pigeonholed' in such an anthology as this, a position we respect and yet enormously regret. Tom Leonard and Peter McCarey are two whom we would have wished to include. Some of the most resolutely unIrish here (such as John Byrne) may seem to some readers to protest too much, for it is out of the collision of urban Scots and Irish grandiloquence or blarney that much of the richest writing in the book emerges. In prose we have the demotic energy of Des Dillon at one extreme and the graver, more considered tones of Anne Donovan and Andrew O'Hagan at the other.

Of course, the polarities of attitude and belief could not forever stand between immigrant and native people. 'Mixed marriages' represent a passionate but often awkward blending of cultures which can also spur children into writing, conscious of discrepancies and words unspoken, or else articulated within different ranges of meaning. Willy and John Maley are brothers who, writing together and apart, have responded to the contradictory identities offered by those closest to them. Christopher Whyte takes his sense of difference further than most, into a newly learned language, Scottish Gaelic. The gay writing of the last two writers named provides another challenge to family pieties offered or withheld.

Ulster presbyterian voices are heard here too, in the poetry and reflections of Angela McSeveney, Helen Lamb, Magi Gibson and Hamish Whyte, although these voices may be echoing from a long way back. Alan Spence's short stories, which have been compared with Joyce's, were first collected in 1977 under the title *Its Colours They Are Fine*, a quotation from the Orange song 'The Sash My Father Wore'. Much of his work, from this collection to his recent novel *Way To Go*, deals with the Orange milieu in Scotland in a way so well observed and so well written as to command a respect no other treatment, to our knowledge, has accorded it. This subject has been sensitively dealt with on the Irish side by Joan Lingard. We are reminded how Northern unionists look increasingly to the Scottish lowlands for linguistic and cultural validation. 'Ullans', their version of 'Lallans', is a prospective counterweight to the Irish. Burns's poems and songs and the ballads balance the nationalist community's music. Liam McIlvanney and others have shown how marked and lasting the influence of Burns has been, first of all on the weaver poets of Belfast, then right down to John Hewitt, Tom Paulin and other writers brought up in the loyalist tradition.

On this side of the water, Scots and Irish Gaelic still reveal the ancient continuities of our now different cultures. That one of the Irish-born writers in this generation, Rody Gorman, first came to prominence as a writer of Scots Gaelic is a sign of the currency of those ancient links. Such to-ings and fro-ings continue. Campbell Armstrong, Alan Warner and the songwriter Mike Scott are ensconced in Ireland. Gerry Loose, Hayden Murphy, Freddy Anderson and Bernard MacLaverty are over here, their presence revealing the still surprising ability of the Irish to grace Scottish literature by being at home in it. Yet Donal McLaughlin expresses the rawer experience of one who arrived here from Derry as a child in flight from the continuing Troubles. And Donny O'Rourke's reflection and poetry catch well that combination of unease and celebration, of violence and peace at the troubled heart of Scots-Irish relations.

In part that tension derives from our proximity. Entering upon the 'white martyrdom' of exile in what is now (but was not then) Scotland, St Columba had to establish a cell from which his native land was not visible. Iona's principal charm lay in its lack of such a nostalgia-inducing vista. On a clear day, from Islay or Arran or Kintyre, Ireland seems very near indeed.

Near, but not necessarily close. Perhaps ultimately it is our shared music that speaks most clearly of the continuities. Across the world people respond to the power of Celtic music to make connections between cultures that politics drives apart. Young people who would have viewed matters differently a generation ago are to be found savouring Irish music on disc, on air, on stage, often in Irish theme bars which would make 'real' Irish folk cringe.

From signs saying 'No Irish Wanted' to signs in Gaelic adorning pubs specialising in Irish kitsch is quite a change. Celtic is cool. Is this a modern echo of the character in the nineteenth century song 'Erin-go-bragh'? – Duncan Campbell though from Argyll is proud to be taken for an Irishman.

There may be a Celtic (with a hard C) connection too in the way we play and watch sport in Scotland, with a bloodthirstiness about the big occasion reminiscent of accounts of hurling matches in the Irish myths, and an intricacy about the style of football heroes (like Jimmy 'Jinky' Johnstone) that recalls the art of Celtic carving, all arcane loops and spirals. It may not be the most efficient or even effective way of playing, but on the right day it can move the heart with its deftness and bravura.

> Scots steel tempered wi' Irish fire
> Is the weapon that I desire.

Thus the borderer C.M. Grieve (in *To Circumjack Cencrastus*), whose profound, romantic and acquisitive fondness for Gaeldom was such that he awarded himself a Celtic nom de plume and guerre. Scarcely a page of this anthology is without a flicker of that fire. Mongrels that we are, there's a glint of steel too. Calvinism and

Catholicism, the best, or worst, of both worlds, that's the antisyzigal birthright of many of those assembled here.

This diaspora is not the Emerald Isle continued by other means. On this side of the water alchemy occurs, a catalysis that puts the emphasis on the *ish* in Irish: Irishish, not Irish pure and simple, but some impure, complicated Hiberno-Scottish hybridity that makes Dublin and Edinburgh, Glasgow and Belfast seem piquantly alike and yet dissimilar to the point of foreignness. That shared cultural (and biological) DNA, the sense of so near yet so far, the same yet different, makes kinship complex. Our book is intended to make things more satisfyingly ambiguous, not less. The last word on the Irishness of Scotland won't be heard any time soon.

Across the Water is a beginning, an invitation to a kind of ceilidh/ceili of ideas. Neither borders nor identities are fixed, not in life, not in literature. All the writers collected here are as Irish as they feel. Without the Irish, Scotland would be a less joyful, vital, raucous place. Some of us have made a song and dance about being Irish; others have contributed a quieter, graver grace. Much about the new Scotland reminds one of the old Ireland the bards once praised. An expatriate is not a former patriot. A former Paddy is not an ex-Pat!

Ireland exerts a notorious pull. Every writer constructs a personal mythology and the Irelands mapped out here are different one from the other as the writers are. More than 40 shades of green. We hope this book represents a coming of age, not just for writers with some connection to Ireland – whose differently accented writing gathered here for the first time can clearly now speak for itself – but for everyone in Scotland with ties across the water. It is published at a confidently inclusive moment when Scotland seems at last to be healing itself, undergoing its own peace process. May we dedicate *Across the Water* to peace, understanding and mutual respect on both shores? *Slàinte*.

James McGonigal
Donny O'Rourke
Hamish Whyte

Patrick MacGill
(1890–1963)

Born in Donegal, Patrick MacGill escaped to
Scotland from a life of drudgery. He worked
as a labourer and wrote a novel of navvy life,
Children of the Dead End (1914). In 1930 he
migrated to the USA .

Back from Kinlochleven

And the place that knew him, knows him no more.

THE waterworks are finished and the boys have
 jacked the shovel,
See, the concrete board deserted, for the barrow squad
 is gone,
The gambling school is bursted, there is silence in the
 hovel,
For the lads are sliding townwards and are padding it
 since dawn.
Pinched and pallid are their faces from their graft in
 God-shunned places,
Tortured, twisted up their frames are, slow and
 lumbering their gait,
But unto their hopeful dreaming comes the town with
 lights a-gleaming,
Where the bar-men add more water, and the shameless
 women wait.

Eighteen months of day shift, night shift, easy, slavish,
 long or light shift,
Anchorites on musty bacon, crusty bread, and evil tea,

Sweated through the Summer till grim Winter came a
 hoary pilgrim,
Chasing from the meagre blanket the familiar,
 flighty flea.
Then the days when through the cutting came the
 death-white snowflakes drifting,
When the bar was chilled and frosted, and the jumper
 seared like hell,
When the hammer shook uncertain in the grimy hands
 uplifting,
And the chisel bounced uncanny 'neath the listless
 strokes that fell.

But to Him give thanks 'tis over and the city fills the
 distance,
On the line of least resistance they are coming sure but
 slow,
How they wait the trull and harlot, jail-bird, vagabond
 and varlet,
For there's many a bob to squander and the city ravens
 know!
Parasites from pub and alley welcome in the grimed and
 greasy,
Gather round with wail and plaudit, eager for their
 dough and gin,
They are coming from the muck-pile and they mean to
 take it easy,
They have pals to share their joy and incidentally their
 tin.

They are tabid and outworn, unpresentable, unshorn,
Occupants of many a model, wooers of the harridan,
Workers of the wildernesses, dressing as the savage
 dresses,

Crawling in the rear of progress, following the march
of man.
Where grim nature reigneth lonely over gelid places,
only
Known to death and desolation, they have roughed it
long and hard,
Where the chronic river wallows in the refuse of the
hollows,
And the thunderbolt is resting on the mountain tops it
scarred.

But 'tis over for the moment, and the heel-end of
creation
Vomits back the men who roughed it to the town that
sent them forth,
They who face the death it threatened with a grim
determination,
They who wrestled with the slayer incarnated in the
North –
Go and see them primed with lager, drain them of the
coppers sought for
In the depths of desolation, in the byways of the beast,
Go and bum them of the ha'pence that like maniacs they
wrought for,
For they bear the famine bravely, but can never stand the
feast.

They are coming to the city, soon you'll see their rants
and quarrels,
See them marching off to prison, see them drinking day
by day,
In the dead end of their labours they forgot your code of
morals,
They are ne'er intoxicated in the super-saintly way.

You will know them by their reeking shag, you'll know
    their way of speaking,
You can spot them by their moleskins and their bluchers
    battered down,
They are wild, uncultivated, maybe rather under-rated –
But at any rate you'll know them by their curses when in
    town.

                  from Songs of the Dead End (1912)

EDWARD GAITENS
(1897–1966)

Born in Glasgow and grew up in the Gorbals,
background of much of his fiction. Imprisoned as
a conscientious objector in World War I. He used
material from *Growing Up* in his novel *Dance of
the Apprentices* (1948).

Growing Up

T HE boy lay awake all night in the light of dreams about the
adventure of his first job. He was fourteen years old. It was
only a month since he had reluctantly left school, but he forgot
now how bitterly he wept when his mother told him he must go
to work and contribute to the family income. Because only last
night his father had asked him: 'Would ye like tae come wi' me to
the shipyards tomorrow, son?' and his mother chimed in: 'Aye,
take him wi' ye. Mebbe ye'll get him a start wi' big money.' And
the boy nodded eagerly: 'Oh, yes, da!'

His father, who had been a long time unemployed, had
suddenly addressed his wife with unusual optimism. 'Ye know, Mary,
I've a feelin' I'll get a start tomorrow for sure! They're layin' a big
ship down at Clydebank. They say it'll mean a year's work for
hundreds o' men.' The wife looked sceptical, but the boy believed
his father would find work and that he, himself, would get his first
job in the shipyards, away out where the Clyde neared the sea!

His father had washed and shaved to avoid a rush in the
morning, for they had to be up at half-past four, take a hurried
snack and cup of tea and catch the five o'clock tramcar. The boy
washed also, exulting as he laved arms, neck and face, and went
through the lobby to the concealed bed in the front room, his
glow of anticipation burning away desire for sleep.

A job in the shipyards! He had often listened intensely to his father and brothers talk of those worlds of fabulous energy and mighty achievements where thousands of men and boys toiled night and day and the clang of hammers never ceased. He would see battleships launched and immense ocean liners. He would help to build one and earn big money! He dazzled with pride.

Night and the wonder of quiet was ending; he heard the homeward footsteps of nightshift workers and day workers going forth, then the hum of the first workmen's tram from afar, as dawn stared at the window, innocently entering, filling the drab room with beauty of light. Slow-fading silence, the slow growth of clarity and rising tempo of sounds, thrilled and awed him. Soon he would hear, through the wall, from the set-in bed in the kitchen, where his parents slept, his mother saying: 'Eddy, will ye get up, now! It's half-past four!' and his father exclaiming: 'Eh! Wha-a-at? My God! Eh! What's up?' and jumping agitatedly to the floor, as he frequently did. Then, the boy was aware, it would be hardly after four.

'She won't have to wake me!' he boasted to the silence, smiling at the cracked, blistered whitewash of the bed-ceiling. He would be up and dressed before his da! He regarded his two elder brothers who were sleeping with him with condescension. They would be abed for three more hours, then James the eldest son, would return from nightshift at seven, have breakfast, read a newspaper and retire to the yet warm bed at eight o'clock. But he did not envy them!

Quivering with eagerness he rose, pulled on his flimsy tweed trousers and slung minute braces over his boyish shoulders, disappointed that he hadn't moleskin trousers, a thick, leather, heavy-buckled belt and big hobnailed boots, like his da. He was still enjoying the novelty of his first pair of long trousers. Aye, he was a man in these! And they were more comfortable, too. They didn't chafe him above the knees like the short breeks he had thrown off a week ago! He heard the kitchen window-blind whirr up and the clang of a tin kettle planked on the stove. That was his mother up. Wouldn't she be surprised when she called him and he was all ready! Perhaps he had better say a prayer to the Blessed Virgin? She would get him a job! Quickly he put on stockings and cheap boots with papery uppers, and kneeling at the bed held forward clasped hands to a coloured china effigy of the Madonna, gracing the centre wall. Unaffected by the raucous snoring of John, he muttered two very quick, devout 'Hail Marys', then, half-ashamed, added the improvisation: 'Hail, Queen of Heaven, the Ocean Star, pray for me and get me a job this day!' He rose pleased, happier, firmly believing the 'Holy Mother' would intercede with the powers that dole out work to men, and went into the kitchen.

His father was leaning against the bed pulling on his trousers, his mother, at the gas-stove, was frying thick slices of bread in dripping for their snack, and the kettle whistled a plume of steam into the room. While he stood by to let his father wash first, in the iron sink at the end of the dresser, his mother turned, pouring boiling water in a large enamelled teapot, and said, half-sullenly: 'Ye'd better put yer collar on. Go an' clean it. An' don't spit on it! Wash it properly wi' soap an' flannel. Ye must be respectable!'

He returned to the parlour, his eagerness dimmed by her sullenness, and lifted a celluloid collar and stringy brown cotton tie from a glass dish on the sideboard where he always placed them when undressing. He had wanted to go like other apprentices, like his da, with a knotted muffler or nothing at all round his neck, and he regarded the collar indignantly. That wasn't like a working man! Did she take him for a jessie or a message-boy?

While his father dried himself he washed the collar at the sink, rubbing it vindictively with a piece of red flannel, then washed himself, anxiously hoping his parents wouldn't quarrel. They were often sulky and short with each other, and sometimes he had been wakened at this hour by a brutal altercation, when his father had struck her and rushed out, crashing the door, and she had yelled after him she hoped he'd be killed at his work. He could not understand the real cause of the strain between his parents – their thin love blasted by the worry of recurring unemployment; his mother's suspicion that her husband didn't try hard enough to get work and his offence at her distrust.

Their tea was ready and he ate the hot, fat-soused bread and drank the bitter brew deliciously, his appetite big with excitement and pleasure. They stood to eat, his father glancing continually up at the clock. His mother said: 'Yer pieces and tea and sugar are ready, there!' At the corner of the table lay two lunches wrapped in newspaper, a huge one for the man, a smaller one for the boy, and on top of each a penny Colman's Mustard tin filled with dry tea and sugar. The boy felt manly as he regarded it; he had begged it from his mother, who had made up his tea and sugar the night before in a screw of paper, and, in good mood, she had emptied the newly bought tin into an egg-cup, gratifying his wish to be as possible like his father. They were ready to leave and stuffed their pieces into their jacket pockets, the boy imitating his father's movements.

His father begged the loan of sixpence and the wife answered complainingly: 'Och, shure I lent ye sixpence yesterday! Could ye no' walk some o' the way?' but she took her purse from under her pillow, where she kept it to prevent him filching coppers while she slept, and gave him the coin unwillingly. Suddenly he exclaimed: 'Isn't that Saint Peter's bell just striking the half-hour? Och, ye've got us up too soon. We could have slept longer!' Unperturbed, she answered: 'Well, ye're better to be early. Ye'll have time tae say an Our Father an' three Hail Marys for a job!' He slung his cap irritably on a chair and knelt in unprayerlike mood at the bed, making the sign of the cross. The boy, palpitating to be off, was almost in tears. 'You say a wee prayer, too,' advised his mother. 'Och, maw, I said two Hail Marys before I came ben!' he grumbled. 'Say another two an' make sure!' she answered obdurately. He knelt beside his father and while their mumbled 'Aves' ascended to holy images on the bed walls, the woman sat to drink a cup of tea. The man cocked an eye frequently at the clock and suddenly crossing himself, rose, donned his cap and said: 'We'd better be gettin' away now!' The boy rose simultaneously and as they went out his mother warned her man to do his best and not be too late home!

The boy was aware of an outreaching sense of freedom when they emerged from the narrow entry. At last they were away! As they boarded a tram he ran before his father to capture a front seat and leant forward gallant and unenclosed as a charioteer, while the packed tram passed all stops. He saw smoke jut from hundreds of chimneys, blinds shoot up, curtains parted and here and there a woman leaning akimbo on a sill four storeys high, contemplating the street. He tried to see into rooms, but speed blurred his vision and he laughed at the phenomenon. Ah, this was better than rising at eight and crawling to school at a quarter to nine. This was rare! And perhaps tomorrow or next day he would be dashing along like this while his former schoolmates were asleep. And when the tram stopped at a crossing where services went all ways, the names CLYDEBANK, YOKER, SCOTSTOUN, ANNIESLAND, DALMUIR, DUMBARTON, glowed with romance, magic as the names of foreign lands to him who only knew back-streets. And here they were in Dockland! The funnels of liners and masts of sailing ships above the warehouse roofs, the flags of many nations afloat in the warm breeze.

Shortly the shipyards' region surrounded him with new wonder. His father decided to call at a firm ten miles out, and as it was still very early they sauntered about the vicinity till starting-time. The boy glued his eyes on great cranes rearing over housetops like figures in a monstrous ballet, and his spirit followed their rhythm while he fired shrill questions at his father, who answered in his detailed, laborious manner. Then at a minute to six they followed the last worker going through the wicket door of the immense gates, and his father craved an attendant commissionaire's permission to enter and interview various foremen. The personage let them pass and immediately the boy was stunned in an ocean of sound, then as soon, struck by a tragic stillness. A procession of begrimed, bareheaded workers, bearing two stretchers, wended towards the ambulance-house at the gate. The boy's father stopped; other men paused a moment, removing their caps, then hurried to their work. The procession passed, the man on the first stretcher gallantly smoking a cigarette, smiled at the boy, but the face of the body on the following stretcher was covered.

The father removed his cap, bowing his head; the boy copied him. 'My, there's been a man killed already! It's terrible. Terrible!' The boy looked up, asking: 'Do they not stop the works when a man's killed, da?' His father answered, 'No, the work goes on, son. The work goes on!' The shipyard ambulance appeared, the bodies were placed within, a nurse closed the door and the vehicle sped through the gates.

The boy forgot the dead man as they went on through the yard amid mammoth sights and sounds. He saw a warship near completion, the mere ribs of ships just begun, liners in repair dock and the pathetic end of a worn vessel in the hands of the breakers. All men seemed midgets here, the riveters' catchboys everywhere in the skeleton ships, like imps, handing red-hot rivets from portable fires to the holder-on, and his small self had never felt so insignificant. Then in pride at being here, he strutted along cloaked in rare distinction. 'Ye can smell the sea here!' said his father, but he only smelled rust, iron and steel, machine-oil and the smoke and heat of furnaces.

All the while seagulls decorated the air, but their cries were unheard in the symphony of Labour. The boy crouched within himself as cranes swung overhead steel plates vast as two floors of his tenement home, and his father showed him a steam-hammer pounding gargantuan objects of molten steel. 'I've seen a hammerman place an egg there and bring the hammer down to rest on it and not break it! They get so skilful!' The boy marvelled, breathless with questioning, while his father hurried to interview foremen in various shops and the holes and corners of ships – great, strapping men who shook their heads distantly or spoke amiably, and canny little gaffers with frowsy moustaches, glasses and peaked caps, who sized up his father shrewdly.

None had jobs to offer, and when the breakfast-time buzzer blew, his father took him to the smiddy's shop, unhitched a tin can from his belt, filled it with water and boiled it on a smiddy fire. Never had he seen so many smiddy fires gathered in one place, nor water boil so swiftly as he worked the bellows handle and his father held the can on a rod. They washed down their food with milkless tea, sitting on a great anvil, while his father discussed with the blacksmith the chances of work in another shipyard.

Crossing by ferry to the opposite shore was the next brilliant event. Now the river was mad with sunshine and against passing and anchored ships the water splintered like golden glass. Amidstream, his father pointed out famous shipyards. 'Yon's Fairfield's away back, and there's Harland & Wolff's. That's John Brown's where we're going next, and yonder's Beardmore's! Yon's the highest crane on the Clyde!' and the boy looked far through smiling space at the goliath moving with relentless deliberation at its task.

And once again they were at shipyard gates, hanging about till the dinner-hour, when his father rushed forward to intercept a little man in a dungaree suit, spectacles and a sailor's cap among the hundreds of men streaming out. While the interview proceeded the boy could not take his eyes from the man's ardent red nose, abnormally small, above his grey moustache. 'Weel, I'm no sure!' said the foreman, 'I'm no sure! I'm pretty full up the now. But see me here tomorrow at six! And is this yer wee laddie? Will ye be wantin' a job for him, too? Weel, bring 'im wi' ye! One o' my platers wants a boy. Ye'll be puttin' him to a trade later on?' and walking in a queer, staccato style, he left them without waiting reply.

'God be praised!' the boy's father exclaimed jubilantly. 'That means a start for me tomorrow! He wouldn't tell me to come if he hadn't a job for me! An' you'll get a job, too, son, wi' fifteen shillin's a week!' The boy couldn't believe it. Fifteen shillings a week! Fifteen shillings a week! Immediately he was rich and in imagination scattering money right and left, buying long-desired things for himself, presents for his mother, father and brothers, making fabulous plans. They walked along with more inspirited step. 'Ye'll have a pay-poke on Saturday the same as me!' said his father, and the boy set his cap a little rakishly, plunged his hands into his pockets manfully and looked at life with tremendous satisfaction!

They could not afford to buy tea in a coffee-shop, and his father took him to a lodging-house where he could boil his can on the hot-plate. They turned down a side street into a narrow lane. From a distance the boy read the black letters on a white-glassed, antique lamp over the narrow door: GOOD BEDS FOR MEN, 4D AND 8D PER NIGHT, and when they reached the place, THE THISTLE HOTEL above the entrance.

They passed into a hot, low-roofed room, with settles and a long, narrow table at which two shirt-sleeved youths played cards with a dog's-eared pack. The place stank vitally of foul life; on a form against the wall a powerful, barefooted negro lay asleep. The boy was amazed at his cavernous mouth, slackly open, exaggerated by full, negroid lips, then his frightened glance fixed on an elderly tramp with one raw, blear eye, the other large and glowing, huddling against a brickwork stove which occupied an entire end of the room, shivering, scratching himself and unwrapping dirty toe-rags from his feet. He stared hypnotised at the brilliant orb as the old man ogled him with a toothless grin.

'You sit there, sonny,' said his father, placing the tin of tea and sugar on the table and going to fill his can at a hot-water tap on the stove. The boy waited timidly, afraid to look about the villainous surroundings, and he started, alarmed, as a thick-set, apish man who leant against the stove reading a newspaper padded across on rope-soled slippers and stood over him. The boy's glance travelled slowly up his loose, greasy trousers and recoiled at the black hair, thick as a dog's, on his enormous arms and breast, showing through his open shirt. The man's little red eyes regarded him with savage contempt, and as the young face turned away he calmly lifted the mustard-tin, turning its oval in his fingers. That moment the boy's father turned and shouted: 'Hi, you! Put that down! That's mine! Put it down!' The brute swung round, deliberately removed the lid, poured the contents on the table and threw the tin at his feet.

The boy was transfixed by that black-and-white spill, a lurid insult, like a spit in his father's face. He jumped back as his father leapt, his left hand seizing the bully's shirt, his right followed by all his weight smashing into his face. He heard a crack and a ripping sound and waited, petrified, certain the big man would beat the life out of his da, that all here would set on him! The two youths started up, the negro shouted, swaying, staring like a sleepwalker, the tramp cackled like a crone: 'Heh, that was a rare smack ye gied 'im! My, that was a guid yin! Right on the chin! Right on the point!' But no one interfered and the big man sprawled back on the table, breathing heavily, then sat up dazed, rubbing his jaw, his torn shirt slopping between his thighs, hair showing down to his paunch. The boy's father pranced, shaping up to him. 'Come on, ye bastard! I'll beat the jelly out o' ye, big as ye are!'

They all turned as the dosshouse proprietor, a stout, carroty-haired man, rushed in tucking a soiled white apron at his waist, shouting furiously: 'What's goin' on here? What the bloody hell! Here you! Get to hell out of here! Come on, out you go! You don't pay for a bed here! What's yer bloody game, comin' here to use my hot-plate without payin'?' The boy's father faced him defiantly, inclined to fight him also, but he only said: 'All right! Keep yer shirt on, man! We're goin'! Come on, sonny!'

In the lane his father hitched up his belt arrogantly, pleased at besting the dosshouse bully. 'Did ye see that, sonny? One good right, straight from the shoulder, an' down he goes, the get! I bested the cur!' He went through the fight again, shooting out his fists, then swaggered along at tremendous pace, thumbs in his waistcoat armholes. He put an arm round his son's shoulder. 'Eh, we're a couple o' rare fighters! They can't best us!' he chuckled and walked faster, looking slyly down. The boy strove to pace him till his heart pounded and he fell behind. His father slackened with a great laugh. 'My, ye're a rare wee walker, sonny!' and the boy smiled, breathing hard. How proud he was of his da! He was the best da in the world! 'Come on!' cried his father. 'We'll eat our dinners down by the water. Damn the tea!'

They walked by the river along the grassy banks. The boy clutched at his father, crying excitedly: 'I can smell the sea now, da!

I can smell it!' He lifted his head and inspired and the adventurous tang filled his little breast. They ate their pieces and his father smoked a clay pipe, then lay down with a big, white-spotted red handkerchief over his head. And the boy sat beside him watching river-life – barges, yachts, pleasure-boats, tramps and great liners from all corners of the world, going along the sun's path of gold, always to the accompaniment of riveters' hammers, clanging on bulkhead and deck. 'Oh, da, look at yon bonny boat! It's like a swan, isn't it, da?' and he pointed at a suave steam yacht, white as snow, anchored midstream, its brass-work and gold paint flashing as it bowed to the smooth flow. His father said: 'Eh! What's that? A swan? Ay, a swan!' and fell asleep, snoring outrageously, and the red handkerchief burbled on his face.

And the boy's happiness rose with the waning day. This warm, light-hearted May day seemed eternal, and he could have sat here for ever, watching life, listening to the echo from shipyards across the water, sending his heart to follow the wild gulls. He was not lonely because his father slept. In this hour all life was his. He was content. He thought how the river widened to the ocean, and only then felt lonely for a bit as a sense of the world's immensity overawed his tiny comprehension. Then a liner from India in tow of pilot tugs crawled past, shutting the white yacht from view for several minutes. A crowd of half-naked lascar sailors leant on the ship's rail, chattering, laughing, singing an Eastern song. One waved a bright scarf to him and he waved his cap. He had often watched lascars shopping in the slum markets. Why were they always happy and laughing? The liner passed. At once the world was friendly, all his happiness was restored and he smiled again at the white yacht.

His father started awake when the sun was some way down, and exclaimed: 'My God! It's late! Yer maw'll be mad wi' us. We'd better get home!' The boy was in a state of sheer bliss with all he had seen that day. No boy had seen the wonders he had witnessed, and all the long ride home he fought sleep, wishful to miss nothing. When he had gulped down his tea he rushed into the back-court to tell his tenement friends. They were rooting for any objects of interest housewives might have thrown into the communal midden, which was beginning to exude its summer stink. They rallied, a charmed, envious circle, while he narrated, a little Homer of the back-streets. He had seen a dead man and the highest crane on the Clyde! His da had knocked a man 'right oot' over a table! – by now his father's adversary had attained prodigious proportions – and he had got a job in the 'Yards' with 'big money'. Suddenly he broke off importantly with: 'Well, I'll have to be gettin' home now. I've got to be up gey early for my job, ye know!' and swaggered away.

There was unusual tranquillity in his home that evening. His mother was pleased because all her menfolk would be in jobs, and she and her man were almost friendly. The boy tried to read a book, but the print danced and he could think of nothing but his fine job with big money. He would give his mother every penny. Keep nothing for himself. He would be a good son to her. She would see! He stumbled to her where she sat smiling, knitting a sock. 'Ye won't let me sleep in tomorrow, will ye, maw?' he said. She tousled his hair. 'No, son. I'll call ye fine an' early.' His father shook his shoulder ruggedly. 'Ye're a fine standing-up man, sonny! Ye'll soon be as big as yer da!' He staggered through to the parlour bed, drunk with the sweet opiate of healthy fatigue, hearing his mother say: 'Puir wee soul! He's gey tire't!' and his father: 'Ay, he's had a long day for a wee laddie.' Immediately he fell asleep, thinking vividly of the morrow's job, smiling, with the cries of seagulls in his ears.

All night he dreamt of exalted shipmasts and tall cranes bowing, proudly lifting, swinging their loads, while wild birds circled around them in brilliant sunshine. And the gallant Clyde, pursuing its historic journey to the mountains and the sea, flowed through his dreams.

from Growing Up And Other Stories (Cape 1942)

Seán Rafferty
(1909–1993)

Born Applegarth, Dumfriesshire, attended
Edinburgh University and although he
published poems in *The Modern Scot* in the
1930s, remained unrecognised until recently.

In May the month of miracle
flower on the black bough
flower on the green leaf;
in May the flower the frost the fall
the month of May is all my grief.

The white hawthorn the lilac massed
to dwarf my mourning where I passed;
they were like alien angels come
before their time to greet her home.

Too early come the cruel frost
that claimed my love too early lost
their promise for a tribute gave
and wept their flowers into her grave.

In May the month of miracle
flower on the black bough
flower on the green leaf;
in May the flower the frost the fall
the month of May is all my grief.

The nights you walk my love my sleep
I waken from the dream
into that dreadful ward of death
where you must die again.

Am I the culprit ghost whose feet
steal on forbidden ground?
I would not have it so or sleep
unless the dead sleep sound.

How could I know you now my love
from any other one
or you know me, for life can do
more things than death has done.

But come tonight before I sleep
I shall not speak or cry
but we shall take as midnight strikes
a formal, strange, goodbye.

This moment where I fill the glass
holds neither life nor death
but we shall drink so I have read
the wine and the wine's breath:

and in that fragrance heard and seen
surrounds us at the end
streets squares and gardens where we walked
and every flower and friend.

    May absence be as kind and clear
    as midnight air between
    the moon and the moon's image
    in the still stream.

Who walk this side of silence still?
long since to sleep a day's work done
across the fields over the hill
the harvesters are home and gone.
Who walk this side of silence still?

The harvesters are home and gone;
their meadows sleep till early light
the water sleeps beside the stone.
Who calls this late their last goodnight?
the harvesters are home and gone.

Who call this late their last goodnight?
their roads are dark, how far their bed?
Listen. Beyond our blindfold sight
are they the living we the dead.
Who call this late their last goodnight?

from Poems (Etruscan Books 1999)

GEORGE FRIEL
(1910-1975)

Born Glasgow where he worked as a
teacher. Published five novels set in his home
city including *Mr Alfred* MA (1972). Joyce's
Dubliners was the model for his short stories.

The Boy Who Wanted Peace

HUGH O'Neill and Shaun O'Donnell, two big broad Glasgow
Irishmen who claimed to be descended from Niall of the
Nine Hostages who was King of All Ireland when the ancestors of
the English aristocracy were grubbing for nuts in the forest, bumped
into each other getting off the same bus at Parkhead Cross just as
the pubs were opening. The sky was blue, the syvers were littered,
and there was the clinging smell of decaying refuse that goes with
a warm spring evening in the east end of the city. They were parched,
hot and sticky after a hard day's work, and with a little jerk of the
head and a question in their royal blue eyes they understood each
other at once and went into the Tappit Hen for a brotherly crack
over a quiet drink before going home for their tea. They were only
a couple of workers from the Yards who built more ships talking
shop of an evening at the bar than ever they built in a year's work,
but their conversation on this occasion may throw some light on
the events that began the same evening, though they themselves
were of course unaware of the coincidence.

'What'll ye have?' O'Donnell asked since he happened to be
the first through the swing doors.

'A glass and a pint,' O'Neill answered, raising one hand high
to salute the barman. The shade and coolness of the place were
pleasant to him after the heat and dust outside. He liked pubs

especially when they had just opened. At that time they were as dim and quiet as a church. A man could be at peace there with a drink in front of him, and the gantry was a kind of altar. Certainly it held on its glass shelves the expensive liquid that made life bearable and sometimes even enjoyable – uisgebeatha in the language of the Gael, the water of life in the language of the Saxon.

'A glass and a pint!' O'Donnell repeated in alarm, his Irish eyes reproachful. 'Do ye think I've been robbin a bank? Ye'll have a half and a half-pint and like it.'

They stood in reverent silence till they were served.

'Funny you saying robbing a bank,' said O'Neill. 'I was just reading in the paper there coming in on the bus. See the Colonel's deid.'

'Oh aye, the Colonel, aye, so he's deid, is he,' said O'Donnell. Not until he had put a little water in the whiskies did he try to understand what they were talking about. He frowned. 'How do ye mean, the Colonel?'

'The Colonel I mean,' said O'Neill. 'Him they got for the Anderston bank robbery. He's deid.'

'Oh, I see, God rest his soul,' said O'Donnell with routine sorrow in his flat voice.

'The paper was saying he died in jail,' said O'Neill. 'Well, no' in the jail exactly, it was in the infirmary, but he was still in jail of course because it was eight years he got.'

'Funny,' said O'Donnell. 'That other bloke they got for the Ibrox bank robbery, he died in jail last month as well.'

'Aye, it makes ye think,' said O'Neill. 'He was a Canadian.'

'No, he was an Australian,' said O'Donnell. 'Or his pal was an Australian or wan o' them was an Australian but no' a Canadian.'

'No, he was a Canadian all right,' said O'Neill.

'No, an Australian,' said O'Donnell, finishing his whisky and elevating his beer.

'Ach, ye're thinking o' the Ibrox bank,' said O'Neill. 'That was the Major, no' the Colonel. The monocled Major they called him. He was an Australian but it was his pal that died no' him. But the Colonel was a Canadian so he was, it was the Major was an Australian.'

'That's what I'm saying,' O'Donnell complained. 'He was an Australian, him or his mate. Wan o' them.'

'Funny how these blokes come to Glasgow,' said O'Neill. He shook the dregs of his whisky glass into his beer.

'Ach, there's a lot o' folks come to Glasgow for the country roon aboot,' said O'Donnell. 'They've heard o' the bonnie, bonnie banks o' Loch Lomond.'

'It's no' the banks o' Loch Lomond they fellows came for,' O'Neill retorted, pouting over the half pint he was raising to his lips. He sipped and went on. 'It's the Royal Bank and the Clydesdale Bank and the Commercial Bank and the Bank of Scotland and the British Linen Bank, that's what they came for. Ye know, there's been a wheen o' bank robberies in Glasgow in the last five or six year. Just you think back.'

'Ach, I don't know,' said O'Donnell. 'See the Bhoys is doing well the now. Were you there on Saturday?'

'Aye, I was there,' said O'Neill. 'But they're no' that clever. The polis aye catch up on them sooner or later so they do. The trouble with the Bhoys is they never keep it up. They go away and let the Thistle or the Thirds beat them when ye least expect it.'

'I don't mind so long as they beat the Rangers,' O'Donnell replied nonchalantly, offering his mate a cigarette. 'Here! But the polis are no' that clever either. They get them but they don't get the money.'

'Ye're right there,' said O'Neill. 'It says in the paper there's thirty thousand pound still missing. But the Bhoys has got youth on their side, that's mair nor the Rangers have. You can see it in the paper there for yourself.'

O'Donnell looked at O'Neill's paper.

'Funny,' he said. 'It was just the same wi' the Ibrox robbery. Forty thousand it was they didn't get. But I'd never take the Bhoys in my coupon.'

'Oh naw, neither would I,' said O'Neill. 'And then there's

Napper Kennedy. Maryhill. They got him in Dublin but they never got the money. Oh naw, I'd never take them in the pools. Ye canna trust them.'

'They got some of it did they no'?' said O'Donnell. 'Somebody left a suitcase in the left luggage. It was his brother wasn't it in the Central Station?'

'Aye, they got five thousand,' said O'Neill. 'Nothing much. There was mair nor thirty thousand they never got yet. And there's Charlie Hope, him that done the Partick bank. He never got as far as Dublin. They got him in his club in St Vincent Street. A bridge club he called it, some bridge club. But they got damn all else but the smell o' his cigar. That was another thirty or forty thousand job. They boys have something to come out to so they have.'

'Ach, they'll never get near it,' said O'Donnell. 'What I say is, the Bhoys ought to spend money on a good inside forward. They've got a lot o' good young yins but the young yins need an auld heid. They'll no' even get gaun to the lavatory without somebody on their tail.'

'Ach, I don't know about that,' O'Neill shrugged. 'They've got ways and means I'll bet you. They don't go to all that trouble for nothing. Where would ye get a good inside forward anyway? They've spent good money before this and it's been money wasted. They're better sticking tae what they've got.'

'Trouble, aye it's trouble all right,' said O'Donnell. 'Eight or nine years they get, every time. But you're right enough I suppose, some of their best servants was players they got for nothing.'

'Well, so what?' O'Neill asked. 'Would you no' do eight or nine year to come out tae thirty or forty thousand?'

'Aye, if I was coming out tae it,' said O'Donnell. 'But that's what I'm arguing, they'll no' come out tae it. The minute they touch it they'll be lifted.'

'But they've served their time, haven't they?' said O'Neill. 'They canny put them in jail twice for the wan offence.'

'That's murder you're thinking of,' said O'Donnell. 'Robbery's different. Sure they'd take the money from them, wouldn't they?

They'd never let them get away wi' it. That would make it too easy. I'd do it myself for eight or nine year.'

'But suppose somebody else has been keeping it to feed it back to them when they come out, ye know, in regular payments, quiet like.'

'Who could they trust to keep thirty or forty thousand for them?' O'Donnell asked derisively. 'Would you trust anybody wi' that amount o' money if you were inside for eight or nine year?'

'I don't know,' said O'Neill thoughtfully. 'I've never had that amount o' money. Maybe ye could if ye made it worth their while. What'll ye have?'

'Just as a matter of interest, how many is that now?' O'Donnell asked.

'It's only yer second,' said O'Neill. 'You put the first wan up when we came in and that's all we've had. Do ye want the same again?'

'Naw, no' the drinks, the bank robberies I mean ye're talking about,' said O'Donnell. 'Anderston, Ibrox, Maryhill, Whiteinch, that's four at least.'

'Oh, there's been a lot mair nor that,' said O'Neill. 'And tae think it's a' lying somewhere! They're a' inside and the money's outside. Thirty thousand here and forty thousand there and the same again and the same again and mair. It would break yer heart just thinking about it.'

'Aye, it would be a bit of all right finding even wan o' they stacks. Will ye be up seeing the Bhoys on Saturday?'

'Aye, ye could find it but would ye have the nerve tae spend it?' said O'Neill. 'Och aye, I'll be there all right.'

'I'll see ye here at two o'clock then,' said O'Donnell. 'I like seeing the Bhoys when they're doing well.'

'But I'll see ye before then,' said O'Neill. 'Ye'll be in here the night aboot eight, will ye no'?'

'Och aye, sure,' said O'Donnell. 'The Bhoys is drawing big money the now all right.'

'Forty-five thousand there last Saturday,' said O'Neill.

They took no more after O'Neill had returned O'Donnell's hospitality. They were two steady working-men, and they went straight home for their tea after their second drink. They knew they would be back in the same pub in a couple of hours. And besides Glasgow's plague of bank robberies there was the state of the Yards on the Clyde to discuss, and there was the Celtic football team to talk about. For two Glasgow Irishmen that was a topic as inexhaustible as the weather to two Englishmen.

from The Boy Who Wanted Peace (John Calder 1964)

FREDDY ANDERSON
(b 1922)

Born in County Monaghan and has lived in
Glasgow for some fifty years. A poet,
playwright and songwriter, he won an *Irish
Post* award in 1991.

On the Celtic Fringe

I first visited Glasgow, en route to Padgate RAF Training Station in
Lancashire, almost sixty years ago. I settled here permanently (so
to speak) three years later. I found it difficult – for a few months at
least – to understand what's called the Glasgow 'patter'. I do not
understand Dr John Moore's concern lest the English and others
might not understand the dialect of his correspondent, Robert
Burns. He advised him to write in English: Robbie sensibly ignored
Moore's advice. Reading Burns in Ireland in the 1930s, I could
understand his meaning a lot clearer than I could the new lingo of
the Anderston tenements. I also found some of Hugh MacDiarmid's
archaic Lallans much more quaint and difficult than Burns's poems.

I found Glasgow to be much more in the shadows than Dublin. War-
time rationing, the recent slump of the 1930s, plus the ever-present
slum tenements created this atmosphere. Yet Glasgow to me was a
cheerier city by far than glum, dour Belfast, or the snobbish, almost
Anglified, Edinburgh. I was an Irish writer by origin but I realised,
though I was only partially fluent in Gaelic, that I had a strong
cultural affinity with the fairly large Celtic fringe, both Highland and
Irish, with roots of many centuries in the Scottish Lowlands.

I in no way found myself at odds with the aspirations of the most
progressive of the Scottish people – they were striving for world
peace, for better housing and social conditions generally. An 'Ivory
Tower Brigade' (the Art for Art's sake junta) still existed in almost
every country even after the terrible War – but not far beneath
their precious idealism one could detect quite distinctly their acute
desire for fame – to be followed, of course, by riches. I took an
almost opposite direction. I was Irish and Celtic, yet international
and not the vague uncertain cosmopolitan – that very conceited,
self-important lone rider of our day.

On Erin's Green Valleys

IT was several years later. Winter was past and the bright days of spring shone on Erin's green valleys. Saint Patrick's Day was only a week away when the Holy Terror sent Oiney along the ditch to find shamrocks on the road to Cootehill, that same little flat town in the north of Cavan where some villains had murdered Nell Flaherty's drake. Near the old Boiler House at the crossroads, where the Quakers made the controversial soup in the Famine times, the young lad met Terry Doogan of the Hills, driving an ass and cart into Creevan. He was quite a tall man, with a slight stoop and a glossy brown beard; he spoke poetry and riddles with a loud deep voice. He often broke off in his conversation to recite a line or two from one of the patriotic ballads of Ireland.

'Is it true, Terry,' Oiney asked innocently, 'that you don't go to chapel?'

Terry paused for a minute. 'As true, God bless us,' he said, 'as the cross on that ass's back and it got that cross implanted as a token of favour for carryin' Christ from the wilderness into Jerusalem on Palm Sunday. "Into our town-land on a night o' snow rode a man from God knows where. . ." And that's a fact.'

'Why don't you go, Terry?' Oiney persisted.

'Ah, sure God himself only knows. Maybe it's the lingerin' smell o' the incense or the pungent smoke o' the snuffed candles, but a great sickness comes over me when I cross the chapel door, a terrible nausea indeed, and I seem to be trapped in the temples o' the ancients. But sure "my cathedral is the glory of the skies, the heat of noon or the first sun-rise. . ." I'm on me way, son, but good luck to you in your search!'

A little further up the road Oiney met a lean, dark young man in a trenchcoat and a hat tilted low over his brow. 'You are from Creevan?'

'I am,' said Oiney.

'Tell me something!'

'Tell you something? If I can.'

'About Doyle the publican in the Market Square. Is he dead yet?'

'No,' said Oiney, 'but he's got the Last Rites an' they've taken him to Monaghan hospital.'

The lean man chuckled.

'The Last Rites, did you say? Good.'

'Why?' asked Oiney, a little puzzled by the stranger's glee.

'Why? Ah, why? That's the question you might say. Well now . . . I see . . . Won't it be a great comfort to his crossin' the unknown boundaries o' the Great Divide?'

The man took his leave, but in days ahead Oiney had cause to remember that strange encounter.

In searching the ditch for shamrocks, to his delight, he found not only many sprigs of the famous plant but down in the deep grass a shining half-crown and a penny piece. His granny steeped the shamrocks in water and let him keep the penny. 'We'll send the half-crown to the Missions,' she said, 'an' buy a black baby. And if you're good, I'll take you on the pilgrimage to Lough Derg. . .'

'Lough Derg, granny? What's Lough Derg?'

'It's an island.'

Oiney looked puzzled.

'An island? I thought you said it was a lough.'

'My God, didn't they learn you anything at all at that school on the hill? There's a holy island on Lough Derg, where the great Saint Patrick himself, Apostle of Ireland, prayed and fasted in a dark cave for forty days an' forty nights. . .'

'What did he do that for?'

She gave her grandson a look of great scorn and then mimicked his voice. 'What did he do that for? What did he do that for? Wasn't he lookin' for paper to wipe his arse with? What did he do that for! Wasn't he prayin' for the conversion of the Irish, you,

you amadhuan. An' God answered his prayer except for them bloody Orange crew up north — God revealed Himself to Patrick.'

'He did what?' said the open-mouthed Oiney.

'Shut your gob or you'll be catchin' flies, gasson! God appeared to Patrick in a spinning white light. He told the saint that on a dark day ahead the lovely green valleys of Erin would slowly sink under the waves o' the Atlantic. An' that Patrick himself would have the privilege of sittin' in judgement on the Irish race!'

'He did not!'

'He did or else I wouldn't be tellin' you! Why else would the great pilgrimages of Lough Derg in Donegal be made for throughout the centuries? Prayin' an' fastin' an' sayin' the Stations in our bare feet. Three days an' nights with nothin' but a crust o' bread an' black tay an' the flint cuttin' your feet an' you chitterin' with the cold, with the bitther winds from the wild Atlantic crossin' the bleak, bare hills o' Donegal. . .'

It sounded so dreadfully forlorn and incredibly weird that Oiney, bored by the long winter in Creevan, felt a great desire to visit the strange place. So, for some weeks, he kept close to the house and ran the messages. He fetched buckets of water from the familiar old lion-headed fountain on the brae, and scoured all the little bottles which ailing neighbours sent in to his granny for a taste of the cure, when it came, from the holy island. One bottle in particular which his granny warned him to rinse well with lashings of soap and water and elbow grease was an empty whiskey bottle sent in by old Terry of the Hills, who she said, God forgive him, never crossed a chapel door. 'Scour it well,' she ordered the boy, 'for the evil dregs o' whiskey will polluther the holy water somethin' awful, an' instead of a cure cause a calamity.'

One morning in June, the slow train drew the Lough Derg pilgrims westwards to Donegal. . . Oiney, carrying a well-rinsed and scrubbed lemonade bottle, sat beside his granny and eyed the others in the carriage. Like the old woman, many were saying their rosary beads, while others dreamed as they looked out of the windows at the grazing cattle in the lovely, patchwork of green and corn-gold fields of Ulster, in by Fermanagh where 'the Erne shall run red with redundance of blood, the earth shall rock beneath our tread. . . ere you shall fade, ere you shall die, my dark Rosaleen. . .'

Oiney, with his own innate kindness and love for his people, gazed innocently into the eyes of the other pilgrims and saw not sin nor selfishness, but instead a little bit too much humility, he thought, and the strain of overwork and worry. These were not the brash sinners that the brimstone missionaries should thunder at from the pulpits raised high above the poor. There was scarcely a soul among them knew what real sin was. These were people more sinned against than sinning, but still afraid of the loss of their invisible souls, as Oiney was afraid.

'Tickets, please!' The powerful voice of the Inspector boomed along the corridor so loudly that Oiney was amazed to discover that its possessor was in fact quite a small man in uniform, crowned by a shiny peak cap. Just then a sharp elbow dug into the boy's ribs, and he heard his granny whisper in alarm, 'Pull your trousers above your knees, gasson! Quick!'

Oiney could scarcely believe her command. 'What, granny?'

'D'you as you're bid,' she shouted frantically, 'for I only got you a half-fare ticket! For Jaysus sake, hurry!'

Oiney's face went scarlet to match his hair almost and he fumbled in embarrassment with the empty lemonade bottle, passing it from one hand to the other. Before he had time to make his mind up what to do, the ticket Inspector stood in their section of the carriage. The old woman, now the picture of piety, handed him the two tickets. He punched one of them and then looked at the other over and over again. Lifting his eyes from the ticket, he looked at Oiney, measuring him up, then back to the ticket again and finally at the empty lemonade bottle, as though it played some mysterious role in all this. 'What age are you, son?'

The old woman was ready to pounce on him. 'Is there anyone askin' you your age, is there?'

The wee man stood his full five-feet two-inches tall,

officialdom triumphant. 'I would like to inform you, madam, that I am an Inspector of the Great Northern Railway.'

'I don't give a damn if you own the Great Northern Railway. Fetch me a real Inspector that respects people's rights, an' us pious pilgrims, no less, doin' penance on the way to the holy Lough Derg!'

The other passengers had their faces turned to the windows, desperately striving to show that they had no connection whatsoever with this awful woman. But the Holy Terror had had so many sharp rebuffs in life that she shrugged off this latest one. 'What are you anyway, you impudent get,' she snapped at the official, 'that you come bursting in on top of me rosary beads? Are you a haythen heretic or worse still a bitther Orangeman that you disturb the peace of a Christian carriage? Have I asked you what religion you are or what you had for breakfast? If you don't go this minit, I've a mind to summon you before the Stipendiary.' She had a liking for these nineteenth-century words; they sounded so important they frightened people off.

The Inspector, realising that he had an impossible case on his hands, thought it wiser to make a safe retreat, but he fired a parting salvo.

'You can be up for defraudin' the Great Northern Railway. . .'

She was on her feet again. 'If you don't lave me sight this instant the Great Northern Railway will be minus an Inspector before we reach the next station! We hanged a wee fella like you in Carrick during the Land War!'

For the remainder of the journey Oiney could not say that he enjoyed the ensuing peace. His granny's tongue rattled away at a great rate. The entire carriage-full of penitents seemed to be staring at his hot, blushing face, making him feel guilty of the terrible crime of belonging to the scourge of Creevan.

This was only the beginning of his penance. From the small jetty at the lough-side, they could see the lone bleak island with its basilica, guest house and other buildings. For well over a thousand years, pilgrims from Ireland, Scotland, England and the Continent had stood on these ancient shores. Soon a medium-sized ferryboat was carrying them across the waves to be welcomed on the island pier by Dean Keown. Oiney saw the Dean give his granny a very strange look, for he knew her well, and probably anticipated a rough time of it.

It was not long before the old woman and the boy began their rounds of the Stations – or beds, as they were called. There were several of these bleak, stony circles, and the barefoot route of the pilgrims lay across sharp-edged flintstone. Oiney picked his pious way very gingerly, but his granny made ample atonement for his avoidance of pain by falling on top of him at regular intervals and accompanying these falls with loud shrieks of 'Oh, Christ, me corns,' 'Oh, Jesus, me bunions'. For Oiney it was like two or three extra penances, and no one on that island was so glad to see the ferryboat arrive to take them all back to the mainland. Dean Keown saw them off and once again Oiney noticed that peculiar look in the priest's eyes as he made sure the boy's granny was safely on board. Dean Keown seemed to give vent to a great sigh of heartfelt relief.

It was a different ticket Inspector on the train home and for a considerable time nothing disturbed the peace and contentment. After the long spells of vigil on Lough Derg, most of the pilgrims fell asleep. Oiney's exhausted grandmother lay back, snoring quite loudly, while the lad counted the passing telegraph poles. Then, for no apparent reason, he suddenly became conscious of the lemonade bottle in his hand. For days he had been carrying it from place to place almost unaware of its very existence. Now he sat stunned, looking at its emptiness. In the midst of the confusion and anxiety on Lough Derg, he had forgotten to fill the bottle with holy water. Nor had his granny noticed the empty bottle either.

He sat for quite a while, really dismayed by the awful discovery. Terry of the Hills, the Widow Murtagh, Mrs Coyle, and the other poor suffering neighbours would be bitterly disappointed. Oiney had brought no holy water home to pour into the little miniature bottles. It was surely bad enough, he thought, to deprive his poor neighbours of a cure for their pains. But to have to hold up his empty bottle and to look in their sad eyes was more than he could bear.

Then suddenly, he had a flash of inspiration, a flash of genius. It was not the fault of the leprechaun of the fountain this time, but the train happened to be passing through the territory of smugglers and the like just then, and who knows but Old Nick himself had a hand in it?

Now ordinary tap water is the same as holy water as far as the layman is concerned anyhow. It has the same transparent colour and the same consistency. So, thought Oiney, in this emergency, only in this emergency, if Terry of the Hills and the others get their miniatures filled with ordinary water, they will not be any the wiser. Of course, reasoned Oiney, ordinary water will effect no cure, but then even the best holy water from Lourdes in France will not always produce a cure. And thus the poor sufferers will not blame Oiney. It was deception, downright deception indeed, but in a worthy cause, and as the Jesuit sophists might say, the end justifying the means.

His granny, thank heavens, was still asleep, and the rest of the pilgrims resting back on clear consciences, when Oiney crept forward along the corridor. No one present, had they looked, would have dreamed in a million years that this small, freckled, pious and innocent boy had an empty bottle stuck up his jersey. He sneaked quietly into the toilet, snibbed the door behind him and filled the bottle with good clear train water from the sink tap.

Old Terry of the Hills, the Widow Murtagh and Mrs Coyle were highly delighted, as were all the others. Oiney stood, blushing with guilt, as they expressed their warm thanks. They mistook his blushes for shyness. A week later his embarrassment was even greater when they came from all parts to thank his granny for the powerful 'cure' she had brought them. 'Thanks be to God an' His holy Mother,' said Mrs Murtagh, 'for I've never felt as good in a month of Sundays. Me spots have disappeared an' not only that, but me daughter, Peggy, is coughin' betther.' She patted Oiney on the head and never even noticed that his freckles had disappeared in a huge crimson blush.

'Bless his wee soul,' she added fervently, 'but who knows he's got the makin's of a holy Bishop in him yet.'

Oiney nurtured silently his terrible sin until the autumn when the missionaries roared into Creevan. Previously he had been afraid to tell his heinous sin in Confession in case the priest recognised him. There were few local lads who had ever been to Lough Derg. At least the missionaries for all their sulphur and brimstone carried your sins back to Dublin with them and well clear of the Parish. Waiting until the queue was clear, Oiney went into Confession: 'Bless me Father for I have sinned.'

'How long is it since your last Confession?'

'It must be three or four months, Father.'

'That's a long time for a lad like you. Well now, let's have your sins!'

'Well, Father, it's like this. I went to Lough Derg, but I didn't take home any holy water at all. I took train-water.'

'Drain water,' said the priest, who was hard of hearing. 'Tell me more about this drain-water! Were you digging drains in Donegal?'

'No, Father, it wasn't drain water; it was train-water.'

'Oh, I see. Rain water. I see. But tell me, how did you take home rain-water from Lough Derg?'

'Father,' said Oiney, almost giving up hope, 'I filled the bottle full of water from the sink tap in the train.'

The missionary tried to get a glimpse of this strange penitent. 'And what in God's name did you do that for?'

'I pretended it was holy water, Father.'

'But sure,' said the priest, 'that kind of water wouldn't cure.'

'But it did, Father, it did,' cried Oiney almost triumphantly. 'It cured Peggy's cough, an' her Ma's spots an' Mrs Coyle. . .'

'Were you tempting God?' the priest asked suspiciously.

'Oh no, Father, shure I wouldn't endanger my invisible soul,' Oiney assured him.

Quaint fellow this, thought the priest, but basically harmless. 'Say the Stations of the Cross as a penance! And don't put drain-water, or train-water or whatever in holy water bottles again!'

'But Father?'

'What is it now?' said the priest impatiently.

'Father? How did the water cure them when it wasn't holy? How did it do that, Father?'

'Listen, young man, and take my word for it. Sure all the water in Ireland is holy!'

from Oiney Hoy (Polygon 1989)

MATT McGINN
(1928–1977)

Born in Glasgow and worked as a teacher but mainly as a performer of his prolific output of songs. His autobiography and songs were published in *McGinn of the Calton* (1987).

Flafferty's Potatoes

YOU don't spend fifty years on farms without developing your own meteorological office right there in your skull and Brian Flafferty's own little met. office told him that the remaining potatoes had to be lifted today. No doubt about it. That west wind whistling in his ears told him there was stormy weather ahead for the West of Scotland.

Cold and frosty it was with a thick white coat on the potato shaws. 'Right there,' his shrill Irish voice rang out, sending white clouds from his small, slightly twisted mouth. 'Give your dead carcasses a rattle and I want every single spud lifted.'

The boys knew what was wanted and they rushed at the shaws tearing them with cold fingers from the soil. Thankful they were to see the last of the tatties.

'Get them Irish grapes lifted,' shouted Flafferty picking up a long twig and running ahead of the horse and harrow making mock swipes at the boys backsides. 'I'll soon get you warmed up.' His voice assaulted their ears.

Two boys there were to every six yards and the moment the horse passed their pitch they rushed in with their baskets plucking the potatoes with slightly more joy than they had plucked the frozen shaws. Up, down, back, forth, up, down . . . It was back-breaking toil for fourteen and fifteen year olds, untrained in the rigours of the farm.

'There's a moudie,' shouted McEwan, and four boys broke off to chase the mouse whose entire world had just been torn asunder by the harrow. 'Never mind the bloody moudie,' roared Flafferty, taking three quick strokes at McEwan's buttocks the moment he reached the boy, 'And give yourselves a shake the rest of you. Get those backs bent or I'll bend them for you.'

Hard work it was out here in the fields, but hard work never killed anybody, and as for these boys . . . make men of them it would . . . all this fresh air and exercise of the muscles . . . liked his job in Saint Martin's did Flafferty . . . best job he had ever had and Flafferty had had a few in his day, working with pigs and cows and barley and pratties the length and breadth of Ireland and Scotland all his life . . . Finish his days in Saint Martin's, he would, given a chance . . . Well it wasn't like other farming jobs . . . here you had all these sturdy young lads in your charge who could be put to all the jobs you didn't fancy yourself and you were doing them good too . . . but these pratties would have to be in today. . .

'Scrape that soil clean,' he bawled, swishing his twig up and down the field, 'There's a tumshie for the best pair of you when we get this field cleared.' The boys gave themselves an additional shake at the thought of the turnip prize. But Patch Kelly wasn't waiting to be awarded such a trophy; he was already in the next field where the large, juicy tumshies grew and had picked himself a beauty before Flafferty spotted him. 'Come here you thieving rascal,' he shouted, and Kelly, who had dropped the turnip, sheepishly approached the farmer. What excuse could he make? None . . . he would just have to take the punishment which Flafferty would undoubtedly administer. . . 'Bend over,' he heard the small Irishman shout, and was in the process of fearfully obeying when a mouse jumped from underneath a shaw twelve inches from his eyes. Patchy jumped, startled by the rodent and ran screaming to the derisive laughter of the other boys nearby, who nearly burst with fits of laughter at the sight of a big lad like Patchy screaming at a mouse. Flafferty made a rush at Kelly and bent him over. Patchy screamed again as the twig came three times into contact with the seat of his pants, and again the others laughed.

'Now bend those backs and get those potatoes lifted,' roared Flafferty pushing Kelly towards his allotted pitch.

from Fry the Little Fishes (Calder & Boyars 1975)

The Pill

Tune: Kissin' in the Dark

Chorus   *The Pill, the Pill, I'm pining for the Pill,*
I'll never have any more because they're
going to bless the Pill.

I wed when I was seventeen,
I hadn't many brains;
Says I the very thing to do
Is fill the hoose wi' weans.
But when I got the room full
I went to see the priest,
To tell him my man Willie
Was behaving like a beast:

He gave me such a terrible row
My eyes were filled wi' tears:
'How long have you been wed?' says he,
Says I, 'This seven years.'
Says he, 'You'd better give over
All your evil sinful tricks –
You've been married seven years
And you've only got the six!'

I'm coming up for forty,
In my faith I've aye been true;
The very last time I tallied them
I counted twenty-two.
But now I've lost the notion
For we're running short o' names,
Though Willie he would welcome more –
He's fond o' havin' weans:

Now they're talking of the Pill
They've filled my heart wi' hope.
I'm sitting here and waiting
On a signal frae the Pope.
I went along tae buy some
At fifteen-bob a tin –
I hope we hae the Pope's O.K.
Before my man comes in!

from McGinn of the Calton (Glasgow Libraries 1987)

JOAN LINGARD
(b. 1932)

Born in Edinburgh of a Scottish mother and an English father. She has published thirteen adult novels including *Sisters by Rite* set in Belfast and *After Colette* which was shortlisted for the Saltire Award. Her thirty four novels for children include the *Kevin and Sadie* Ulster quintet, her best known books worldwide.

I lived in Belfast from age two to eighteen. All my formative years were spent in the province and inevitably have had a tremendous influence on my life and writing, especially I think on my writing for children. It was in Belfast that I learned to read and to write and where I made friendships that have stayed with me for life. The Belfast speech and its cadences were constantly in my ears, in school and in the street, and even now, so many years later, it is that particular voice that I hear most easily in my inner ear.

It is the territory that is most deeply ingrained in my memory. I know Edinburgh well, I have lived here more years than anywhere else, but it is Belfast, and in particular my own area of East Belfast, that I remember in the smallest detail, down to the look of the paving stones beneath my feet when playing hopscotch, the lamppost on the corner that we used to throw a rope over and swing around, the gospel hall with its exhortations to sinners to repent while time was still available. And of course I remember the murals of King Billy on his white horse on gable end walls, for how could one not, they were so decorative and colourful and they brightened up the drab brick?

We had nothing to do with the Orange Order in our family. We lived in a predominantly Protestant street – it even had Holland in its name – with only two Catholic families amongst us. In Belfast one was always aware of such details. Surnames gave it all away in any case. My mother was a total non-bigot and was friendly with the Catholic family who lived two doors from us. Not everybody was. Both of my parents were unorthodox in terms of religious adherence. My father was a non-believer and a non-church-goer. and there didn't seem to be many of them in the province, which made him an odd man out. My mother and I went to the Christian Science church, which put us even more on the margins. As a Protestant, it was important which group one belonged to. Presbyterians were top dogs, as I saw it, then came the Church of Ireland, followed by the Methodists, behind whom trailed the Unitarians and the Baptists, and after that there were various other sects, the also-rans, such as the Salvationists and the Christian Scientists. It was made clear to me that Christian Scientists were not 'real' Protestants, not with a mother church in Boston and a woman called Mary Baker Eddy as leader. Religion then in all its complexities was a big influence and when I did come to write it was inevitable that I would write about Belfast and its religious heritage.

From the age of eleven I knew I wanted to be a writer and I wrote, but not one word about Belfast. Dull, deadly old Belfast! That was not the stuff of fiction. I had not read any books set in the province, or in the Republic, either, nor was I to do so throughout my schooldays. Irish literature, like Irish history, was ignored. Happily this is no longer the case. When I came into my twenties, and was then living in Scotland, I realised that I had a whole wealth of material from my Belfast years waiting to be drawn upon; indeed, demanding to be drawn upon. My first adult novel, *Liam's Daughter*, was set partly in Northern Ireland and partly in France. My first children's book, *The Twelfth Day of July* was placed firmly in the city of Belfast.

Sisters by Rite

A T CHRISTMAS Aunt Belle's letter said she would be coming home on leave in a few weeks time and she had a notion to go to Dublin.

'Dublin,' mused my mother. 'I think you and I might go with her, Cora.'

Dublin. Sin city! Sodom, Gomorrah, Rome, Dublin. There wasn't much to choose among them, if you could believe Uncle Billy.

'You wouldn't catch *me* going there,' said Rosie. My mother had offered to take her but the McGills wouldn't consider it. 'It's full of German spies,' said Rosie, 'and you'll trip over priests and nuns on every corner and the shawlies have about fifty-five children each and they *smell*.'

I promised I'd bring her back a gigantic box of milk chocolates with hard centres. Not much was rationed in the South, except for clothes and tea. Tea was the great thing. Tea unlocked the magic gates. 'Now you take a good few quarters with you,' said Mrs Jamieson from down the street. She went to Dublin regularly, knew all the ins and outs. 'And pack your case light on the way down, maybe put in an old jersey or two that you can throw out and take a few old labels from Cleavers and the like with you.'

Aunt Belle arrived wearing her ATS uniform, with her hair rolled up like a sausage under her cap, and carrying a kitbag. She was fizzing with excitement. She threw her cap up in the air and tugged at the sausage roll. Hairpins winged in all directions. She had just got engaged to a really nice bloke, a corporal in the Signals, and they were going to get married as soon as the war was over which everybody said couldn't be long now.

'*We're going to hang out the washing on the Siegfried line,*' sang Rosie and I.

Aunt Belle thought she would buy her engagement ring in Dublin. Len had told her she should just go ahead.

The black-shawled women were waiting for us at Amiens Street station. They must have smelt our tea for they advanced with outstretched arms and soon had us encircled. The shrilling of their voices and the stench of their bodies made me step back. Rosie had been right about the children too: they did seem to have dozens of them, in their arms, under their shawls, behind their heels. Fingers grazed my coat and one old woman, toothless, dirt embedded in the lines of her face, touched my cheek and said what a pretty girl I was. I was both fascinated and repelled. But I warmed to the compliment, for it was seldom that I was told I was pretty. I was too gawky and too freckled for that. I smiled at the old woman and she squawked, 'Pretty girl, pretty girl,' and came closer so that her smell invaded my nostrils and I wanted to shove her away. And then I was ashamed for I had been taught to love my neighbour. I pushed my way out of the gaggle.

Aunt Belle auctioned the tea for clothing coupons and the shawlies scattered to seek fresh prey. They moved like a flock of rooks across the station floor. My mother said something about the Roman Church having a lot to answer for. I tugged at her hand.

We stepped into the streets of Dublin. The bright lights astounded me.

'It's like daytime.'

'This is what it'll be like in Belfast,' said Aunt Belle, 'when the lights come on again.'

But I knew that it could never be quite like this. There was an excitement about the city that made me want to skip. The streets swarmed with people who looked as if they were enjoying themselves. Pub doors swung open spilling out light and noise. The restaurants were busy, the shop windows full. I was enthralled.

Aunt Belle bought a diamond ring putting every penny she had left into it, and a few of my mother's as well. 'Go on, Belle, it suits your finger! And you only get engaged once.' How true that turned out to be. The jeweller told us it was a bargain and would cost two if not three times as much in the North. That decided it.

The night before we came home we sat in our hotel room sewing labels from Robinson and Cleaver's and Anderson and MacAuley's into our new clothes. My mother sprinkled a little talcum powder over them, so that the materials wouldn't look so new. 'There now!' She admired a green corduroy dress she'd bought for me. 'You'd never know, would you?'

I was surprised by her – *breaking the law* – but said nothing. There was much that I did not understand in adult behaviour and awaited the day when it would become clear to me.

And now for the ring. Where was that to be put? My mother had an idea: we would bury it inside a quarter pound of butter. Mrs Jamieson had told us that you could bring in one or two small things if you declared them. It was the big stuff they were after.

The compartment was crowded going back. Nobody was saying much or reading the newspapers and magazines they held in front of them. Smugglers the lot of them, I decided, eyeing the bags and suitcases on the racks over their heads. The woman opposite me kept wiping her forehead and the man in the corner had a shifty eye that moved from Aunt Belle to my mother and back again. The customs had their spies everywhere, Mrs Jamieson had warned us.

The train halted at the Free State border. The customs here weren't really interested, we could be taking half of Dublin back with us as far as they were concerned, as long as we had paid for it. We rumbled across no man's land to the British post.

Now, the atmosphere changed. All was hustle and bustle as passengers got up to take down their luggage. The woman opposite stood on my new sandals and didn't even say she was sorry. People were talking loudly in the corridor.

'They're on the warpath,' said a man in a checked suit, putting his head in.

I saw a customs man go by with a fur coat over his arm. Mrs Jamieson had told us perturbing tales of how, if they suspected you, they took you into sheds and stripped the clothes off you. How could I ever stand naked in front of a man? I whispered in my mother's ear.

'Don't be silly, dear.' Unlike everyone else, she was smiling. And Knowing the Truth no doubt, but what the suitable truth would be in this situation I could not imagine. Surely God couldn't approve of us smuggling?

'Right then.' The men were at the door. I didn't like the look of the thin faces under the peaked hats and knew there was going to be trouble. My mother continued to smile and Aunt Belle said, 'Certainly, Officer,' when she was asked to open her case. He ran his fingers through her silk underwear and I felt sick. 'Where did you get this lot?' He looked at the utility labels which she had sewn in so carefully the night before. 'Don't make me laugh!' Nothing would make him laugh, I decided. He lifted the honeymoon camiknickers and petticoats and stuffed them into the sack he was carrying. He allowed me to keep my dress and sandals although I didn't think he was fooled. There wasn't much room left in his bag anyway.

My mother, who had also been told by Mrs Jamieson that it was good tactics to declare something, offered the information that she had a half pound of cheese, a quarter of butter and a box of chocolates, already opened.

'You're not allowed to import foodstuffs into the United Kingdom, madam.' He held out his hand.

My mother faltered, my aunt held her breath, I saw her hold it: her rib cage froze.

'You can't take the butter,' I cried. 'You can't!'

'Cora!' said my mother.

'And why not, miss?'

'You just can't.' My voice faded to a squeak inside me.

'Is there something special about the butter?'

'No. It's just that – I'm very fond – desperately fond – of butter. If you could put a buttercup under my chin you would see how fond.' I felt my temperature rising.

'Cora dear,' said my mother, more softly this time.

'I'm sorry, miss, but the law's the law.' His hand came out for the butter. Perhaps he was fond of it too, would take it home to his wife for tea and she would cut into it and find Aunt Belle's ring and her eyes would shine, like the diamond itself. We watched as his fingers curled round the packet and then rested for a moment, as if he were in two minds, but in the next instant his hand was in motion again swinging up and over the bag and opening it like the jaws of a crane to release its prey.

We travelled the rest of the way back to Belfast in silence. Aunt Belle was brave; she didn't cry or let anyone in the compartment know what a terrible thing had happened to her. I watched the countryside rushing by and the long trail of smoke the train was leaving behind and ate chocolate after chocolate from the opened box until my mother removed them saying I would be sick.

Aunt Belle never did get married. Len was sent to France and killed by a stray bullet just five days before the war in Europe ended. It was as if losing the ring like that had brought her bad luck. My mother said that was nonsense.

'If you ask me,' said Rosie, 'it was because it was a Papist ring.'

Another possibility occurred to me: that Aunt Belle was being punished for doing wrong. My mother did not like that theory either. She said that God was a good God, merciful and forgiving.

'You worry about things too much, Cora love. Why is it that you cannot just accept?'

from Sisters by Rite (Hamish Hamilton 1984)

WILLIAM MCILVANNEY
(b.1936)

Born in Kilmarnock. After Glasgow University
worked as a teacher before becoming a full-
time writer. He has published poems, stories
and novels, including a trilogy featuring
Glasgow detective Jack Laidlaw. His novel
Docherty (1975) won the Whitbread Prize.

By the time I was born the family connection with Ireland was
already a ghost, manifesting intermittently and hazily in old songs
and musty stories. At New Year my sister might sing 'The Donegal
Wedding' or an uncle give us what he remembered of 'Come Back,
Paddy Reilly'. In retrospect my uncle's missing words could be seen
as symbolic of how far time had eroded any living sense of Ireland
among us. Like an old manuscript rotted with age, the oral record
was patchy at best and sometimes completely illegible. Family
anecdotes could be so vague that they sometimes spawned variant
versions of themselves and began to recede into the mist of legend.

One of my favourites told of my great grandfather (on my father's
side) coming over alone to the West of Scotland to labour in the
building trade. He got a job in Kilmarnock and was said to sleep in
one of the builder's sheds until he could save enough money to
bring his family over. I liked that one. Isn't it good to have a bit of
heroic endeavour in your background, then? I'm proud of the great
grandfather and will admit of no variant to that particular story.
(One of the good things about being working class was always that,
the record being so fragmentary, you could always more or less
choose your geneology by selecting the good bits.)

But, vague though it may be, I've always been glad the Irish
dimension is there in me, as it is for so many in Scotland. I've long
believed that the positive contribution of the Irish to the nature of
Scottishness has been sorely undervalued. The two together, it
seems to me, make a seriously lively blend of thoughtfulness and
spontaneity, merging in an ability to confront the darkness of life
and enjoy it at the same time. So while I am, as my mother has
often described herself, Scots tae the backbane and an inch o' the
marra, the fact that there is some residual Irish blood circulating
somewhere in the veins can only be a good thing.

Docherty

THE rocking-chair interested Conn – worn, discoloured, chipped at parts, it somehow conveyed to him a sense of other places as well as other times. Whenever he had the chance, he liked to sit in it, gathering speed, as if it were a means of transport. But he didn't very often get the chance. It was the only piece of furniture his Grandpa Docherty had brought with him and the old man almost lived in it, like a private room. When Tam started to call it 'the jaunting car', Conn was puzzled, until he noticed how often his Grandpa talked about Ireland from it, as if he was still seeing it.

The chair was the last prop for the old man's pride. Hurt by the knowledge that it had taken the family renegade and his Protestant wife to save him from the poorhouse, he continued to convince himself, with commendable inventiveness, that as long as he had the chair he was less a non-paying lodger than a sub-tenant. Swaying gently in it, he would disappear for an hour at a time into martyred silence on which the inscription read: 'Far be it from me to be a nuisance to anyone.' It was precisely at such times that his presence tended to irritate. A question met with a response the tired gentleness of which was a remonstrance. Carefully judged attempts to bring him into the conversation were foiled by the deafness which afflicted him in unpredictable phases, sometimes coming and going by the minute. Tam diagnosed him as suffering from 'politician's lugs'.

Jenny was best at dealing with him. Her success lay in the way she combined a readiness to accord him privileges with a refusal to grant him concessions. Miraculously, she managed to keep him supplied from the housekeeping with money for tobacco and the clay pipes he smoked it in. She didn't buy them for him. Every other day, the money appeared on the mantelpiece, and was enough to get him the occasional glass of beer he took as well. It was never mentioned after the first evening when she told him what it was for, and she never handed it directly to him. It might as well have come from an anonymous benefactor. At the same time, she wasn't inclined to spend a lot of attention on his huffs. Her ability to ignore them made them happen in a void, so that he was glad to come out of them.

When others wanted to complain about him, Jenny would remind them of his hands, as if they were justification enough for any mood. Before, Conn had always been conscious of the hugeness of his Grandpa's hands. Now they were crippled with arthritis, making him unfit for work. Grotesquely gnarled and knobbed, they seemed only distantly related to his arms, projecting from them like pieces of monumental sculpture. 'It's in the breed,' Old Conn would explain. But Tam, who in his wilder moments would have blamed the weather on the wealthy, claimed they were the result of his work with Kerr the builder. There was a certain amount of proxy justice in Tam's statement. Kerr had worked Old Conn for a pittance all his life and, when he couldn't work any more, had dismissed him with a handshake in which all that changed hands was sweat, not Kerr's. When his father was dead, Tam used to say, they should have the hands mounted and presented to Kerr. 'For above his bloody mantelpiece.'

Once settled in, the old man came to seem not so much a new presence as the acknowledgement of one that had always been there, as the figure of a madonna merely locates an already existing influence. With him ensconced every day beside the fire, the mystique of venerability had difficulty surviving the manual clumsiness, the hoasting, the simply boring repetitiousness of his talk.

Only Conn perhaps felt something like awe, for a short time. He was fascinated by the hands filling the pipe, moving separately like misshapen crabs, the small swirl of sound that began somewhere inside, enlarged slowly, broke in a storm of coughing, the complete stillness which the old man could achieve within the motion of his chair. Also, he was the one his Grandpa liked to talk to. Secretly, Old Conn was paying for his keep by being subversive. Indoors, he talked of Ireland to his youngest grandson, trying to convey to him the sense of Connemara, which had become the landscape of his own mind – those miles of unremitting barrenness through which the rocks rise up like headstones. But outside, on the frequent walks when he took Conn 'up the country', he was trying to save the boy from the Protestant limbo in which he lived. He catechised him in the nature of God, spoke familiarly enough of hell to have been there, kept putting the rosary into his hands. Always before they came back to the house, Conn would be reminded of the need for secrecy, as if God were the head of a cabal.

It would all have affected Conn more deeply if it hadn't been for the counter-influence of his Grandpa Wilson. He too, needing to tighten his grasp on something before it loosened forever, moved closer to Conn, like a rival planet. His love of town rather than country exerted more power.

To walk through Graithnock with Mairtin was to be ambushed at every corner by the past. From the fluted pillar inset in the wall of the Old High Kirk 'To the memory of Lord Soulis AD 1444' (of whose murder Mairtin was able to give an eye-witness account) to the house of Alexander Smith in Douglas Street ('a genius wi' words' of whom Mairtin hadn't read a line) the town came alive with ghosts. The industrial school was still to him what it had been – 'The Place', Graithnock House, residence of the last Earl of Graithnock, executed for his part in the '45 Rebellion after having unsuccessfully demanded that the citizens of Graithnock supply him with their arms. Mairtin liked to repeat how the local people had informed the Earl that if they gave him their guns it would be 'with the muzzle till him.' Graithnock, Mairtin said with pride, had always been loyal to the crown.

From Mairtin Conn learned of 'The Soor Mulk Rebellion' of almost a hundred years ago, when housewives drenched baillies and farmers in milk at the Cross, rather than pay the increased prices the farmers were demanding. He discovered who Tam

Samson was. He found out that thirty people had once been crushed to death in the old Laigh Kirk during a panic when the congregation thought the roof was falling in. He memorised, like a mystic message of grandeur, the words: 'Here lies John Nisbet who was taken by Major Balfour's Party and suffered at Graithnock 14 April 1683 for adhering to the word of God and our Covenant – Revn. XII and II. Renewed by public subscription AD 1823.' 'Who was taken . . . and suffered' – the words haunted him.

The best story of all was the one Mairtin told about the Foregate. When he was a boy, he said, there had been a two-storeyed thatched house there. When they were knocking it down, one of the workmen had found a leather pouch concealed under the thatch. As he lifted it out, it burst, and in seconds people were scrambling in the street for the hoard of silver coins that had scattered. The coins belonged to the reigns of Charles I and Charles II. How had they come there? 'Only the grave kens,' Mairtin would say.

With that ability to conjure exotic past out of mundane present Grandpa Docherty couldn't compete. Conn found himself joining with Angus in a conspiracy of mild laughter at the old man. They liked him but got into the habit of not taking him seriously. Angus was inclined to bait him a little, encouraging him to talk about Ireland. He would have done so more often if Mick hadn't been aware of Angus's tendency and stifled it whenever he saw it asserting itself.

Mick was almost certainly the one affected most by his grandfather's arrival. It clarified his understanding of himself and his family. Mick was naturally an accepter of the way things were, not spinelessly, or mindlessly, but just because he believed that was the only way you could make anything of them. He had a capacity for refining the raw shape his life had inherited into a personal pattern, and enjoying it, so that the drab necessity for work, for example, heightened his leisure-time rather than stultified it. Consequently, the discontent of someone like his father occasionally irked him and frequently puzzled him. Through countless long arguments with Tam, which Mick had incidentally enjoyed, he had tried to formulate what he meant, to explain why he didn't share his father's fervour for change. He had never quite succeeded.

But in his grandfather, when he came to live with them, he saw his argument incarnate. Mick admired the old man very much. In everything from his arthritis to his love of Ireland, Mick found the same quality – the ability to accept necessity and make it a part of himself. It didn't matter if you didn't believe that Catholicism was true. Mick himself had stopped going to church because it had come to mean nothing to him. But the point was that it was true for Old Conn, as everything about him was. There was nothing that for Mick could imaginably have been different. He felt his grandfather had become what he inevitably had to be. Accordingly, he lived amicably with himself, the pain in his hands, his poverty, his exile. By accepting his troubles, he was able to extract daily from their bitterness, as by an age-old, secret process, the dram of comfort that made his living worthwhile.

His insight into Old Conn gave Mick a perspective on the rest of his family, he felt. He saw his grandfather as having inherited from his early rural life the talent for enduring as simply as a tree, twisted by the winds, perhaps, stunted even, but still there. What his father lacked, having been born in an industrial town, was that simple acceptance. To Mick, Old Conn had a patriarchal authority, offered a way of life to them, not through his words, which were often almost nonsensical, but by being as he was.

But it was an authority to which Mick's young brothers seemed impervious. There was a brief spell not long after Old Conn came to live with them when their disrespect threatened to become open. It took one of Tam's cauterising expressions of anger to cure them.

Old Conn had been talking about Skibbereen. He did that a lot. It held some obscure but fundamental significance for him that made him invoke it every so often. When someone mentioned present hardships, Old Conn had a habit of saying, 'Aye. How are things in Skib then?' as if that somehow put everything else in perspective. He referred much to the mass grave there and sometimes would allow you to persuade him to sing 'Revenge for

Skibbereen', lack of breath erasing half-lines, garbling words. The effect was of listening to someone far away in a shifting wind.

On this night he talked himself towards a peroration: 'The blight, ye see. But the blight wisny jist in the grund. It wis in the folk as weel. The nabarry. Their leavin's wid've saved lives. But naw. Fur want of a tattie they died.'

Angus and Conn could hardly stop laughing. Apart from the natural tendency of solemnity to induce hysteria in them, there was the fact that Angus had been doing a secret imitation of the old man's expressions and gestures. Conn, trying to swallow his amusement, noticed Angus coming nearer and nearer to the state that his mother called 'Gettin' above yerself'. As if to demonstrate the accuracy of Conn's observation, Angus spoke.

'It wid hiv tae've been an awfu' big tattie. Wid it no', Grandpa?'

Angus brayed once with laughter and Conn irresistibly echoed him.

'Hey!' Their father crumpled the paper he was trying to read. 'D'ye ken who ye're talkin' tae?'

He stared at them steadily. The rain falling beyond the window behind him slicked the room in grey light. Conn felt the charge of shock that meant incontrovertibly they had crossed a border, trespassed where they shouldn't be.

'Dae ye?' He paused, his eyes angry. 'This is a man that kens whit he's talkin' aboot. He's had times when there wis nothin' tae eat but air. An' he came through them. An' if he hadny, you two widny be here. Show them yer hauns, feyther. Show them! Ye see that? Ye ken hoo they goat like that?'

'Workin' wi' the bricks,' Conn suggested.

'Wi' pittin' the bite in ma mooth. An' that means yours as weel. An' don't you forget it. That's a man ye're talkin' tae. No' a bloody bit o' furniture. Ya pair o' yelps!'

'Och, feyther,' Kathleen said. His anger was becoming ridiculously disproportionate. 'Ye've said yerself ma Grandpa goes oan aboot Ireland at an awfu' rate.'

'Whit if Ah have? An' you're another yin. Lady Muck. Ah've heard ye complainin' aboot the mess o' the fire-end wi' him. This is a hoose. No' a hotel. An' if Ah fa' oot wi' him aboot Ireland, well, that's a private argument.' He looked round them all. 'An' jist all of ye remember. He's where ye come fae. An' whaurever ye go, ye'll have tae take 'im wi' ye.'

They sat welded into a group by his words, the rain corroding their silence. Having turned a casual evening into a family manifesto, Tam smoothed out his paper and resumed staring at it. Angus watched him opaquely. Kathleen huffed. The old man rose slowly. 'Well. Ah'm doon the entry-mooth fur a breath o' air.'

When he was gone, Conn remained hypnotised by the rocking of his empty chair. Its motion without presence gave it a quality of mysterious power. By the time it was still, it had impressed the image of itself on Conn with a force greater than works, a part of his personal heraldry.

from Docherty (Allen & Unwin, 1975)

The Graveyard at Skibbereen
'In memory of the victims of the famine 1845-48
whose coffinless bodies were buried in this plot.'

Here's element: the core, truth touching bone.
Pity has locked with hopelessness and holds
A primal stance, engaging hills and sky,
Rain and river in mutual dystrophy.
Here place has reared its own Rosetta stone:
A plaque trying to talk above wind and weather.

Nobody comes. The rain ages the river
But in play. The rocky hill has weathered to a skull.
Nature's a subtle mockery of us,
Shows us symbols of our enduring passion
Which feel nothing. Everything changes,
Nothing is changed.

Nobody comes. Rain rots the gate
The wind creaks open, admitting nothing
To the cold empty centre of it all
With wind for its only borders.
Yet nature observes the rules, even here maintains
The grist of dreams, hawks the heart amulets.
Flowers protest remembrance, although withered.
On the ledge of the sculpted stone a clutch of pebbles
Measures a child's hand, seems to gift innocence.
Rain drips from a straw-twisted crucifix,
Is blood or tears — imagination's choice.

But nobody comes. The game's too sad and complex.
For who could excavate this tumulus

And read these ghosted people from their bones,
Tell strong from weak, whose hands were best to make,
Whose red hair kindled eyes, what shape was growing,
What voices were struck dumb,
What mother's hopes were buried with her body?
The drunken and the sober share each other.
Humanity absolved them of itself.
Because some people lived, these had to die.

Who knows more reason? Who would dare decipher
A meaning from the emptiness, decide
What prejudices kept their need denied,
Whose absences committed a mass murder,
What comfortable arses snuffed the sun,
Whose cultured hands fed gaping mouths with dirt?
They're gone, have turned down private corridors,
Leaving an absent-minded mound of dead.
No doubt they had their worries too, no doubt.

Nature is soothing, shrugs to an innocent hill,
Spreading two feet of grass above the past,
Brings numbness in the intravenous rain,
Making the plaque look silly, shouting at void.
Nothing is here. An old man and a boy
Trot past in a pony-trap. Two perfections of swan
Study their white reflections in the river.

So nobody comes, nor need they, nor should come.
For each in his own sky knows how this grass
Tufts in the wind on its wart of hill and this place
Swells like a tumour.
And we are dying still of Skibbereen.

Brannigan's Song to the Wall of his Room

(While, smiling from his private doom,
The groom's father's cousin, Brannigan,
Irish as Guinness, is practising
In some sealed chamber of his head
Where all his boyhood hopes lie dead
The song, drunk as a skunk, he sings to the wall of his room.)

No woman softens what I feel
No child makes me a home.
I am a house of blazing lights
To which no one has come.
My father ploughed a bitter field
But I am ploughing stone.
I cuddle a great emptiness,
My dreams all live alone.

My dreams all live alone.
I'm married to the shovel now.
It's a heathenish affair.
A roster is my rosary,
Communion's bitter beer.
Give me a horse, I'll show you how —
It's tractors over here —
By Jesus, I could plough.

By Jesus, I could plough.
The field was by the sea.
There was a girl with haystack hair
Once sat across my knee.
I wonder if she's here the now,
I wonder if she'll marry me,
I wonder if she'll have my child.
Tomorrow, then, we'll see.

from These Words: Weddings and After
(Mainstream 1984)

STEPHEN MULRINE
(b.1937)

Born Glasgow, his work includes poetry,
plays, scripts for television and radio, and
translation (especially of Russian drama).
From 1975–95 he was extra-mural creative
writing tutor at Glasgow University.

Reflections

Some years ago, in a Radio Scotland series on immigrant communities, the estimable Billy Kay observed that around 20% of Glaswegians were not only of Irish, but specifically Donegal extraction,
which my own background confirms. My paternal grandfather
arrived in Glasgow as a young sprig from Donegal, just in time to
cut stone for the Mount Florida tenements, and I remember him as
a tall, bent man, with drooping whiskers, unintelligibly rapid
speech, and the patience of a saint, looking on benignly while I
stripped the tomato and pea plants he tended with such devotion
in his Possilpark allotment. He died when I was ten, and he remains
the best of my childhood Irish memories.

As for the rest, the product of a mixed marriage, and the eldest of
five, it was my lot to undergo a Catholic education, while my
younger siblings, the lesson learned, all went to 'normal', i.e.
Protestant, schools. At my primary and secondary both, 'Irishism'
was de rigueur, prescribing allegiances from politics to football, and
I was an early apostate – supporting Partick Thistle was not simply
eccentric, it was heretical. My recollections of that period are
mixed, and the tyranny which passed for pedagogy in the 1940s
and 50s seemed even more oppressive in Catholic schools. The
Lochgelly was particularly fearsome, jerked out from under a
soutane, and the sins it was deployed against included not knowing
the colour of the priest's vestments at Sunday Mass. That was the
subject of an inquisition on Monday mornings, when I survived a
few close calls, thanks to an informative little missal I had been
given, ironically, as a school prize.

Beyond the school gates all my friends were Protestants, and
'outsiderhood', the natural state of the writer, came early. I knew

all the sectarian songs by heart (the necessity to fit in makes for a quick learner), and could probably still do a turn at a Rangers social. Within school, which my heathen chums regarded as a sink of superstition and obscurantism, though they expressed it more succinctly, I acquired a decent education, along with an aversion to black robes, steel-rimmed glasses, and the colour purple. That I still associate with spring term Mariolatry seances, held in a candle-lit classroom reeking of incense, draped in purple velvet, and filled with white lilies. Aleister Crowley would have loved it – I hated it.

Irishness was thus synonymous with alienation, and my mental images of Ireland were all of rural poverty and backwardness – it was a place people escaped from in search of work and the right to think freely, only to acquire fresh grievances, second-class citizen-ship among them, to add to the ancient wrongs. Later, my first encounter with the island itself was Belfast, where I served for a time in the RAF, and formed the conclusion that yes, indeed, there were worse places than Glasgow. My ancestral voices, I now realise, were to a considerable degree muted by those early experiences, and in rejecting them, much was lost. Accordingly, I owe a very great deal to my wife's late mother, born and bred in Co. Longford, for a truer picture of the country, the warmth and natural courtesy of its people, wherever the four winds may have scattered them.

In fact, not until a few years ago did I set foot on the holy ground proper, and became an overnight hibernophile. Prejudice after prejudice melted away, as we criss-crossed the Republic, marvelling at its prosperity and self-assurance, moved by its beauty, and the generosity of its welcome. In Donegal, where at least one of my grandfather's kin hung on to make a go of it, we passed an articu-lated lorry bearing its cargo of 'Mulrine's Soft Drinks', and in the bog country, where my wife still has many relatives, and where people once ate children, the landscape is strewn with dazzling white-painted ranch-houses, like a verdant Texas. I have discovered Ireland late, unfortunately, in the guise of tourist, rather than returned prodigal, but while I speak as a native Scot, I wish no country on earth a brighter future than the land of my fathers. God knows, they deserve it.

Geraldine

BUNCHING firewood, at threepence the dozen bunches, wasn't much of a job. Old Shanks was a noted miser, and his son was almost as bad, even if he dressed better. And if the RSPCA ever got close to that horse of theirs, well. . .

The most disgusting sight Owen had ever experienced was Auld Boaby the horse, with a cold. It was indescribable, unless you wanted to turn people's stomachs, over their hot peas.

Going out on the cart with Boaby, on a Saturday, when the Shanks made their deliveries, was supposed to be a privilege. There was no going rate, but if you'd worked in the yard regularly during the week, and hadn't been carrying on, Shanks would let you ride up, while he swore at everything that moved, between Duke Street and Springburn. He sold firewood to about fifty shops, in three-dozen crates, and at the end of the run there would be a half-crown for the hired hands, in addition to whatever in kind, sweets or comics, they received from the shopkeepers. Good Catholic boys, of course, never stole.

Harry Reynolds had the economics of William Shanks and Son off pat.

'It's exploitation, Owen. Real Shaftesbury stuff. He's gettin twelve bob a crate, and he peys us thruppence a dozen – that's ninepence outlay. Plus he gets the wid fur nuthin, affa demolition sites, ur floatin doon the kinawl. An Aul Boaby's hauf-starved, ye kin see fur yirsel.'

Boaby's ribs, it was true, showed alarmingly, and there never seemed to be anything in its nosebag.

'Barrin you-know-what,' said Harry, with wicked emphasis.

'Whit aboot rent an rates? Overheads.'

The Shanks' yard lay alongside the Monkland Canal, a

ramshackle stockade of old doors and railway sleepers. Yard, and next day's work for the saw, were barely distinguishable. The notion of paying rates on the place, Harry dismissed out of hand.

'Electricity, then.'

'Right, right, I grant you. Enough electricity tae power the saw, an a forty-watt bulb so's us poor sods don't chop wur fingers aff. That's yir overheads. An the rest's profit. Twelve hunner percent, at a conservative estimate.'

Owen thought the Shanks, father and son, unlikely capitalists.

'Don't let the auld claes fool ye. Hiv ye seen wherr they stey?'

'Ay, sure – up a close, same as us.'

Harry snorted derisively.

'Who tellt ye that?'

'Harry, Ah've seen thum. Ah know thur address.'

'Ach.'

Harry spat across Boaby's pitiful rump.

'You're simple.'

'An ye know whit you are, Harry – you're a Communist.'

'That's right. A Socialist. It's ma auld man that writes the *Reynolds News.*'

Harry was a year ahead of Owen at school, and respected no-one. He kept a cobbler's awl in his pocket, for protection, he said.

'It's fur Brother Michael's wanderin hauns. Course hazards.'

Owen couldn't believe him, and Harry shrugged.

'You'll see. Ah'll pass it oan tae ye at Christmas, when Ah leave. Ye'll need it.'

Harry was casually determined to quit school before Highers. The fifth-year sang Mass every Friday, he said, and he was having none of it. He was joining no Confraternity of the Sacred Heart, either, and that was next to blasphemy.

'Course the auld man'll no let us leave, but Ah'll jist convince him. Mess up a coupla exams.'

'Whit're ye gonny work at?'

Harry fielded the question.

'Trapeze artist, same as ma maw. Owen son, it's sheer chance.

If yir name's on the bullet. . .'

He shrugged.

'Ah think Ah'll start ma ain firewid business, gie these two some competition. Coupla hunner yards upstream, skim aff aw the best wid afore it reaches them. Buy a motor – any aul clapped-oot wreck'd be quicker than Boaby – get roon aw the shoaps furst. Ah'll take ye intae partnership. Actually, that's whit Ah'm daein this fur – groanin under the yoke. Ah'm workin undercover, learnin the ropes. D'ye no believe me? Eh? A fellow-traveller, sharin yir breid?'

Harry certainly knew the ropes. Neither of them cared much for the Saturday run. Harry resented humping the crates, for a measly half-crown, and Owen disliked the exposure. Their route skirted Riddrie, and Owen was afraid of being spotted by some of his wealthier classmates. If that ever happened, the Shanks' cart would be as good as a tumbril, headed for a sure agony, on Monday morning.

Still, when it came to chopping and bunching sticks, Harry had no peer. The Shanks never let anyone touch the saw, and one or other, usually Peter, would feed the wood through the saw-guides, across the grain, in six-inch widths: doors, old floor-boards, combustible rubbish of all kinds, as fast as he could lift it onto the saw-table. At the other end, sitting with a hand-axe and a block, the boys received the cut wood and chopped it diagonally, so the sticks would bunch tighter, into a zinc bath. Harry worked so fast, his axe a blur, that he could keep up even with both Shanks, father and son, feeding the saw in tandem.

Once the bath was full, it would be emptied onto a bench, and the sticks scooped up in handfuls to be compressed in a kind of circular clamp, for tying. When the clamp was released, the tightly-trussed bunch was placed in a crate, and the whole operation, twelve times repeated, earned the boys threepence.

It wasn't much of a job, even for part-time, but it paid for illicit cigarettes, the café or the pictures, occasionally even the skating, at Crossmyloof Ice Rink. Owen liked his mother to come to him for a 'tap', besides, after the weekend. It made staying on at school seem less egocentric.

Harry rarely mentioned his parents, except to pour scorn on their ambitions for him.

'A teacher, he says, as if there's no enough a them. Chalk in yir arteries, yir blood turns tae distemper.'

Curiously, he didn't smoke. He had enough bad habits, he said, though he didn't swear either.

'Wan a these days Ah'll get really cross, then ye'll hear.'

Owen never heard, and the only thing that upset Harry was the rats, which infested the yard, being on the canalside. After dark, if you sat quiet for a while, the scuttling and squeaking got so brazen that you half expected an army of them, at any moment, to burst out from behind the dozen or so doors that always lay about the shed, their red eyes glittering with blood-lust. They scared Harry stiff, and he was never silent, chopping or talking without pause, until old Shanks came back from the pub to lock up.

The yard had a regular turnover of boys. The piece-work, and the dismal environment, made it among the least desirable of jobs, worse even than a winter milk-round. It wasn't a patch on fruit-picking, Harry said, either for money, girls, or vitamin C. He had an aunt in Blairgowrie, and he'd picked raspberries there during the holidays.

'Thruppence a pound, Owen. Baith hauns, intae a wee luggie – that's a bucket tied roon yir waist. They make thum intae dye fur sailors' uniforms. Nae kiddin. Navy blue, yir airms navy blue right up tae the oaxters. Ye kin make ten bob in a day.'

And the Perthshire girls, with their brown skins and sing-song voices, were no match for a smart Glaswegian.

Harry had a sister, who went to Charlotte Street School. It didn't sound like a boast, but he was quick to amend.

'They wur gonny send me tae Saint Aloysius, but they couldnae afford anuther blazer. See this . . .' the flashing axe paused, and he laughed. 'This peys fur Geraldine's.'

Owen helped him empty the bath onto the bench, and Harry

went on, generously. 'Ye should come doon fur her some weekend, take her tae the skatin. She's your type, but she needs bringin oot. Don't want they nuns addlin her brain.'

Owen agreed, but the idea of asking any girl out – of making it plain that you fancied them – terrified him. Most of all, he envied Harry's easy way with them, the ones in Silvio's, for instance, just down from the yard, where they sometimes went for coffee, or a plate of peas. Harry could call a girl 'darling' or 'sweetheart', and make her blush, and he always knew the right things to say. They seemed trivial to Owen, though, and envy was tinged with disappointment, both in the girls, and this denatured, fawning Harry. It must have shown.

'Well, ye've goat tae chat them up, brek doon thur innate reserve. Whit d'ye want, Owen, the Immaculate Conception?'

Owen would have settled for the body and blood, but he daren't admit it. Like most Catholic boys, they regarded sex as abstracted from people – the Flesh, with its burden of sin. Protestant co-education, Owen thought, was worth any number of Masses, and there was something desperate about even Harry's performance.

Harry always walked home alone, at any rate. He could take a shortcut through the Necropolis, he said, and Owen wouldn't fancy that. Owen, his nightmares filled with the undead, certainly didn't, and he visited Harry's house only once, keeping to the road, though the circumstances were gloomy enough.

You couldn't easily get the sack from Shanks' yard. Boys drifted in and out, week to week, on a casual basis, bunching enough sticks for five Woodbines and collecting their pay on the spot. And neither of the Shanks took enough notice of their workforce to invite insolence. Old Shanks, beyond the form jibe about 'Tims', or 'left-footers', kept his conversation strictly business. So too, minus religion, did his colourless son. As Harry observed, mock-offended, 'Even Hitler liked kids and animals.'

So when old Shanks terminated Harry's employment it came as a surprise. Owen, a bystander, saw it as a clash of wills, on an icy

Saturday morning, with Boaby frantic on the Drygate cobbles, and too little charity about.

Old Shanks was already a lit fuse by the time he got the cart stopped, at Stanley's General Stores, and in no mood to be summoned, by Miss Stanley herself, after the boys had carried in the usual three-dozen crate. She wanted to complain, of course.

Like most small shopkeepers she kept her returnable empties, bleach, and lemonade bottles, ready for collection behind the door. Harry had been on the point of lifting two, she said, on his way out. True enough, Owen had heard the bottles clink, and it was a common enough ploy – passing them off in another shop, collecting fourpence and two more bottles for the next, relay-fashion. Harry based a theory of economics on it, but he didn't engage, he said, for political reasons.

However, worse than the bottles, Miss Stanley swore there had been money taken – the right money for twenty Capstan and a paper – left on the counter by a customer in a hurry. She'd just turned her back, she said, before ringing it up. The ginger-haired one was last to leave the shop, it must have been him. She was losing stock every Saturday, she said, bottles full and empty, comics, liquorice sticks, what-have-you – firewood was just too expensive at that rate, and he needn't come back. She was practically spitting in old Shanks' face. Firelighters took up less room, anyway, for more profit.

Old Shanks near enough dragged Harry down from the cart. Boys couldn't be trusted, and Tims, with confession to absolve them, were the worst of the lot. Education only made them more arrogant. Peter Shanks, the voice of compromise, was for Harry turning out his pockets. Harry swore at him, refused, and that was that. Reynolds was finished, as far as the Shanks were concerned, and he could count himself lucky not to be talking to the police.

Harry didn't even wait to retrieve Miss Stanley's unwanted crate, and Owen spent a miserable afternoon completing the deliveries with Peter Shanks. The latter, by way of atonement, was almost friendly to Owen, asking him about school and so on, and offering him a cigarette when they had finished. Old Shanks, dry-mouthed, had already gone off to the pub. Boaby was out of harness, and stood pathetically snuffling into a half pail of chopped oats, his Saturday treat. Shanks asked Owen if he could manage earlier on Monday night, Owen said he'd try, and the conversation ran out. After a few more puffs, he reached into his waistcoat pocket and handed Owen two half-crowns. Owen thanked him then, and left, more relieved than grateful.

Outside, on the canal bridge, the thought that his good fortune was at Harry's expense oppressed him, and he stood for a while dropping stones into the water, where sprigs of ice were already lancing out from the banks. Five shillings was a lot, and Harry might, after all, have taken Miss Stanley's money. Disgusted with himself, Owen turned and headed down Castle Street towards the Necropolis, walking at first, then running.

Harry's door, on a gaslit top landing, was the worst in the close, its woodgrain paint a mass of blisters, and an absurd floral pelmet over the fanlight. Through the half-landing window, gravestones and mausoleums rose to the horizon, and Owen imagined scrambling in terror up three storeys, pursued by a legion of fiends, to that tightly-shut door and a bell that obviously rang nowhere.

He was about to give up, and post the half-crown through the letter-box, when he heard the first of three locks being turned. When the door eventually opened, a girl of about thirteen stood in the hall. She looked surprised, and turned away to switch on a light.

Owen didn't speak, and his voice, if he managed to ask for Harry, must have come from someone else. Geraldine, he knew immediately, was the most beautiful human being he would ever see. The experience of a vision, like Bernadette's at Lourdes, could have been no more electrifying, and Owen was ready to believe, in blind faith.

Geraldine had Harry's colouring, the Irish Catholic badge, but her braided coppery hair and perfect skin belonged to a higher evolutionary stage, and Owen could hardly conceive of her walking the earth, let alone being Harry's sister. The modest brown and blue of Charlotte Street expressed her completely, and if she had stood before him in shining raiment, Owen would have worshipped no more fervently.

The vision spoke, and Owen learned that Harry had gone to Crossmyloof, in mid-afternoon. He should have been home for his tea, but he might have gone on to the pictures. She would tell him Owen had called.

While she spoke, Owen's mind raced ahead in panic – he should ask her name, at the very least, what year she was in, did she ever go skating? But he couldn't. She knew his unspoken thoughts, their triteness, what was the point? He thanked her, and she closed the door. At the half-landing, in the eerie light from the broken mantle, he looked out and envied the dead. He had forgotten to give her the money.

Harry was grateful enough, on the Monday; it revived his faith in human nature, he said, and he apologised for being out. He made no mention of Geraldine, Owen thought deliberately, and they went their separate ways in school, like conspirators. . . A few weeks later, at Christmas, Harry left, as he had promised. He found a job as a trainee salesman, in a gents' outfitters, and when Owen next saw him he had applied to sit the exam for Customs and Excise. Owen, meantime, went on to higher things.

He never saw Geraldine again, and except on a rare occasion, never wanted to. There was no need. The damage was done.

from Scottish Review 25 (1982)

ANNE DOWNIE
(b. 1939)

Writes for TV. Broadcast work includes
The Bill, High Road and numerous plays for
BBC Radio 4. She is also an actress.

On Having an Irish Background

As a child I felt confused. Why did we stand up in Holy Cross
Church and sing 'Hail glorious St Patrick, dear saint of our isle.'
Why were we taken to mass on his feast day for a start? Why not
St Andrew? I lived in Scotland, as did my classmates and family. St
Patrick wasn't saint of *my* isle. The only isle I lived on was the
British one and I really didn't feel part of that either. I was Scottish,
before I was anything else. I felt a certain curiosity every year as an
Irish postmarked envelope, varying in size, according to the crop,
came through our letterbox. My farmer cousins never forgot to
send us shamrock. I wore a token sprig and was bemused by some
of my fellow pupils who came to school bearing small bushes in
their lapels, almost trying to outdo one another with their
'Irishness'.

My confusion turned to a faint resentment. My mother, brought up
in Belfast until she was twelve, didn't feel particularly Irish either.
My father was the one who clung to his Irish roots. He was third
generation Irish. The Delaneys (my maiden name) came from
Silvermines, Co. Tipperary, economic immigrants to Scotland. I'm
not sure why we sat through endless Irish dancing festivals, but
some friend or relative of my parents ran the O'Neill school of Irish
dancing and we were dragged along for moral support. It felt alien
to me, but then so did the Mod. I began to feel displaced.

As a teenager I discovered acting. Prior to going to the Royal
Scottish Academy of Music and Drama much later in life, I was in a
Gorbals based drama group, the Greyfriars, in which my father was
a leading light. Most of their early productions were Irish. I was
reared on a diet of 'Boyd's Shop', 'The Far Off Hills Are Green',
'The Righteous Are Bold' etc. The Scottish playwrights were a bit

thin on the ground in the late fifties and Irish plays were received with rapturous applause both by the parishioners of St Francis, to which the group was attached and the wider, mainly Catholic community. Again I was bemused as to why everyone was going on about pretending to be Irish. Where was Scottish culture in all this?

Perhaps it was because we were taken over to Ireland so often on holiday that I almost turned my back on it. Familiarity bred, if not contempt, then a form of indifference but the political strife and killings in the name of religion were anathema to me. I wanted to disassociate myself.

I can remember the moment things began to change. I was sitting in the Theatre Royal watching Brien Friel's play 'Dancing at Lughnasa'. At the moment when the sisters break into wild joyous dance I felt something primeval stirring in me. I wanted to be up there dancing with them. It was as if the cultural inheritance that I had deliberately submerged had come to the surface.

My re-awakened interest in my Irish roots found a corresponding pull for my now Canadian brother who had been over to Silvermines, Co. Tipperary, visiting the birthplace of my great grandparents, who left there for a better life in Scotland. When I read all the disparaging remarks about asylum seekers being branded economic immigrants, as if that was a pejorative term, I think of my ancestors, no doubt meeting with the same hostility when they landed on these shores.

I'm only grateful they persevered.

Deadly Sin

MAEVE raised her leg a fraction off the floor then sat back on her heels to ease the pain. Her hand felt the indentation on her knee where a ridge on the rough stone had cut into the second Sorrowful Mystery. She eyed the distance between herself and the healing strip of carpet in front of the hearth. Two black cats and Dympna, the half-dog, lay stretched out, impervious to the hallowed air around them.

A rebuking finger stabbed her in the shoulder. The girl turned round to find Aunt Bridget fixing her with a disapproving glare while scarcely pausing for breath in the rhythmic chanting of the Hail Mary. Offering her sacrifice up for the Holy Souls, Maeve, once again, placed her knee in the position of torture. By the end of the Rosary, she felt an entire battalion of souls must be winging their way Heavenward, courtesy of her endurance.

'Prayer for the Pope's intention,' said her mother, launching into the 'Our Father'.

'Prayer for Willie Joe McCann,' mumbled Uncle Seumas.

'And Maura McShane, who's overdue,' her sister added, not to be outdone.

'Prayer for King Edward to give up that married woman,' Aunt Bridget intoned, throwing herself into the *Memorare* with a relish totally lacking in religious fervour. That the Duke of Windsor had made his choice many years before was no reason, in Aunt Bridget's estimation, for admitting defeat.

When the spiritual needs of what seemed like half the villagers of Ballymoran and their former sovereign had been attended to, Maeve was the first to rise, rubbing her now misshapen knee.

'Be sure and confess your distraction to Canon Brady!' Aunt Bridget's tight little mouth almost smiled, anticipating the severity of the old priest's penance.

'Indeed and I won't!' Maeve responded spiritedly. 'I was kneelin' on a bump! My knee was in agony!'

'Our Blessed Lord had nails through His!' Bridget's tone suggested, somehow, that Maeve had personally wielded the mallet!

The girl bit back an angry reply. With a sense of victory, Bridget picked up Dympna and tucked the dog under her bony arm. Maeve turned her head away. The dog's mutilated stumps always aroused a feeling of revulsion within her. That dog is disgustin'! She almost spoke her thoughts aloud. It should have been put down right after the accident!

The memory of that day had etched itself deeply in Maeve's young mind, Aunt Bridget's hysterical screams drowning out Uncle Seumas's earnest protestations.

'I didn't see her, Bridget. . . How could I?' . . . then 'You knew I was threshing! You shouldn't have let her run wild!'

Bridget's ears were deaf to his words. The weight of grief and guilt made her sink to the ground. The pathetic bundle of matted fur whimpered in her arms as she rocked back and forth. Seumas turned on his heel and left. Bridget cradled the dog to her breast, wrapping it in her cardigan which was quickly suffused with a bright red stain. A hand reached out for the dog. Seumas was back, hunting rifle under his arm. 'Come on, Bridget! Let me put her out of her misery!' Bridget's cry of rage witnessed that her senses had returned.

Over the next few months, she nursed the dog back to health, lavishing all the love and attention once sealed within her body. A love that might have been given to her child, if she could have overcome her fear of men. Bridget's obsessional devotion was now directed at Dympna. The unfortunate animal was subjected to the changing whims of an ageing spinster, who dressed it daily in a variety of ribbons and necklaces; a fate no whole dog would hang around long enough to endure.

Maeve hadn't actually said she was going to Benediction, she told herself, as she quickened her step past the goose-pen. It wasn't her fault if that's what they all assumed! A hissing noise behind her told her she'd been spotted. She broke into a run as an irate mother, yellow balls of fluff teetering drunkenly in her wake, temporarily abandoned her brood to give chase.

'HERE, JUMP!' a voice shouted as she struggled with the wire catch over the gate post. Her arms were grabbed and she was hoisted over. Charlie let go his grip and grinned at her. On the other side of the gate, her pursuer hissed and spat impotently.

'If that was mine,' said Charlie, indicating the goose, 'I'd have her with spuds!'

'She's O.K.!' Maeve shrugged.

'Is she hell!' Charlie was vehement. 'She near had the ankles off us!'

'She thinks you're after her goslings, that's all.' Maeve walked away, fearful that she could be seen from Aunt Bridget's room, at the back of the house.

'She's wrong there,' he grinned. 'It's you I'm after! . . . Didn't think you'd come!'

'And why wouldn't I?' Maeve's tone was defiant.

'Ah, well . . . you see . . . I'm really dangerous. . . Not just a huffer and puffer like your oul' goose there!'

'Don't believe you!' She looked hard at him for evidence to the contrary.

'And why not?' He pulled her down beside him on the grass. She was grateful for the large oak tree obscuring them from prying eyes.

'Just a feeling.' Despite her words, she edged away slightly, keeping a respectable distance between them.

'You think they put you away for missin' Mass, do you? The smile had left his face.

'They haven't 'put you away'. It's not prison!'

'What would you call Saint Peter's Reformatory, then?' A note of bitterness had crept into his voice.

'Well . . . I mean . . . I don't see any guards over you.'

'Said I needed a pee! There's some things they let you do on your own!'

Maeve's clandestine meetings with Charlie became a nightly occurrence. 'They'll be thinkin' I've a weak bladder!' he laughed. She found it easy to talk to him, and as for Charlie, Brother Dominic would have been amazed! 'A fella of few words' was how he labelled the boy, but with Maeve, he really opened up. He even told her of his crime, something that had been locked in the dark recesses of his mind, for the four years since it happened.

He'd meant to kill his father, no matter what they said! When Charlie heard screams and saw his sisters cowering in terror that night, nothing 'snapped in his fourteen year old mind' as his Defence put it. Instead, he saw what he had to do with chilling clarity. He was a good shot. He had to be! His marksmanship had to put food in the family's belly, since their meat money regularly lined the till in Frank Dougan's public house. He'd killed dozens of rabbits, but a man was different. You had to hit the right spot. He looked at his mother's cut lip and swollen eye, then took quick, but careful, aim, as his father lunged towards him. A line from *Macbeth*, learnt at school, came incongruously into the boy's mind . . . 'Yet who would have thought the old man to have so much blood in him'. His only regret was that the sentence in the Remand Home meant his mother was denied the family's only potential wage earner. She would have to scrape a living for them on her own. But sure hadn't she always done that! His father had squandered what little they had. The family had wanted for everything. At least now, they could live without terror.

It wasn't until Maeve was making up the pig fodder, almost two months late, that she realised retribution for her sin had been exacted. As she squeezed the hot potatoes through her fingers, carefully mixing in the bran, her stomach heaved. She ran out of the boiler room and gulped in lungfuls of fresh air. The sickly sweet smell of the bran mash drifted through the open door, and a fresh wave of nausea hit her.

'What's the matter with you?' Bridget appeared suddenly in the yard in front of her, Dympna tucked, as usual, under her arm.

'Nothing!' Maeve turned away. Dympna's acquamarine beads always reminded her of the poster in Miss McNulty's geography class, 'The Bay of Naples'. She tried to concentrate hard on that beautiful blue-green sea, forcing the memory of the animal feed from her mind.

'Hmm . . . she's a funny colour isn't she, my love?' The dog closed her eyes in complete indifference.

'I'm hungry, that's all!' Maeve crossed the yard quickly, anxious to distance herself from her inquisitor.

'Breakfast's on the table. No thanks to you, Miss. You were supposed to set the table, first thing!' Her aunt hurried to catch up with her, lest her barbs missed their mark. Maeve slipped into place beside Uncle Seumas, who was already wolfing a huge plate of fried eggs, bacon and potato bread. Egg yolk was running down his grizzled chin. Her mother put a plate in front of her. As she looked down at the eggs floating in their little pool of grease, she felt her gorge rise. She was too late to reach the door before the contents of her stomach hit the floor.

She would have to go to Scotland to have the baby! It was the only answer. If the Sweeney family were to hold their heads high in Ballymoran, then not a soul, bar the Canon, must know of Maeve's fall from grace. After the bitter recriminations passed, Aunt Bridget was galvanised into action. She hurried down to Saint Saviour's Church, returning fifteen minutes later with Canon Brady. Seumas excused himself embarrassedly while Bridget and Maeve's mother went into conference in the front parlour, a conference from which the person, top of the agenda, was entirely excluded.

While her fate was being decided, Maeve slipped out of the house. The Reform boys would be working at Willie Burns's farm. She must get a word to Charlie. The father had a right to know! As luck would have it, Charlie, and a younger weedy-looking boy, were smoking behind the hut, which served as a toilet. His face lit up when he saw her.

'Keep a look-out Andy!' he shouted back at the youth, as he ran up the meadow to meet her. He seemed delighted at the news and appeared not to notice her distress. 'A baby . . . our baby! God, that's wonderful!'

'How could it happen, Charlie? We only did it the once . . . and not really . . . not properly!' Maeve was angry at his apparent unconcern.

He held her hands. 'Listen to me, Maeve . . . now listen! I love you . . . d'you hear me? I love you and I'm going to marry you. Our baby's going to have a proper home. I'll be gettin' out of Reform and we'll. . . '

He was cut short by the look-out's hoarse but insistent call.

'Charlie, quick! He's comin'!'

Brother Frederick was striding towards them, an angry scowl on his face.

'You boys there . . . get back to work AT ONCE!'

'Don't worry, darlin'. It'll be O.K.,' Charlie whispered, as he walked away. Brother Frederick stared disapprovingly after Maeve's retreating figure.

Charlie's assurances now seemed hollow to Maeve, as she leaned over the deck-rail of the ship, trying to get a last glimpse of the Irish coastline. They had kept her at home until she began to 'show'. Uncle Seumas ran her to the ship, hardly exchanging a word throughout the journey. His silence, she was sure, was embarrassed rather than censorious.

Glasgow seemed a grey noisy place after the fields of Ballymoran. As they rattled through the streets in her Uncle John's van, narrowly missing two fat women, who seemed, in common with a number of its citizenry, to have some sort of death-wish, he blethered on, in sharp contrast to the journey she'd passed with Seumas.

'Ah jist wish you could stey wi' us, hen! You'd be very welcome. You know that! But we huvnae the room!' He was right! Maeve was mortified when she saw her three little cousins cramped in the one bed, to accommodate her overnight stop.

'Don't worry about that, darlin'. Sure they enjoy it,' her

mother's sister reassured her. Despite her assurances, Aunt Teresa spent a great part of the evening trying to stop their 'carry-on'. The sound of sharp smacks added to their guest's discomfiture.

Maeve found it impossible to sleep. Her aunt's house was on a busy main road. Tramcars clanged past the bedroom window half the night. It sounded as if they were driving around the room. She got up to close the window, which was level with the passengers on the trams' top deck. She thought they couldn't see her in the darkened bedroom, but one cheery young lad blew her a kiss, which sent her scurrying back to bed. His smile reminded her of Charlie's, and the memory brought hot stinging tears to her eyes.

She felt exhausted in the morning, as Uncle Jack ran her to the convent, her home for the remainder of the confinement.

'Noo, if you need onythin', Maeve . . . onythin' at aw, jist ring this number. It's the work. The foreman'll make sure I get the message!' He embraced her roughly and handed her case to the young nun who opened the door.

'She'll be hunky-dory! Won't she, Sister?' The nun smiled in silent affirmation and glided off down a corridor, Maeve in tow. The place smelled of a peculiar mixture of wax polish and incense. The young nun showed her to a simply furnished room. Its only decoration was a picture of Jesus in his dying agony, a crown of thorns on his head. She thought at first the eyes were closed, but when she looked again, they appeared to open. There was an inscription underneath which read:
NO MATTER WHERE YOU STAND IN RELATION TO THIS PAINTING, THE EYES OF THE SAVIOUR WILL ALWAYS FOLLOW YOU.

That's about all I'm needin'! Maeve thought, wearily.

The time there passed slowly. Maeve was grateful when the nuns agreed to let her help out in their hospital. Giving out magazines and tea made the long lonely days endurable. The convent grounds were beautiful, though. The nuns had built a simple grotto where various statues to the saints were housed, each with its own small patch of shaded garden. You could sit there amongst the scent of flowers, with only the bees for company, and imagine you were hundreds of miles from the city.

It was while Maēve was sitting in Saint Joseph's own little horticultural haven that her waters broke. She was early! True, she'd been feeling twinges, but she'd been experiencing so many different sensations lately, that it was hard to differentiate between them. She'd been feeling the baby pushing against the limits of its cramped space for some time now, and used these private moments in the grotto to talk soothingly to him. She felt certain he was a boy! She had been in the midst of one of those secret conversations when the floodgates opened, quite unexpectedly. She felt a sudden terror, as if the baby was going to be washed away in the tide coming from within her. An elderly nun, Sister Cecilia, busy hanging out the washing, heard the girl's cries and hurried towards her as fast as her arthritic feet would allow.

The next few hours were a confusion of pain, bright lights and sheer exhaustion. Nuns shouted conflicting instructions at her . . . 'Push. . . No, don't bear down just yet. Hold on. . . Come on now, one FINAL PUSH. . . and AGAIN. . . that's it!'

Then a feeling of immense relief, as if years of constipation were at an end.

Maeve heard her baby cry, a weak but insistent sound. She struggled to raise her head, in time to see a masked and gowned nun, carrying the wrapped bundle, now crying lustily, from the room.

'My baby! I want my baby!'

'Now, now, my dear,' a kindly, but unfamiliar nun's face loomed over her. 'It's for the best!'

It was then that she gave way to the tears that had been welling inside her for nine months. She was never to see her baby. She'd agreed, albeit unwillingly, to give him up.

'You're only sixteen, now, Maeve. Your whole life is before you!' the Canon had argued, in a voice unused to being challenged.

'Best that it goes to a good Catholic home!' Aunt Bridget had declared firmly. There was absolutely no way she was going to have their shame paraded before the whole parish! Bernadette Flynn, President of the Union of Catholic Mothers, and Maura Divers, second cousin to His Grace, the Archbishop, no less, (and didn't she let you know it) would have a field-day! Maeve's mother, fully dependent on her sister-in-law's charity for the roof over their heads, had wrung her hands, but turned away from the girl's silent plea.

'Now the sisters know of many well set-up couples, whom God, in His wisdom, has chosen not to give the blessing of children,' Canon Brady had said finally, as he patted her hand.

'They'll give the babby all the things it needs!'

They wouldn't give it what she could! Its own mother's love. At that thought, she cried, as though her heart would break; terrible racking sobs that shook her whole body and left her feeling exhausted and bereft.

Charlie was fully aware of the risk he was taking, but he had to see her. Now that it was Spring, they were back helping with the lambing.

'We won't be doing the Sweeney farm, this time round,' was all Brother Dominic had said. There wasn't much more he could have told them. Bridget had merely sent a brief note, saying 'as they were using other local help', the boys' services would no longer be required.

'I see Maeve Sweeney's back,' Charlie had overheard the fella who did the chicken sexing say to Willie Burns.

'Aye! I don't think Scotland was to her taste,' their employer had answered.

No mention of a baby there! He had to find out for himself! Charlie had never had anything of his own. The mere thought of seeing his own flesh and blood had sustained him through the last few months. He bent low, as he skirted the hedge between the Burns and Sweeney farms.

He was crossing the yard when Bridget saw him. Dympna had let out a half-hearted bark, which died away quickly, as if the effort had been too much for her.

'Hey, you there! Just a minute! Where d'you think you're goin'?'

'I'm lookin' for somebody!' Charlie peered in the farmhouse window, at an empty room.

'You're a Reform boy, aren't you? You've no business to be here! Get off our land! . . . D'you hear me?'

Charlie crossed and looked in the byre. 'Not till I've seen Maeve!'

A look of dawning realisation came over Bridget's face.

'Jesus, Mary and Joseph! YOU'RE the one!'

Charlie spun round and gripped her arm fiercely. 'Where is she? And where's my baby?'

'Your baby!' Bridget almost spat the words at him. 'What right have you to call a baby yours?'

Maeve was in the dairy, churning the butter, when she heard the voices, raised in anger. It couldn't be. . . She ran out, scattering squawking hens from her path, and saw Charlie facing Aunt Bridget, fighting desperately to control the rage building within him. He turned and his face changed as he saw her.

'Maeve. . . Maeve. . . are you all right?'

'Charlie, they wouldn't let me keep the baby. She made me give him away!'

Maeve broke down in tears.

'YOU BITCH!' Charlie shouted at Bridget. 'YOU BLOODY BITCH! What right had you. . .'

'Every right!' Bridget cut him short, a steely glint in her eyes. 'You're a criminal, a common criminal! Just thank God your son has a home with people fit to look after him!'

'I'll get you for this!' Charlie's face was white with anger.

'Don't threaten me!' Bridget was now in control. 'You took advantage of an innocent girl. If you come here again, I'll make sure they lock you up and throw away the key!'

'I'll get you!' Charlie shouted over his shoulder, as he ran out of the yard. 'You better watch out! D'you hear me!'

For the next few days, Bridget never let Maeve out of her

sight. Charlie's threats did not scare her. What really frightened her was the thought of her niece committing deadly sin. . . with a Reform boy! The Blessed Virgin would weep tears of blood at the very thought. As a self-appointed moral sentinel, she stuck closer to Maeve than her guardian angel. When Maeve went to collect eggs, Bridget was right there, holding the pail. When she went down to the long meadow to fetch the cows for milking, Bridget came too, almost running to keep up with her niece's long strides.

'Where are you off to?' Bridget stopped in her search for Dympna whom Seumas's black and white collie, Finn, had been persistently sniffing round. The girl was turning out of the yard.

'Goin' for water,' Maeve replied. 'The pump's actin' up again!'

Bridget had to make a quick decision. To seek out the dogs from whichever barn they were bespoiling, and boot Finn to ensure he finally got the message, or keep up her vigilance.

'You shouldn't lift any weights till your insides have healed!' She took one of the pails from the girl's hand. The dogs could wait! Maeve was unsure whether her aunt was being genuinely solicitous, believing as she did that childbirth was a form of illness. Or was this just another attempt to keep her under surveillance? Not that it mattered! She was beyond caring.

They entered the meadow, where the pool, used as their emergency supply, was situated. The water was brown and brackeny but providing you boiled it long enough, the tea it made was drinkable. Maeve hung onto a bush with one hand and bent over the pool, pail in hand. Something bright and blue, like the Bay of Naples, was glinting on the bottom. Bridget saw it at the same time. Before Maeve could stop her, her aunt plunged waist deep into the murky water. Bending forward, she thrust her arms below the surface, then uttering a terrible cry like an animal in pain, she held aloft the pathetic form of Dympna, water cascading from the dog's lifeless body.

Polygon 1986

John Byrne
(b.1940)

Born Paisley. Playwright, artist, director and stage designer. As well as *Slab Boys* trilogy set in a carpet factory in 1957, wrote the highly praised TV series *Tutti Frutti* (1987) about an ageing Glasgow pop group.

I have very mixed feelings about my 'Irishness' inasmuch as I have always, and with good reason, considered myself to be died-in-the-wool Scottish. . . then again, that sort of Scottish – three grandparents Irish immigrants (my South Queensferry-born paternal grandmother had the maiden name of Quinn) – was very familiar to me. The register call at the six or seven schools I went to in Glasgow and Paisley had a fair smattering of Bagans, McDades, Killens, Gilhoolys, McCormacks, O'Briens and none of them was remotely Irish. When I left school I palled around with Raffertys, O'Hares, O'Donnels, O'Neills and they were every bit as Scottish as I was. It was really only at New Year or when some cousin came over from America to my grandmother's house in Cardonald and there was a big get-together where every song (apart from my father, Paddy's party pieces 'Old Faithful' and 'Bathing in the Sunshine') was an Irish music hall number – e.g. 'The Rose of Tralee', 'I'll Take You Home Again, Kathleen' and 'Hullo, Charlie Tully' to the tune of 'Hullo, Patsy Fagan' – that, in hindsight, marked us out from our genuinely died-in-the-wool Scottish neighbours such as the Lavelles and the Girisoles.

If the truth be told I have a deep loathing for the Irish. I loathe their easy 'charm', their forelock-tugging to the English (I exempt the IRA from this), their 'blarney' and their general all-round foulness. Those who made it to Scotland did themselves and their offspring a big favour, in my book.

Mind you, they didn't have it easy. I'll always remember my old Dad saying how determined he was never to call a son of his Paddy for the simple reason that Paddies got all the dirty jobs in Scotland. England too, I dare say.

I do have a yen though to visit the Ould Sod (I have been on several occasions, one time to Dublin when the car got broken into and my typewriter and only suit was knocked, which didn't endear the bastards to me) and perhaps exorcise this vile antipathy towards my forebears. They did, after all, supply me with plenty of ammo (the Catholic faith with its extraordinary imagery into which I was baptised and confirmed) for the assault against the arse-numbing 'worthiness' of Scottish plays in the late 1970s.

But that aside, all that I hold dear – the 'stuff' I'm made of – is entirely Scottish. Paisleycentric. Parochial. Died-in-the-wool, if you like. Hail, Glorious St Patrick!

The Slab Room

JACK: This is the Slab Room where the powder paint is ground and dished for the Designers. . . you saw the paper patterns out there. The lads here divvy up some colour . . . rose pink, magenta, persian yellow. . . dump it onto these marble slabs. . . add some gum arabic. . . do we have some gum arabic, anyone? [There is no response] Then it's just a matter of grinding. . . to get rid of the impurities. . . [Demonstrates] Okay? Would someone like to dish that? [There is no response] Quite a diff from the studio, Eh? You'll be relieved to hear you won't be having too much contact with these unsalubrious surroundings. You'll be helping Bobby Sinclair. His department's a bit more wholesome than this one. . .

SPANKY: When ur ye off, Jack? No' wantin' tae rush ye ur that. . .

PHIL: Aye, Plookychops. . . them boils ae yours is highly smittal.

JACK: Here, there's no call to get personal. [Advances on Phil]

PHIL: [Drawing back in alarm] Keep away fae me! Hector. . . fling us ower the Dettol.

JACK: Jealousy will get you nowhere, McCann. Just because I'm on a desk. . .

SPANKY: S'a bloody operatin' table ye want tae be oan! That face. . . yeugh!

PHIL: Ye can pit in fur plastic surgery, ye know. . . oan the National Health.

SPANKY: Ur a 'Pimplectomy'.

PHIL: It'd only take aboot six month. . .

SPANKY: . . . an' a team a surgeons. . .

PHIL: . . . wi' pliers.

JACK: I'll have to go now, Alan. . . Sorry. There's a couple of trials I've got to have a look at. I'll be back. The Boss would like you to show the chap here what goes on in this place. . . in the way of work. . . so. . . See you later.

    [Exits]

SPANKY: Get a brush an' some rid paint, Heck.

HECTOR: Whit fur?

PHIL: Tae paint a cross oan the door, stupit. . .

SPANKY: . . . tae warn the villagers.

HECTOR: Whit villagers?

SPANKY: Och, shuttit.

PHIL: Right, son. . . whit'd ye say yur name wis again?

ALAN: Alan. . . Alan Downie.

PHIL: Okay, Alma. . . let's show ye some ae the mysteries ae the Slab Room. Mr. Farrel. . .

SPANKY: Yes, Mr. McC?

PHIL: I'm just showing Arthur here something of the intracacies of wur work. I wunner if you an' the boy there wid staun tae the wan side an' keep oot ae the road?

SPANKY: Certainly. Hector. [Beckons Hector off to the side]

PHIL: Thank you. Right, Alec. [Leads him over to the sink]
. . . this. . . is what we cry a sink. S-I-N-K. . . Now, I
don't expect you to pick up all these terms immediately
but you'll soon get the hang of it. And this. . . [Grabs
Hector's lapels] . . . is what is called a 'Slab Boy'. . .
You say it. . . [No response from Alan. . . just a slightly
embarrassed smile] . . . Slab Boy. . . good. And here. . .
[Grabs Spanky's lapels] . . . is another one. . . another
one? Good! Note the keen eye. . . the steady hand. . .
the firm set of the jaw. . . they're forced up under
cucumber frames, you know. . . Note, too. . . [Lifts up
Spanky's coat tails] . . . the arse hingin' oot the
troosers. . . This last because the Slab Boy. . . you say
it. . . [No response except black look from Alan] . . .
Good! The Slab Boy is expected to put in a full eight
hours sweated labour a week for a few measly shillings.

SPANKY: . . . an' aw the gum crystals he can eat.

PHIL: Hence the firm set of the jaw. Thank you, Mr. Farrell.

SPANKY: Don't mention it.

PHIL: Don't you wish you was one of this happy breed,
Andrew? Grinding out the spanking shades for our
Designer chappies. . . so that they, in their turn, can
churn out those galy little rugs that one sees in our
more select stores. Don't you wish you was a Slab
Boy?

SPANKY: [With feeling] Oh, aye. . .

PHIL: Well, Amos?

HECTOR: Aye, ye don't know whit yur missin'.

SPANKY: Nae'er ye dae. . . ya lucky bastart.

ALAN: I wouldn't mind working in here. . . it sounds fun, but
Mr. Barton's putting me in with Bobby Sinclair.

PHIL: Much ye gettin'?

ALAN: Three pounds a week was suggested.

SPANKY: Three poun' a week?

ALAN: Round about that.

SPANKY: That's mair than the three ae us pit thegither.

PHIL: Is Wallace Bathroom yer uncle or whit?

HECTOR: Auld Barton. . . the Boss.

ALAN: What d'you mean? Course he isn't.

SPANKY: Must be some kinda blood relation tae start ye aff at three poun'. . .

ALAN: It doesn't seem an awful lot to me. I've got a young brother who's earning that and he's only sixteen.

PHIL: Whit is he? A brain surgeon? Three quid? Wheeewww. . .

SPANKY: Much did ye get in yur last joab?

ALAN: I haven't had a job before. I'm at the Uni.

[The Slab Boys exchange quizzical looks]

University. I've only left school.

SPANKY: Whit age ur you?

ALAN: Nineteen.

PHIL: Did ye get kept back a loat?

ALAN: Stayed on to get my Highers.

SPANKY: Whit school did ye go tae?

ALAN: The John Neilston.

SPANKY: Aw, another wan.

ALAN: Oh, did you go there too?

PHIL: Naw, Albert. . . whit Spanky means is yur another wan ae them. . . a Mason. . . ur yur auld man is. Place is fulla Masons. . . 'cept fur me an' Spanks.

HECTOR: Don't listen tae them, Alan. Thur always gaun oan aboot Masons. Jimmy Roaberton's a Mason. . . Bobby Sinclair's a Mason. . . Wullie Curry's a effin Mason. . .

SPANKY: He's a effin Oaringeman.

HECTOR: Well, if everybody's either a effin Mason urra effin Oaringeman how come you an' Phil's workin' here? Eh? Tell us that. . .

SPANKY: Ah lied aboot ma age an' Phil there swore tae Waddell Bathtaps he'd flush his Rosaries doon the pan if he could only get tae be a Slab Boy. Aw, naw. . . when Mr Bathtub took me intae his office, grasped ma haun. . . strangely but firmly. . . an' offered me wan poun' seventeen an' six a week. . . Ah went straight hame an' set fire tae ma scapulas. . .

PHIL: An' don't think it wisnae sare. Ah wis there when he done it. Soon as Father Durkin heard we wur workin' here.

SPANKY: Phil's Auntie Fay goat beat up by the Children of Mary.

PHIL: Gie'd hur a right doin'. . .

SPANKY: She hud tae go tae Lourdes. . .

PHIL: An' the entire faimily wur refused entry tae Carfin Grotto.

SPANKY: An' that really hurt. They wur oot there every Sunday . . . doon oan thur knees. . .

PHIL: . . . draggin' the ponds fur money.

SPANKY: Huvvin' a quick burst oan the beads. . .

PHIL: Ready? [Together] In the name of the Father, and of the Son. . .

HECTOR: Aw, cut it oot, you pair. Don't pay any attention tae them loonies, Alan. . .

ALAN: But I'm not a Mason. . . honestly. . . I don't know what you're talking about.

PHIL: Aw, naw? Tell us this, then. . . When ye wur in at Wardle's oaffice this moarnin' ye shook hauns, didn't ye?

ALAN: Yes, but. . .

SPANKY: An' did it feel like ye wur in the grip of a man that
was throwing a mild epileptic fit. . . ?

ALAN: I don't really see. . .

SPANKY: An' said ye'd be workin' wi' Bobby Sinclair?

ALAN: Yes, but. . .

PHIL: At three quid a week?

ALAN: Yes, but. . .

SPANKY: Told ye he wis a Mason!

PHIL: Definitely!

SPANKY: Furst day us poor sods wis handed a packet a nuts an'
telt tae report tae the Slab.

PHIL: No' even a pat oan the bum.

SPANKY: Look at that boy there. [Grabs Hector] He wis
gonna be a Capucci monk. Look at him noo!

HECTOR: Hing aff! [To Alan] Ah went tae Johnstone High.
Ah'm no'a bloody Pape!

PHIL: Nae sense denyin' it, Heck son. Show the boy yur
kneecaps. Thur aw caved in fae prayin' tae St Wilton
furra desk! Prodissant school. . .

HECTOR: Aw, shuttup! Yur always gaun oan aboot gettin' oot
the Slab an' oantae a desk. Some hope! Jack Hogg wis
four years in here afore he even goat a sniff ae a desk.
We've aw goat a couple a years yet.

SPANKY: Thur wis a loat mair Designers in Jackie's day. . . Luk
at it noo. Gavin's away tae Australia. . . Billy McPhail's
in Kidderminster. . . an' Tommy Devine's goat T.B.
Thur's hunners a desks oot there. . .

HECTOR: Aye, but they'll bring in somebody fae ootside. . .

SPANKY: Well, Ah'm askin' Wullie if thur's a desk fur me. . .

PHIL: Ask if thur's two.

HECTOR: Whit aboot three?

SPANKY: Ach, Heck. . . why don't ye resign yursel'? You're in the Slab Room till Vince Eager gets intae the Tap Twinty.

HECTOR: Ah wis only. . .

SPANKY: Ah can see ye noo, Hector. . . unemployable. . . scoffin' Indian ink wi' the auld men fae the Moadel. . .

PHIL: . . . gaun roon the doors wi' claes pegs. . . Chokin' weans fur thur sweetie money. . .

SPANKY: A flopperoonie! So don't go gettin' any big ideas aboot askin' furra desk, kiddo. . . you're lucky tae be in a joab.

SPANKY: Whit'd Ah be daein' wi' a pinsil?

PHIL: [Taking out newspaper] Aw. . . come. . . on. . .

ALAN: Here, you can borrow my pen. . . [Takes out Parker Fifty-one]

PHIL: [Grabbing pen] Gee! A Parker Fifty-Wan! Whit's a slip ae a boy daein' wi' a pen like this?

ALAN: Belongs to my Dad, actually. He lets me borrow it sometimes.

PHIL: Better no' brek it then [Starts writing] Aaach. . . the nib's fell aff!

ALAN: [Panic stricken] Jeeesus Christ!

PHIL: Ah wis only kiddin'. An' less ae the bad language, you. A bit of decorum, sonny boy.

SPANKY: That's right Phil. . . you tell the young turk. Don't think ye can let rip wi' that kinda talk in the Slab Room. We fought two World Wars fur the likes a you. That lad there loast a coupla legs at Wipers. . . so that the world wid be a cleaner, better place. . .

PHIL: Where a man could walk tall. . . legs ur nae legs. . .

SPANKY: Show him where the Gerry grenade went right up
yur. . .

PHIL: Indeed I wull not! I only ever display that oan Poppy
Day. [Peruses newspaper] Ach, Ah'm no' in the
prizewinners this week either. Tch. . . Heh, know whit
the furst prize is this week?

SPANKY: Naw, whit?

PHIL: [Reads] 'First prize. . . Two matching hampsters.'

SPANKY: Eh? Hamsters? They allowed tae gie away livestock?

PHIL: Whit ye talkin' aboot? 'Two matching picnic hampsters. .
. handy for beach and country walks.' Nae mention a
livestock. . .

SPANKY: Ach, it's the Paisley Express. . .

PHIL: Here's wan. . . twinty three across. . . Says it's an
'anagram'. Whit's an anagram?

SPANKY: S'like a radiogram but no' as high aff the grun. How
d'ye no gie up, Phil? Yur never gonnae win it. . .

PHIL: Came pretty close last time. Three oota forty-eight. Ah'll
win them hampsters yet.

SPANKY: An' whit ye gonnae dae if ye dae?

PHIL: Breed them an' train the pups tae turn a big wheel an'
grind up aw this bloody paint. Heh, where's Sadie wi'
that trolly? Ah'm ravenous. Alvarro, whit time is it?

ALAN: [Consulting chronometer] Almost quarter past. . .

PHIL: An' whit speed ur we daein'? You'll gie yursel lockjaw
humphin' that aboot. . .

SPANKY: Ye gaun tae the canteen the day, Phil?

PHIL: Nae option. . . nae pieces.

ALAN: What sort of menu do they have?

PHIL: They huvnae goat a menu, son. S'aw chalked up oan a
big blackboard. Thur's yur 'Scotch Pie Hawaiian'. . .

SPANKY: Yur 'Link Tartare'. . .

PHIL: 'Saps in a Basket'. . .

SPANKY: Bit messy that. . .

PHIL: Ur if ye really want somethin' special. . .

SPANKY: 'Tortoi a la King'.

PHIL: Ye eat it oot its shell.

ALAN: I might give that a try. . .

SPANKY: Healthy appetite, the boy. . .

ALAN: What are all those jars and things up there?

PHIL: Gosh, Alfred, I thought you'd never ask! [Crosses to shelf and takes down jar] This yin here contains the mortal remains of one Joe McBride, the oldest Slab Boy in the long history of this illustrious company. Going on for eighty four was Joe when he goat word that he wis tae start oan a desk. He' been in the Slab Room, man and beast, fur nigh on sixty years. . .

SPANKY: Sixty five.

PHIL: Thank you. . . as I was saying, Aldo. . . they eventually pit the poor aul' bugger oantae a desk. . . made him a designer. The shock of course was too much fur the elderly chap. When the cleaners arrive oan the Monday mornin' they fun the veteran Slab Boy slumped over his newly acquired an' greatly prized desk. . . stone dead! His hoary auld pate in a jar. . . a freshly ground jar of indigo. An' ye know whit they say, Arthur. . .

ALAN: [Wearily] What's that?

PHIL:

SPANKY: When you indigo. . . you indigo!

from The Slab Boys (1978)

SEÁN DAMER
(b. 1940)

Born and brought up in Edinburgh. Books include
From Moorepark to Wine Alley and *Glasgow: Going
for a Song*. Currently working on a film script
about World War II resistance on Crete.

Memoirs of a Catholic Boyhood

Ireland was an unavoidable component of my Edinburgh childhood.
My paternal grandfather – whom I never met, because he lived in
Canada – was a Catholic Irishman from County Waterford. My
father told me many stories about Ireland, the piano-stool contained the words and music for many Rebel Songs. One of the very
first books I ever read was *The Irish Twins*. Three out of seven
primary school teachers were Irish nuns, many of the other
teachers in both primary and secondary schools had Irish backgrounds, two of the three priests in the parish were Irish. We sang
hymns like 'Hail Glorious Saint Patrick' in church, the Hibs and
Celtic football teams were integral parts of the cultural landscape,
we went to Ireland on a family holiday once, we were aware of,
and played, Irish traditional music, and we sang Irish songs. So by
the time I left secondary school in 1958, Irishness was an inescapable aspect of my identity.

However, this Irishness was of an opaque nature. First of all, it was
inextricably interwoven with the Jansenist Catholicism of Central
Scotland, riddled as that was with superstition, Mariolatry, and
paranoia. Secondly, its version of history was highly partisan. In
other words, it was highly romantic. The beginnings of the break
came when I moved to Glasgow in 1968 after graduating. There, I
became involved in the Folk Revival, and played a great deal of Irish
fiddle music, and listened to a great deal of Irish song. I should also
say that while I supported Celtic in a dilettante manner, identification with the team to the exclusion of other ways of identity
formation was not for me. Nonetheless, I began to educate myself
in Irish literature, history and politics, a process which continued
apace when I became the first established lecturer in sociology in
Trinity College, Dublin, in 1971. When I moved to Dublin, there
was perhaps a sense of 'going home.'

I soon realised that the version of Irishness which had been inculcated in me in school and at home was of the Mickey O'Mouse variety. Further, the contemporary events in Northern Ireland made a strong impact, and I strongly identified with the Nationalist community, especially after Bloody Sunday. But I also immersed myself in traditional music, and was to be found every Saturday night in O'Donoghue's Bar listening to John Kelly and Joe Ryan. So my 'Irishness' became both more politicised and more culturally rooted throughout the early 70s; I also became involved in socialist politics. As a result, my antipathy to Irish Catholicism increased exponentially, with all its reactionary triumphalism, wilful obscurantism, and to me personally, systematic anti-women practice. The church's stand against divorce, contraception and abortion sickened me.

When I involved myself in public debate about these issues, I was cheered on by my Irish friends. But I noticed that not one of them would support me in public. So when a chance to leave Ireland came at the end of 1975, I was glad to take it. I had had enough of the Ould Sod; it was definitely not my home. I should also say that I made a conscious decision that my three daughters, all born in the 1960s, would not be brought up in any kind of sectarian atmosphere. I did not want them to go to a Catholic school, I did not want their heads filled with Bally-in-the-Bog banalities, and I wanted their upbringing to be secular and humanist – although I might not have put it as clearly as that at the time.

Thereafter, my 'Irishness' centred round an ongoing interest in the politics of Northern Ireland, in which several personal friends were heavily involved, and traditional music, which I continued to play. But a holiday in Crete brought me a new interest: Greece, and Greek history, culture, society and politics. These days, 'Greekness' is a much more important part of my identity than 'Irishness'. I speak good Greek; I do not speak Irish Gaelic. It is quite likely that I will in fact settle permanently in Greece. There is no chance of me settling in Ireland.

I retain a not-very-active interest in the politics of Northern Ireland because I want to see a just peace. I retain an interest in Irish traditional music, but do very little about it. And I retain an interest in Irish literature – but then, I have always had an interest in all literature.

So to sum up: I am a Scottish person, with my roots firmly in Glasgow, where I chose to plant them, even although I was born and brought up in Edinburgh. I am happy to acknowledge that a part, a small but real part, of my background is Irish. But I, and no one else – and certainly not clerics, or gombeen men or women in any shape or form – will define what that part comprises, and how important it is in my life. As someone who likes to think of himself as an internationalist, my 'Irishness' is now a small part of a multi-faceted, plural, Scottish identity, which I will celebrate in my terms, when I want to, if I want to. By the way.

'Hail, Hail!' is a chapter from an unpublished novel, *Connolly*, about a streetwise Tim private eye, Kate Connolly, who has a Ph.D. in Criminology. She and her widower father, Pat, are very close, and are both season-ticket holders at Parkhead.

Hail, Hail!

FIVE-ONE!! Celtic Park was bouncing, and Kate and Pat bounced with it, singing deliriously: 'There's only one Henrik Larsson.'

Kate and Pat joined the jubilant fans in the Albert Bar. The war-songs of Celtic rang round the walls. The five goals were analysed and re-analysed in forensic detail. Eventually, when the racket had subsided to a mere din, Kate was asked for a song. Pat called for order, and the din subsided to a hubbub. She put down her pint of MacLay's, composed herself, looked far away, and sang:

As I went a-walking one morning in May,
To view yon fair mountains and valleys so gay,
I was thinking on those flowers, all going to decay,
That bloom around yon bonny, bonny Slieve Gallion braes.

The pub erupted into applause. Kate smiled her thanks, took a drink of her pint, and glanced at Pat. Tears were streaming down his face as he looked sightlessly at the wall. Kate had learned the song from her mother; it had been one of her favourites. Kate took her father's arm gently, and led him slowly from the pub. Once outside, Kate took some tissues from her bag, and gave them to Pat. He dried his eyes, and blew his nose mightily.

'Thanks, love,' he said. 'I'm sorry. That song, it just, it just reminded me of your Ma. I can remember her singing it.'

'I know, Dad,' said Kate, 'I know. It's alright.'

They decided to go for an early curry, and took the subway to Partick. Pat recovered quickly. So Kate was not surprised when Pat said as they ate, 'The bhoys done good!'

'No, Dad,' said Kate. 'The bhoys done brilliant.'

'Aye, I know, love.'

'A famous victory,' said Pat. 'A Fontenoy of a victory.'

Kate laughed. 'Fontenoy? Gies peace.'

'Hey, I know my Irish history, girl.'

Kate groaned. 'I know, Dad, I know.'

'Well, there's them as don't want to know,' said Pat. 'And there's them that want to forget that history. I mean, look at the bould Fergus McCann. I mean what does he think he's doing banning these old songs from Celtic Park, Kate?'

'It's 1998, Dad. Old IRA songs have no place in a modern non-sectarian football club.'

'You'll be telling me next that Celtic's no a Catholic club, like that gobshite McCann?'

'I think what McCann meant was that Celtic has never been a sectarian team, in the sense that it always signed Protestants as well as Catholics.'

'Aye, that's true, but it's always been a Catholic team in terms of its support.'

'In the main, yes.'

'And most of these Catholics came from Ireland?'

'Or were of Irish descent, yes.'

'And Ireland fought for its freedom. Like my father did.'

'Yes.'

'So what's wrong with singing 'The Boys of the Old Brigade'?'

'Dad, we're more than three-quarters-of-a-century on from the Boys of the Old Brigade. They're all dead and buried now.'

'But they still fought for Ireland's freedom, and should be honoured for that.'

'Yes they should. But a football club in Glasgow in 1998 is not the place to do it.'

'You'll be telling me next that the Provisionals weren't fighting for Ireland's freedom either, Kate.'

'The PIRA fought alright, Dad. But I'm not sure that they knew what they were fighting for. And if the way they fight is an insight into the Ireland of the future, I don't want to know.'

'That's a fine way to honour Bobby Sands.'

'That's a different issue and you know that fine well. Insofar as I'm interested in a United Ireland of the future, it's in a socialist Ireland. And the Provos couldn't spell 'socialism'. They've no politics except killing and bombing the Brits out of the Six Counties. And people like that don't make good politicians in a democracy.'

'They had to defend their people, Kate.'

'For sure. But indiscriminate bombing in London and Manchester is attacking other people, innocent people.'

'There was a lot of indiscriminate killing of innocent people in Derry on Bloody Sunday, Kate.'

'Two wrongs don't make a right. I'm not going to be forced into a phoney identification with the Provos because I happen to support Celtic Football Club.'

'And what about Ireland, Miss Smarty-Pants? I suppose you've got no identification with the Ould Sod either?'

'Dad. Ireland doesn't enter my waking dreams from one month's end to another. I am perfectly well aware of that part of my background which is Irish – you made damn sure of that – and I will celebrate it on my terms, how and when I want. Neither Gerry Adams nor Martin McGuinness are going to tell me how to think. I was born in Scotland, educated in Scotland, and live in Scotland. And I work here. Quite frankly, you can stuff the Boys of the Old Brigade. As a matter of . . . '

'Kathleen. Kathleen. You're shouting at me. That's out of order.'

'I'm sorry, Dad. But I've got some politics, you know. Women's issues mean far more to me than Republicanism, old or new. Sinn Fein may have a smart-looking women's programme, but I suspect the only women they really care about are Kathleen ni Houlihan, Roisin Dhu and the Shan Van Voght.'

'Och Kate, you and your politics.'

'Och Dad, you and your lack of politics. You still see the world through green-coloured spectacles. That's obsolete. I want to live in a secular, non-sectarian Scotland where religion doesn't matter. Do you know that in Ireland, divorce and contraception and abortion are still illegal?'

'And so they bloody well should be, Kate.'

'That's not what the women of Ireland think, Dad.'

'Well, like you said, Kate. I'm a dinosaur. Och aye. Dinosaurs never die, they only fade away.'

Kate had to laugh. She signalled for the bill.

it wasnt that he was a diehard oh no he had in fact read james connolly and was if anything a natural sticky but then on the other hand his fathers past died hard that old irish tendency to reach for the gun when you couldnt sustain an argument or think of something new to say men bloody men but of course the brits would murder and torture and lie in cold blood about anything to do with ireland bunch of ignorant racist bastards but how you can defend men that go around battering weans with clubs with nails sticking out of them doing the brits black propaganda for them its the obverse of democracy thats what it is but Im buggered if I can see whats going to happen next peace process is good news but where will it lead if the orangemen have nothing to say except no surrender as long as the brits cant read the lessons of history oh yes another martyr for old ireland another martyr for the crown whose brutal laws may kill the irish but cant keep their spirit down och bollox its about time Kevin Barry was subbed

previously unpublished

Tom McGrath
(b. 1940)

Playwright and poet, McGrath is also a
jazz musician and associate director of the
Royal Lyceum Theatre Edinburgh. His play,
The Hardman (1977) is based on the life of
Jimmy Boyle.

Scots Folk Irish Folk

I was born in Rutherglen, in Lanarkshire, in 1940, and considered
myself a Scot, even though my grandparents on my mother's side
were from Italy, and those on my father's side from Ireland.

I spent most of my early years living in my Italian grandfather's
house where I learned to do very unScottish things like drinking
chianti and eating spaghetti, which the boys at school called worms.

My Irish grandparents lived down in Mill Street, up a close, in a
two-roomed flat with the main bed in the kitchen. I was a frequent
visitor in my preschool years and my grandmother filled my head
with tales of Ireland – nothing mythological, more personal
memories of her own – about how she sang in the choir at chapel
and what a great time they all had until the bishops cracked down
on the music as too ornate and forced them to be simpler.

She was obsessed with the voice, my grandmother, Margaret. My
father's cousin was the actor Leonard Maguire, and, though we
never ever met him, she insisted that we listen to him on the radio
so as to hear his 'beautiful speaking voice.'

The songs she sang to me were standard Irish fare – 'I met her in
the garden where the pretties grow. . .' – which made Ireland in
my mind a slightly odd place where people said pretties instead of
potatoes. But she also had a selection of small records – smaller
than EPs – which she'd play me, introducing me to the characters
and sounds of the music hall. 'With his 'ead tooked, oonderneath
his arm, he waawks the bloody tower. . .'

My Irish grandfather was called Tom McGrath, just as my father
was called Tom McGrath, and I was Tom McGrath. It felt like one of

those infinite regress mirror effects – look back in time and there was a long endless line of Tom McGraths. There must have been a first one, the original Tom McGrath, but I was the most recent, which, even at that young age, felt like a responsibility.

I knew that my grandfather had come from Ireland and got work on the railways. He was a signalman, by the time I knew him, recently retired. He kept chickens in a hutch down in the back green, and he used to do fretwork but it was bad for his asthma. He had a wee Scotch terrier called Sheila and he dug a garden plot on the way up to Cathkin. He smoked a pipe and used a spitoon – which horrified my sisters but gave me a respect for his accurate aim. Like lots of old Irishmen he had a fiddle. Sometimes he would take it out from its case and it looked as if he might play a tune, but he never did. He wore a suit with a waistcoat and a gold pocket watch, occasionally a bowler hat. Photographs of him and my grandmother going 'doon the watter' on one of the Clyde steamers, matched easily with the image of my Italian grandfather riding the top deck on the first Ru'glen tramcar. As far as I was concerned, both sides came from somewhere that was neither Ireland nor Italy – a place I called 'the olden days.'

My father was more modern. When he talked of Ireland it was about his summers spent there fishing for trout when he was a boy. He told me how he had to hide in a ditch whenever the Black and Tans came along. He didn't explain what the Black and Tans were, except I knew they were some kind of malign soldiers. It was many years later that I read more about them. Then I wanted to question him, but it was too late, he was gone.

What was there about my father that I would say was Irish? He had red hair. Even though he was an electrician, working in a leather tannery, he loved books and music. When he was sixteen he had learned the piano. He worked as a pianist semi-professionally, playing the soundtracks in the silent films cinemas, accompanying singers, playing in bands. When his friend Freddie Gallagher – a Hoover salesman – came around with his fiddle, it wasn't Irish jigs they played together, but Benny Goodman numbers, all that jazz. Likewise he met my Italian uncle who was playing saxophone in a dance band. Maybe the American sounds of the dance halls provided common ground for everyone to stomp and blow on, wherever they came from.

At home we'd have musical evenings, with friends and neighbours dropping by to sing all kinds of music. We'd hear excerpts from operas – arias, duets – and my father would sing most nobly about going down to the sea again, the lonely sea and the sky. Mr Hall from across the road – undoubtedly a Scot – would regale us with Eileen Oag, oh that my darlin's name was. . . and we'd all laugh whenever he mentioned Big McGrath the cattle jobber. It was an Irish song, we all knew that, but again it was like a picture book reality, something strange and in the past. In the small burgh of Rutherglen, politics were rarely mentioned, and Irish politics not at all. There'd be differences in religion with many of our Scottish neighbours – they were Protestant, we were Catholic – but apart from hearing about the Orange band stopping and playing right outside the Chapel on the Main Street, it never amounted to any kind of conflict. Perhaps it was the experience of the war which made it feel as if people had more in common than there were differences between them.

●

In my early teens, the Irish thing got a hold of me in a different way. On the one hand there were the priests – so many of them Irish in Glasgow – on the other hand James Joyce, a writer so filthy and sacrilegious, it seemed, he would be forever on the Index for Forbidden Books.

The Irish priests were a source of great amusement to myself and my sex-obsessed buddies. Every Sunday, at the end of Mass, when your toes were curling to get up off of that kneeler and out of the chapel, the Irish priest would go to the foot of the altar steps and bellow out something, in a resounding Irish brogue, which, being translated, was 'Prayers for the Conversion of Russia.' Then he'd launch into the Hail Holy Queen at a cracking pace which even Mary, the Mother of God, would have been hard put to decipher. Irish priests thought they had a personal line to her, of course, and it was only many years later, when I visited Notre Dame in Paris that it was driven home that she was not an exclusively Irish invention. 'Lust,' snarled Father Joseph, the Passionist Priest, and banged the desk. 'Sheer lust!' It was his comment on our teenage sexual habits. One by one we were forced to go and confess to him. 'Touching myself. . .' When I read the sermon in *Portrait of an Artist*, James Joyce became my hero.

All through a summer, it seems, on Wednesday evenings, me and my pals would walk over to Parkhead to watch Neilly Mochan score goals to win the Coronation Cup for Celtic. All through that summer, it seems in my memory, the green, gold and white of the Irish tricolour fluttered above the stand. It always made me feel good just the sight of it, but it meant nothing to me in terms of nationality or politics. The whole crazy Rangers/Celtic, Protestant/Catholic thing was just something that had come our way after the ration books. It didn't feel as if it had any necessity. Just another phenomenon in a fruit and nutcase world. Of course, if I saw a bunch of Gers supporters coming towards me, I'd nick down the nearest sidestreet and get out of their way. It might not have much meaning, but it could have consequences.

I learned what we called the Irish rebels songs – Sean South, Kevin Barry – at the same time as I learned all the 'dirty' things that were available in the Quartermaster's Stores – (guides at penny rides) – and soon taught myself to bear the bitter taste of Guinness in the State Bar off Sauchiehall Street.

At the Athenaeum (the old drama college), I saw and heard the work of Sean O'Casey. 'The whole world's in a terrible state of chasis. . .' On the radio, I heard Patrick McGhee read from the novels of Samuel Beckett. Meanwhile, at home, Hugh MacDiarmid was laying it off about the Scottish Renaissance, with a very aggressive attitude which made me feel that I wasn't really Scottish after all, and, whatever the drunk man had to say to the thistle, it was not meant for the likes of me. Irish writing became a refuge point, along with the American Beats and the French existentialists, with the Irish always closest to me – like blood relations.

When I met and was married to Maureen Herron, who'd grown up in Maryhill, Glasgow, but was born in County Monaghan, right on the border between North and South Ireland, it felt like a suitable match. We honeymooned in Dublin, our first time in an airplane, my first time in Ireland.

We found a room on Baggot Street, frequented by Luke Kelly, Kieran Burke and Barney McKenna of the Dubliners. We'd gone for a couple of weeks but we stayed for months. We visited the Martello Tower out on the coast along towards Bray where I paid homage to Chapter One of *Ulysses*. 'Stately plump Buck Mulligan. . .'

He'd raised his shaving mug to heaven as if it contained the sacred host. We drank in McDaid's alongside Paddy Kavanagh.

When we visited the old farmhouse up outside of Monaghan, it felt as if I had come home. The well, the thatched roof, the old woman sitting in the gathering gloom, Uncle Tom squeezing a tune from his accordeon. This was the origin of everything, and this was where it would end. How did I recognise this place I had never seen in my life before? Why was it all so familiar to me? Back in Dublin, Maureen's aunt declared of me, 'Thinks he's a poet, does he? Wait till he can write like W. B. Yeats, then he can call himself a poet.' A challenge is a challenge, but, to this day I call myself no such thing.

And Scotland? In the sense of feeling located as a writer, when did I start to find a kinship here? It had always been there, of course, with fellow writers in cities, particularly Glasgow, and, once let loose in the theatre, all sorts of new possibilities for contact and communication opened up. *The Hardman*, written in Glaswegian, co-authored with Jimmy Boyle, is a script peppered with Irish names and backgrounds. Though I had not intended it so, the struggle it depicts between the prisoner and his jailers – the naked prisoner covered in shit – reflects the sorry history of Ireland in modern times. Perhaps, though, this was not personal to me. Maybe the nightmare side of Ireland has laid claim to us all.

I still haven't answered my own question. When did I begin to feel at home here? When did I find kinship with what might be called 'Scottish writing' in a wider sense? The answer is specific. It was when I was adapting Neil Gunn's *The Silver Darlings* for radio. Working with the character Kirsty, I had the uncanny feeling that I knew who she was, had actually met her. Only when I thought about it more did I realise she was my wife Maureen's Auntie Molly. The characters in *The Silver Darlings* seemed to dance a jig along the Caithness coast on my desk before me. Was it an Irish jig or a Scottish jig? It made no difference. The Scots, the Irish. They're all the same folk.

there was that time charlie tully

there was that time charlie tully
took a corner kick
an' you know how he
wus always great at gettin thaem
tae curve in, well charlie takes the corner
and it curved in and fuck me did the wind
no cerry it right intae the net, but they
disputit it, and the linesman hud the
flag up an they goat away wae it and tully
hud tae take it again. you should've
seen it. just seemed tae go roon
in a kind o' a hauf curcle, above their heids.
fuckin keeper didnae know where tae look.

and there was that time john cassidy
went into the toilet
and there was no lightbulb
and he just had to fix up
with some water he found in a bucket.
and here it was piss.
he didnae discover it
until it was actually in him.
he was very sick after that.
he goat very bad jaundice.

Mr McCafferty

Mr McCafferty
went tae the laughterty
aw just fur some fun.
Religion wus menshuned
and aw his intenshuns
wur wurth nae mair than
a Hoat Croass Bun.
Said Mr McCafferty,
hame frae the laughterty,
an oor or two later oan,

"bunch o effin papish baskets,
see if ah see that reidheidit wan
aboot next Seterday ah'll no miss him,
ah never furget a face,
especially no a Catholic face."

Then he sat down and drank some saki.

Excerpt from **Dream Train**

[Lecture Theatre]

[Baron is giving a lecture]

BARON: As an insomniac of several years standing – or should I say laying on one side then the other, finally flat on my back – I have always taken a great interest in the various methods people have devised for themselves in the cause of trying to get a good night's sleep - everything from counting sheep to a cup of Horlicks. [Yawns] Of these none has fascinated me as much as the famous Goldberg variations of the great composer, Johann Sebastian Baa Baa Black Sheep. . . [Yawns, struggling against sleep]. . . it was a Count who commissioned them. A very rich man. An insomniac. And his idea was that whenever he couldn't sleep, which was each and every night, give or take a knap-sack, I mean a catnap. . . [Yawns]. . . whenever he couldn't sleep, then someone could come and play the music Baa Baa had composed for him. [Yawns. Falls asleep for a moment. Jerks awake.] Goldberg was Baa Baa's most accomplished pupil.

It was he who turned up each night and played for the Cunt, I mean the Count. And of course he was [Yawns] well-paid [Yawns] for his efforts [Yawns] for the Count [Yawns] was a very rich man. [Slumps forward, head on chest. Snores a little. Wakens.] Please do excuse me, ladies and gentlemen. It's always the same when I try to give a lecture. I become overwhelmed by sleep. . . . [Face falls on to the lectern. He sleeps.]

[Music. A few moments later. Enter Julie. She looks at the Baron as he sleeps.]

[Baron wakens and sees Julie.]

JULIE: I'm sorry. I didn't mean to waken you.

BARON: Please don't apologise. Were you at the lecture?

JULIE: Yes.

BARON: How was it?

JULIE: Brilliant. As ever. You always shed such light.

BARON: Really? You've heard me speak before?

JULIE: I never miss an opportunity. Every lecture you have given on the subject of the great composer, I have been there.

BARON: Truly?

JULIE: Truly.

BARON: But doesn't it irk you that I always fall asleep?

JULIE: No, no. That's the whole point, you see. With everyone else, they lecture and their students fall asleep. With you it's the opposite way round. You know, I feel embarassed to say it to a man of such great intellect, but it's really cute.

BARON: Cute? You think I'm cute?

JULIE: Yes. And oh so interesting. Because, you see, with you there is no predicting. You never know exactly when you will fall asleep, or what you might be saying at that point. It makes it so. . . intriguing. . . so full of implications. You see, it's not so much what you say as what you don't say. New thoughts come into the minds of all who fail to hear you.

BARON: And there I am snoring away.

JULIE: A snore conveys profundity.

BARON: It's most gratifying to hear you say so. Just goes to show. Here I am close to despair because of my failure to communicate, yet I have been communicating all the time without my knowing it.

JULIE: Such humility!

BARON: What time is it?

JULIE: Almost half past two.

BARON: What time did I fall asleep?

JULIE: One twenty five precisely.

BARON: Then I've been asleep for almost an hour.

JULIE: I'm so sorry to have wakened you. I know you find it difficult to sleep the rest of the time.

BARON: How do you know that?

JULIE: I've studied you. I'm very interested in you, you see.

BARON: You've been here all the time I've been sleeping?

JULIE: I went away but I returned.

BARON: Had you forgotten something?

JULIE: I came back to see you. Tiptoed in. Because I wanted to count your wrinkles.

BARON: My wrinkles? I didn't know I had any. I don't have a mirror at home, you see.

JULIE: The marks of wisdom. Do you mind if I touch?

BARON: No.

[She smooths his brow. He closes his eyes, enjoying it. Music.]

previously unpublished

BERNARD MacLaverty
(b.1942)

Born Belfast where he worked as a lab
technician before studying at Queen's
University. Moved to Scotland in the early
1970s, lived on Islay and then in Glasgow where
he is a full-time writer of novels and short
stories. *Grace Notes* is his most recent book.

When I think about music and painting one of the things that
continually arises is the inability to articulate what is happening in
the art form. Typed bits of paper beside good works in Art
Galleries are often daft verbiage. When a composer talks about his
music it is brow furrowing to say the least. So when a writer comes
to talk about the fictions he has so carefully constructed should he
be any better? I hope the complex and intelligent response is in the
fiction.

Because a writer uses words does not mean he is analytically gifted.
His gift is in story telling. Not in writing papers about his stories.

What can I say about Ireland in my work? It's the place I grew up. It
is my place of experiencing. I am still writing about it. My answer to
the question – about the part an Irish background has in my writing
– would be to hand over the books. Let the reader decide, let
them work out the complex issues. It is too difficult to write in a
paragraph what took hundreds of pages to explore.

The Wake House

AT three o' clock Mrs McQuillan raised a slat of the venetian blind and looked at the house across the street.

'Seems fairly quiet now,' she said. Dermot went on reading the paper. 'Get dressed son and come over with me.'

'Do I have to?'

'It's not much to ask.'

'If I was working I couldn't.'

'But you're not – more's the pity.'

She was rubbing foundation into her face, cocking her head this way and that at the mirror in the alcove. Then she brushed her white hair back from her ears.

'Dermot.'

Dermot threw the paper onto the sofa and went stamping upstairs.

'And shave,' his mother called after him.

He raked through his drawer and found a black tie someone had lent him to wear at his father's funeral. It had been washed and ironed so many times that it had lost its central axis. He tried to tie it but as always it ended up off-centre.

After he had changed into his good suit he remembered the shaving and went to the bathroom.

When he went downstairs she was sitting on the edge of the sofa wearing her Sunday coat and hat. She stood up and looked at him.

'It's getting very scruffy,' she said, 'like an accordion at the knees.' Standing on her tip-toes she picked a thread off his shoulder.

'Look, why are we doing this?' said Dermot. She didn't answer him but pointed to a dab of shaving cream on his earlobe. Dermot removed it with his finger and thumb.

'Respect. Respect for the dead,' she said.

'You'd no respect for him when he was alive.'

She went out to the kitchen and got the bag for the shoe things and set it in front of him. Dermot sighed and opened the drawstring mouth. Without taking his shoes off he put on polish using the small brush.

'Eff the Pope and No Surrender.'

'Don't use that word,' she said. 'Not even in fun.'

'I didn't use it. I said eff, didn't I?'

'I should hope so. Anyway, it's not for him, it's for her. She came over here when your father died.'

'Aye, but he didn't. Bobby was probably in the pub preparing to come home and keep us awake half the night.'

'He wasn't that bad.'

'He wasn't that good either. Every Friday in life. Eff the Pope and NO Surrender.' Dermot grinned and his mother smiled.

'Come on,' she said. Dermot scrubbed hard at his shoes with the polishing-off brush then stuck it and the bristles of the smaller one face to face and dropped them in the bag. His mother took a pair of rosary beads out of her coat pocket and hung them on the Sacred Heart lamp beneath the picture.

'I'd hate to pull them out by mistake.'

Together they went across the street.

'I've never set foot in this house in my life before,' she whispered, 'so we'll not stay long.'

After years of watching through the window, Mrs McQuillan knew that the bell didn't work. She flapped the letter-box and it seemed too loud. Not respectful. Young Cecil Blair opened the door and invited them in. Dermot awkwardly shook his hand, not knowing what to say.

'Sorry eh . . .'

Cecil nodded his head in a tight-lipped way and led them into the crowded living-room. Mrs Blair in black sat puff-eyed by the fire. Dermot's mother went over to her and didn't exactly shake hands but held one hand for a moment.

'I'm very sorry to hear . . .' she said.

Mrs Blair gave a tight-lipped nod very like her son's and said, 'Get Mrs McQuillan a cup of tea.'

Cecil went into the kitchen. A young man sitting beside the widow saw that Mrs McQuillan had no seat and made it his excuse to get up and leave. Mrs McQuillan sat down, thanking him. Cecil leaned out of the kitchen door and said to Dermot, 'What are you having?'

'A stout?'

Young Cecil disappeared.

'It's a sad, sad time for you,' said Mrs McQuillan to the widow. 'I've gone through it myself.' Mrs Blair sighed and looked down at the floor. Her face was pale and her forehead lined. It looked as if tears could spring to her eyes again at any minute.

The tea, when it came, was tepid and milky but Mrs McQuillan sipped it as if it was hot. She balanced the china cup and saucer on the upturned palm of her hand. Dermot leaned one shoulder against the wall and poured his bottle of stout badly, the creamy head welling up so quickly that he had to suck it to keep it from foaming onto the carpet.

On the wall beside him there was a small framed picture of the Queen when she was young. It had been there so long the sunlight had drained all the reds from the print and only the blues and yellows remained. The letter-box flapped on the front door and Cecil left Dermot standing on his own. There were loud voices in the hall – too loud for a wake house – then a new party came in – three of them, all middle-aged, wearing dark suits. In turn they shook hands with Mrs Blair and each said 'Sorry for your trouble.' Their hands were red and chafed. Dermot knew them to be farmers from the next townland but not their names. Cecil asked them what they would like to drink. One of them said,

'We'll just stick with the whiskey.' The others agreed. Cecil poured them three tumblers.

'Water?'

'As it is. Our healths,' one of them said, half raising his glass.

They all nodded and drank. Dermot heard one of them say, 'There'll be no drink where Bobby's gone.' The other two began to smile but stopped.

Dermot looked at his mother talking to the widow.

'It'll come to us all,' she said. 'This life's only a preparation.'

'Bobby wasn't much interested in preparing,' said the widow. 'But he was good at heart. You can't say better than that.' Everybody in the room nodded silently.

Someone offered Dermot another stout, which he took. He looked across at his mother but she didn't seem to notice. The two women had dropped their voices and were talking with their heads close together.

One of the farmers – a man with a porous nose who was standing in the kitchen doorway – spoke to Dermot.

'Did you know Bobby?'

Dermot shook his head. 'Not well. Just to see.' He had a vision of the same Bobby coming staggering up the street about a month ago and standing in front of his own gate searching each pocket in turn for a key. It was a July night and Dermot's bedroom window was open for air.

'I see your curtains moving, you bastards.' A step forward, a step back. A dismissive wave of the hand in the direction of the McQuillans'. Then very quietly, 'Fuck yis all.'

He stood for a long time, his legs agape. A step forward, a step back. Then he shouted at the top of his voice, 'Fuck the Pope and. . .'

Dermot let the curtains fall together again and lay down. But he couldn't sleep waiting for the No Surrender. After a while he had another look but the street was empty. No movement except for the slow flopping of the Union Jack in Bobby Blair's garden.

Cecil came across the room and set a soup-plate full of crisps on the hall table beside Dermot.

'Do you want to go up and see him?'

Dermot set his jaw and said, 'I'd prefer to remember him as he was.'

'Fair enough'

The man with the porous nose shook his head in disbelief. 'He was a good friend to me. Got my son the job he's in at the minute.'

'Bully for him.'

A second farmer dipped his big fingers in the dish and crunched a mouthful of crisps. He swallowed and said to Dermot, 'How do you know the deceased?'

'I'm a neighbour. From across the street.'

'Is that so? He was one hell of a man. One hell of a man.' He leaned over to Dermot and whispered, 'C'mere. Have you any idea what he was like? ANY idea?'

Dermot shook his head. The farmer with the porous nose said, 'When Mandela got out he cried. Can you believe that? I was with him – I saw it. Big fuckin tears rolling down his cheeks. He was drunk, right enough, but the tears was real. I was in the pub with him all afternoon. It was on the TV and he shouts – what right have they, letting black bastards like that outa jail when this country's hoachin with fuckin IRA men?'

He laughed – a kind of cackle with phlegm – and Dermot smiled.

The signs that his mother wanted to go were becoming obvious. She sat upright on the chair, her voice became louder and she permitted herself a smile. She rebuttoned her coat and stood up. Dermot swilled off the rest of his stout and moved to join her on the way out. The widow Blair stood politely.

'Would you like to go up and see him, Mrs McQuillan?' she said.

'I'd be too upset,' she said. 'It'd bring it all back to me.' Mrs Blair nodded as if she understood. Cecil showed them out.

In their own hallway Mrs McQuillan hung up her coat and took an apron off a peg.

'Poor woman,' she said. 'Did they ask you to go up and see him?'

'Aye.'

'Did you go?' Her hands whirled behind her back tying the strings of the apron.

'Are you mad? Why would I want to see an oul drunk like Bobby Blair laid out?'

He went into the living room and began poking the fire. Their house and the Blairs' were exactly the same – mirror images of each other. His mother went into the kitchen and began peeling potatoes. By the speed at which she worked and the rattling noises she made Dermot knew there was something wrong. She came to the kitchen doorway with a white potato in her wet hands.

'You should have.'

'Should have what?'

'Gone up to see him.'

'Bobby Blair!' Dermot dropped the poker on the hearth and began throwing coal on the fire with tongs.

'Your father would have.'

'They asked you and you didn't.'

'It's different for a woman.'

She turned back to the sink and dropped the potato in the pot and began scraping another. She spoke out to him.

'Besides I meant what I said – about bringing it all back.'

Dermot turned on the transistor and found some pop music. His mother came to the door again drying her hands on her apron.

'That poor woman,' she said. 'It was bad enough having to live with Bobby.' She leaned against the door jamb for a long time. Dermot said nothing, pretending to listen to the radio. She shook her head and clicked her tongue.

'The both of us refusing. . .'

As they ate their dinner, clacking and scraping forks, she said, 'It looks that bad.'

'What?'

'The both of us.'

Dermot shrugged.

'What can we do about it?'

She cleaned potato off her knife onto her fork and put it in her mouth.

'You could go over again. Say to her.'

'What?'

'Whatever you like.'

'I don't believe this.'

She cleared away the plates and put them in the basin. He washed and she dried.

'For your father's sake,' she said. Dermot flung the last spoon onto the stainless steel draining-board and dried his hands on the dish towel, a thing he knew she hated.

He slammed the front door and stood for a moment. Then he walked across the street, his teeth clenched together, and flapped the letter-box. This time the door was opened by a man he didn't know. Dermot cleared his throat.

'I'd like to see Bobby,' he said. The man looked at him.

'Bobby's dead.'

'I know.'

The man stepped back then led the way into the hallway. The farmers were now standing at the foot of the stairs. The one with the porous nose was sitting on the bottom step swirling whiskey in his glass.

'Ah – it's the boy again,' he said. The man led the way up the stairs. Dermot excused himself and tried to slip past the sitting farmer. He felt a hand grab his ankle and he nearly fell. The grip was tight and painful. The farmer laughed.

'I'm only pulling your leg,' he said. Then he let go. It was like being released from a manacle. Somebody shouted out from the kitchen. 'A bit of order out there.'

In the bedroom the coffin was laid on the bed, creating its own depression in the white candlewick coverlet. The man stood back with his hands not joined but one holding the other by the wrist.

Dermot tried to think of the best thing to do. In a Catholic house he would have knelt, blessed himself and pretended to say a prayer. He could have hidden behind his joined hands. Now he just stared – conscious of the stranger's eyes on the back of his neck. The dead man's face was the colour of a mushroom, his nostrils wide black triangles of different sizes. Fuck the Pope and No Surrender. Dermot held his wrist with his other hand and bowed his head. Below the rim of the coffin there was white scalloped paper like inside an expensive box of biscuits. The paper hid almost everything except Bobby's dead face. Instead of candles the room was full of flowers. The only light came through the drawn paper blinds.

From downstairs came the rattle of the letter-box and the man murmured something and went out. Left alone Dermot inched nearer the coffin. His father was the only dead person he had ever seen. He pulled the scalloped paper back and looked beneath it. Bobby was wearing a dark suit, a white shirt and tie. Where his lapels should have been was his Orange sash – the whole regalia. All dressed up and nowhere to go. Dermot looked up and saw a reflection of himself prying in the dressing-table mirror. He let the scalloped paper drop back into place. Footsteps approached on the stairs.

Two oldish women were shown in by the stranger. One was Mavis Stewart, the other one worked in the papershop. Mavis looked at the corpse and her lower lip trembled and she began to weep. The women stood between Dermot and the door. Tears ran down the woman's face and she snuffled wetly. The woman from the papershop held onto her and Mavis nuzzled into her shoulder. She kept repeating, 'Bobby, Bobby – who'll make us laugh now?' Dermot edged his way around the bed and stood waiting. The women took no notice. Mavis began to dry her tears with a lavender tissue.

'I never met a man like him for dancing. He would have danced the legs off you. And he got worse when the rock and roll came in.' Dermot coughed, hoping they would move and let him pass.

'And the twist,' said the woman from the papershop. 'I think that boy wants out.'

Mavis Stewart said, 'Sorry love,' and squeezed close to the bed to let him pass. Dermot nodded to the stranger beside the wardrobe. 'I'm off.'

'I'll show you out.' The stranger went downstairs with him and went to open the front door. Dermot hesitated.

'Maybe I'd better say hello to Mrs Blair. Let her see I've been up. Seeing Bobby.'

He knocked on the living-room door.

'Yes? Come on in.'

He opened it. Mrs Blair was still sitting by the fire. She was surrounded by the three farmers. Dermot said,

'I was up seeing Mr Blair.'

'Very good, son. That was nice of you.' Then her face crumpled and she began to cry. The farmer with the porous nose put a hand on her arm and patted it. Dermot was going to wave but checked his arm in time. He backed into the hallway just as young Cecil appeared out of the kitchen. It was young Cecil who showed Dermot out.

'Thanks for coming,' he said. 'Again.'

from Walking the Dog (Penguin 1994)

HAYDEN MURPHY
(b.1945)

Born in Dublin, now lives in Edinburgh.
As well as writing poetry, he is an arts critic
and journalist.

Within

Mnemonic for an Imagination: No. 54
for Trevor Royle

Ireland was distant and Scotland was different to H in 1966. Yet a
poetry reading astride a ladder in a Forrest Hill Road bookshop
induced the familiarity of conceit. An audience. A pub nearby. New
friends. The Tom-Toms of Buchan and McGrath talking. The
Dubliner was at home even then within Edinburgh.

Snowball Fighting
for Stewart Conn

An unshaped snowball on a cobbled street
Flattened by traffic. No hand-holding
Life. A shape in the eye. A round memory
Of white inside fingers kneading
The flour-coloured pearl rosary
Hung round the face free of hair.
Then a cold slap makes eyes blink.
Mouth is wounded into splitting silence
By the aim behind thrown whiteness

Almost shrouded

By dark oiled wheel marks of delivery
Vans moving furniture out of doors.
Dampening veins. Blue-black raised

Berries with blobs of freckled thorns.
Etched weapons melting. Inside a shaped
Snowball there is no life. Nothing
But a dull oblivion of whiteness

Unpealing to pale. . .

In 1972 the Common Room in Trinity College Dublin reverberated as Sorley McLean chants for and of our common and cruel century. H meets Trevor who wisely distracts Caitlin Maude. Envy creates companionship to become enduring friendship. Later in '72, post murder in Derry, H brings to Edinburgh a rondal on Yeats: *The Foul Rag And Bone Shop Of The Heart*. It brings circus ambitions down but conjures up the myths of applause that were to lead H to annual attendance for devotional purposes to Festival.

He has become a reviewer even when he had thoughts of himself as a critic.

Festival Inscapes
for Bill Patterson

Edinburgh seas have a landscape
Where one can be blown
Into a Gaelic air. Hear
Stars talk as they swim
Between greydusted waves.
Beat monotony on Sundays.
Recognise the weekdays

Inside their moon. Voices
Sit with the sun and talk
Of squalor and farewells.
Mindsnail shells gather
Skulls of natives with
Speechrhythms inside
People they saw on good
Days before they withdrew

To the weatherstorm's edge
Of an icicle. The hammer
Is in an auctioneer's
Hand pausing to sell inland
To a salesman a thought
That Divine Revelation
Could be turned on a page.
A folded spine tickled
By numbers or prices stuck
On during the Mime of Creation.

Edinburgh seas had a landscape
Where one can be blown
A hero into a green conversation.
The heart to the heat of a moment.
Withheld for a doubt is a thought.
Maybe the sea is the place to create
Our occasion for Inscape's invasion.

Pact upon promise. Words within rhyme
Caught in heat of heart where we all
Wear green conversations to be blown
To a home where Edinburgh sea may have

A landscape.

Straying from London and the well-Plough of publishers Martin, Brian & O'Keeffe H becomes two bottles a visit to Chris/Valda Grieve in Biggar. The purpose to get the sometimes absent poet Hugh MacDiarmid to see to the proofs of a two volume *Complete Poems* of a lifetime. It often led to disasters but also willing subjection to the ultimate dictatorship of literature.

A decade later H is front-of-house for Henry Stamper's *Between the Wars* and learns to commune with the ethereal spirit that is Harry. H is also to attend this one-man show's curtain call in Dumfries in 1992.

Time for Felling
for Pearse Hutchinson

Time for felling the trees.
Combing the sea into sand-curls.
Clipping the hedges of blight.
Closing the window. Creasing the air.
Time for painting the railings.

Ashes float on water.
Mouth gapes. Glass spins.
Colour flakes sun's gleam.
Movement flecks distract silence.
Ashes snow on the fish's flail.

In trees beetle mates with squirrel.
In goldfish bowls the sky turns grey.

In the country of the blind that is memory the selective ear welcomes echoes. In a plain place on an island off the West Coast of Scotland poet Michael Hartnett sings. He continues to do so from Saturday into Sunday. Where once silence was devotional a new dawn brings familiar but refreshing rain. Tears. H listens. In Glenstal Abbey, near both their childhood's Limerick, a Scottish Presbyterian Precentor lends his voice to the plain chant of the happy Benedictine monastic 'clowns'. Hartnett embraces the common grace notes. H hears.

Closing the Ears
I.M. Michael Hartnett: 1941-1999

Closing the ears of the dead
Was harder when eyes were blind
To all but funeral's affectation.

A fly parades its vanity on the faces' vain.

Tightening the hands together
In an unsaid prayer. Embracing
Music's colour. A hill of knuckles

Turning white. The harmony of blasphemy.

A street flood pausing to climb
Over nameless faces. Proceeding.
Following. Instincts killing.

Guilt is patterned. Distanced.
Seamed with taut threads pulling
· Ever towards the distance of difference.

Scotland becomes altered as Ireland evolves. Anthony Ross in early days taught H to learn to accept there are differences between people. Recognition of this removes the need for barriers or borders. Suffering from obedience H knows he has still to accept that foresight is as useless as hindsight unless he can be still learning from within. Ireland is the familiar colony of conscience while Scotland is still invading.

Edinburgh: October 12–30, 1999

Botanic Gardens: My Shapeless Net
for Sean Hutton

The glasshouse cairn of Glasgow.

You turned away rather than leave.
The memory of sounds shared became
A secret, a single shadow lingering.
One shape to another. Thoughts
Of smouldering fires pyred up.
Eyes recovered from the nights
When other spirits joined the talk
Of words and countries left behind

Sometimes one would think you were
Struggling with a dead language
                    Beckett: *All That Fall*

On the other side I turned away
The leaving as yet another moment
Memory could betray, and lines
Contort into a fragment caught
In my shapeless net of lies.

Edinburgh's precipitious canopy of shades.

Belfast
for Brian Rooney

The girl
Became a woman who had cried
Aloud in dull confusion when she found
Senses left outside had pigment grey.
Fear confounded in a pitch-cap mind.

The woman
Wore clothes the wind had wound
Around streaming sores of eyes and mouths
That failed to see stars, hear echoes, connect
Voices to vice. Blanched she became pale by discontent.

The creature
Created by erosion of those two.
Nature's dreary comet.   Now
An interrupting star, announced
A birth's arrival. Mind's painful

Silhouette.

from Exile's Journal (Goldragon Press 1992)

James McGonigal
(b. 1947)

Born in Dumfries, now lives in Glasgow and works in the Faculty of Education at Glasgow University. Has published poetry, short stories and critical work on Ezra Pound and Basil Bunting.

I avoided visiting Ireland until I was in my late forties. This might have been because mentioning the place was avoided in my family home. It was a sign of difference betweeen my parents, I think, which they coped with by silence. Growing up, even the surname was an embarrassment to a word-sensitive teenager – I was called after the world's worst poet, and in the old pen-and-ink sketch in *Poetic Gems* he actually looked like my granny! Something else to keep silent about.

On my first trip there in the early 1990s, I was somewhat abashed to find myself more at home in the North than the South, maybe because it contained violent antipathies that I recognised as familiar from Central Scotland. The red-white-and-blue kerbstones, the forbidding Red Hands of Ulster and the smoky grey camouflage of armoured cars and police stations were abhorrent, but at least the houses and fields were trim and the road system worked well enough to let us drive through it at speed, not looking sideways as we headed for Dublin.

Crossing the border was like having blinked through a tunnel and emerged somewhere in southern Europe: everything was so relaxed as to be precarious and unnerving. Cars seemed to be steered like unruly horses, or backed without warning from green lanes out into dual carriageways. The statues of virgins at street corners and saints on shop counters, the sagging telegraph lines and dusty windows all reminded me of Catholic schools I attended in 1950s Scotland: cosy, claustrophobic, slightly crazy in the eyes of Protestant neighbours.

Of whom there were many, since I grew up in Dumfries, although my father came from a mainly Irish-Catholic mining village in

146

Lanarkshire and my mother, a convert, came from Edinburgh. Both were teachers. They had come to this country town mainly to cure the effects of my father's tuberculosis, endemic in his childhood environment. My mother's own family, those non-Catholic uncles and aunts, pretty clearly shared a view of the oddness of her marriage and its remorseless fecundity, with ten children finally to be fed and clothed. At a deep level, however, I think she retained much of her East Coast Presbyterian value system, and that I must have sucked in a fair measure of it – the parts that make me hard to live with, all work ethic and aspiration, dourness, determination.

So I was shocked by Ireland at first acquaintance, by its easyoasy mix of charm and scandals, its ready acceptance of the unplanned social occasion (including traffic jams), its seeming lack of any sense of proportion in physical or mental or spiritual life. That shock too may partly have been one of recognition. Just as in Ireland you see at every turn in the road a face or a name or a stance familiar from the streets of Glasgow, so there may be aspects of the Irish temperament which are still mine too, even though my father's family of McGonigals, McConnachies, Valleleys and O'Rourkes have been in Scotland now for almost 150 years. They worked then in foundries, pits and mills in brutal enough conditions; their descendants work as geologists, systems analysts, teachers, nurses, doctors, lawyers, economists, trade unionists, philosophers. There's still a wild, dislocated side to them, however, a sense of difference, and a tendency to blur its nagging hunger with food or drink.

Not much prayer, so far as I can see, but who can tell? Recognition of just how much Catholic schools and churches did to maintain those original migrants' sense of humanity in the face of bitter religious and racial opposition in Scotland (which had its own bloodsoaked historical roots that are also, with hindsight, 'understandable') keeps me as faithful as I can be to Catholicism and its spiritual way. This is not to say that I am blind to the flaws to be found in the Church as a multinational and local organisation, and in my own practice. But I have occasionally been mistaken for a priest, and once for a Dominican novice-master. Religious imagery is one of the codes I think and write in. I like psalms, gospels, miracles, jam-packed with paradox and poetry.

In both Catholic Scotland and Ireland, of course, there is now a widespread reaction against organised religion among younger people. Sometimes vegetarianism or animal rights tend to replace it; sometimes hedonism or fanaticism; often a real and generous social concern. What is lacking seems to be a sense of irony, which develops as a useful survival mechanism in handling religious doctrines or values which are not seriously negotiable, but which makes for funny and irreverent conversations in groups sharing a Catholic background, in my experience – the very opposite of both po-faced piety and defiant rejection.

I've returned on holiday to Ireland with my wife and children several times over recent years and sometimes think that I could easily go native and be buried there. The landscape is less stark and beautiful than Scotland's, and its history even sadder. Yet what uplifts me always is the alternative which it holds out to us. In its language, its politics and its writing, Ireland declares that things can actually be done differently, without seeking or getting guidance from London, and without necessarily having to pretend to be acceptably rational and earnest. This last has been the fate of many of the Irish in Scotland, though I suspect that most of us are still at least half crazy after all these years.

I've never learned to speak comfortably the protestant discourses that appear everywhere in Scottish intellectual and social life. Arriving at a meeting with professional colleagues and being cheerily invited to come 'into the body of the kirk' makes me feel alien and surly, even though part of me knows fine that they are just trying to be friendly, God help them. For my part, I am aware of a tendency with relative strangers to be inappropriately charming and confessional, expecting always to be forgiven my trespasses. There is no sacrament for that in Scottish life, unhappily.

Irish charm in others I accept and enjoy in the spirit in which it is offered, as both false and true at once. Like the Irish, I find it difficult to answer questions with a simple yes or no. Irish Gaelic had no word for 'no' so political negotiations with the colonising English since Tudor times have fostered the myth of native deviousness: it was quite literally almost impossible for the Irish, lacking a negative, to give an answer that rang straight in translation. This linguistic tendency may carry over into Irish English, and enrages Scots-Ulster unionist politicians of the present day, who favour simple answers to complex questions. Yet the tendency also seems to endow the Irish with consummate political skills. The European

Community suits them down to the ground: and that, in some eyes, merely confirms the deviousness.

Returning from a holiday in Waterford last summer I found myself, to my own surprise, writing a series of poems 'for translation into an abandoned language'. I thought then that I meant Scottish Gaelic, but Rody Gorman chose to translate them into Irish. They were written because I had got fed up reading the right-hand page translation of Gaelic poems first and then gazing over at the original with more hope than enlightenment, knowing no more than a dozen words in that language, which is yet so close in its forms and phrasing to the language spoken by my Donegal ancestors, and abandoned by them and their children as they turned into Lanarkshire Scots. So I decided to write the Scots-English versions first, and let my ancestral spirits check out the translations in eternity. And I hope and expect that they enjoy the ironies and forgive any inaccuracies or harshness that they find in the words, since my experience and language have been so different from theirs.

Seeing the Light

of aurora borealis bamboozingly far south
last night as we drove to our evening class
under a sky the colour of blood oranges

that pulsed as if the fruit could fizz
through pith and rind and then inhale
again to perfect segments

as if a doctor's hand had moved
under the flesh of air to turn
the unsuspecting foetus of a star.

A brightness where the pain of many prayers
was anchored. The Firth of Forth opened
and closed its mouth at this orange walk

across the sky beyond the high flats –
where folk like us, housekeeping in infinity,
tapped out their codes, tapped out and in

their testament of clothed and naked lights.

Urban Peasantry

Moss beds and grass make an altar of sorts to it –
we lay tired bodies down there in the end.
You'll see it in the way we rework soil
and litanies: odd buds from broken ground.

Leaving no bottle half empty surely reveals it.
Just before falling asleep the one prayer
two bodies whisper is often remembered.
But we can fall awake as quick, into open air

before the sun has time to wipe mist off his face.
Educated, our heads hold thoughts promiscuously,
plants and coiling weeds entwined illuminate
the mind's manuscript, often fantastically

beside the point. Horses and women we like. Birds
and their native languages (which holy mothers
taught their sons to speak) we've learned
to read at least, inscribed in air.

Those swallows, for example, being foreigners always
spell 'flight' with a circumflex, the sign
of rising-falling voicing on a vowel.
Midges learn too late what this can mean.

Each year we drive towards harvest, find our place
in the History of Remembrance and Forgetting.
Another summer's growth burnt off by frost.
Ice polishes its teeth for bloodletting.

Driven Home

I am the angel charged to take you home.
I have nothing to look forward to. You have.

You think you nodded off for forty winks:
big boy, you have been dozing for a hundred years.

And here we are on Purgatory's M8
blinking awake by floodlit Kirk o' Shotts

where rusted tv masts and riding lights
pitch above Central Scotland's forest's waves.

Here's Holytown and Newhouse. Sing the one
about your father's many mansions. Hope it's true.

They're gathered at the door to see you in.
Loosen your seatbelt. There's our Maker – no,

that bloke with silver stubble on his chin
and five scenes from your famous childhood
tattooed on each forearm. On you go.

from Driven Home (Mariscat 1998)

Turning Over in a Strange Bed

Living with women is like turning
over in a strange bed at night
and trying to find your watch
and trying to read its face

or like living in a landscape
which is Donegal to your Galloway
with something like the same hills
with nothing like the same water

splashing down to a greener sedge.
Alongside your road they run like a river
your road follows valleys carved out by water
that is still peaty enough and cool

to quench your daily thirst.
Their blood is legendary and their sweat
on the right occasion never to be forgotten
while their tears remain unpredictable

by any instrument you will ever possess.

Ag Casadh Thart i Leaba Choimhthioch

Is ionann a bheith i do chònaì le bean
agus a bheith ag casadh thart i leaba choimhthìoch san oìche
agus a bheith ag iarraidh d'uaireadòir a aimsiù
agus a bheith ag iarraidh a èadan a lèamh

nò a bheith i do chònaì
mar a bhfuil dreach na tire cosuil le Tìr Chonaill seo agat
i gcoinne Ghallobhagh seo agam fèin
le mòràn na cnoic chèanna
agus gan a dhath den uisce ceanna

ag stealladh anuas go cìob gur glaise.
Le gruaimhìn do bhòthair fèin
ritheann siad mar a bheadh abhhainn ann
bìon do bhòthar ag reachtàil gleannta a snaidheadh leis an uisce
atà fòs mòintiùil go leor agus fionnuar

le do thart laethùil a mhùchadh.
Tà cliù agus càil ar a gcuid fola
agus a gcuid follais ag an tràth ceart nì dèantar dearmad air go bràch
agus a gcuid deor nì feidir a innseacht cèard ata ì ndàn dhòibh

e glèas de chineàl ar bith a bheas agat ariamh.

*from Poems Written for Translation
into an Abandoned Language*
trans. Rody Gorman

ALAN SPENCE
(b.1947)

Born Glasgow. Poet, playwright, novelist and
short story writer. Currently writer in
residence, Aberdeen University. Won
McVitie's Prize in 1996. Latest novel,
Way To Go (1998)

I've never been to Ireland. (Apart from hours spent in the no-place
of Shannon Airport en-route to New York.) Strange, I suppose, for
someone from the West of Scotland, where we all have an
ancestor or two from over the water. (In my case, my father's
grandmother who married a Scot from Campbeltown and that was
that.)

For my father it was where he'd spent his one and only holiday
outside Scotland, camping in Donegal one magical summer he
always remembered. A mythical place.

Ireland for me as a child, growing up in 1950s Glasgow, was a litany
of placenames to be sung with clenched fists punching the air.
Derry, Aughrim, Inneskillin, the Boyne. Long-ago battles over God-
knows-what. Rallying cries. No Surrender. Remember 1690. Uncles
inculcating the attitudes. I've catalogued it in my stories and novels.
Fed up writing about it. The madness. Atomisation of the prole-
tariat right enough, with a vengeance. I wrote it out of my system.

Over the years I was inspired by the sonorous mysticism of Yeats,
the ebullience of Joyce, the bleak humour of Beckett. Voices in my
head. But I was reading them alongside Basho and Hesse and Kafka
and Neil Gunn. I wanted to be open to all of it.

And Ireland's still a place I've never been.
(Sounds like a song. Sing to the tune of Galway Bay!)

Its Colours They Are Fine

BILLY pulled on the trousers of his best (blue) suit, hoisting the braces over his shoulders, and declared that without a doubt God must be a Protestant. It was no ponderous theology that made him say it, but simple observation that the sun was shining. And a God who made the sun shine on the day of the Orange Walk must surely be a Protestant, in sympathy at least.

From the front room Lottie mumbled responses he couldn't quite make out, but which he recognised as agreement. Over the twenty three years they'd been married, she had come to accept his picture of God as a kind of Cosmic Grand Master of the Lodge. It seemed probable enough.

Billy opened the window and leaned out.

The smell of late breakfasts frying; music from a radio; shouted conversations; traffic noises from the main road. A celebration of unaccustomed freedom. Saturday had a life and a character all of its own.

Sunlight shafted across the tenement roofs opposite, cleaved the street in two. A difference of greys. The other side in its usual gloom, this side warmed, its shabbiness exposed. Sun on stone.

Directly below, between a lamp-post and the wall, a huddle of small boys jostled in this improvised goalmouth while another, from across the road, took endless glorious corner kicks, heedless of traffic and passers-by.

One of the most noticeable things about a Saturday was the number of men to be seen in the street, waiting for the pubs to open, going to queue for a haircut, or simply content to wander about, enjoying the day. For them, as for Billy, a Saturday was something to be savoured. He would willingly work any amount of overtime – late nights, Sundays, holidays – but not Saturdays. A

Saturday was his. It was inviolable. And this particular Saturday was more than that, it was sacred. In Glasgow the Walk was always held on the Saturday nearest the 12th of July, the anniversary of the Battle of the Boyne. It was only in Ulster that they observed the actual date, no matter what day of the week that might be.

Billy closed the window and went through to the front room, which was both living-room and kitchen.

Lottie was laying out his regalia in readiness for the Walk – the sash, cuffs, white gloves and baton. She had laid them out flat on a sheet of brown paper and was wrapping them into a parcel.

'Whit's this?' he asked.

'Ah'm wrappin up yer things. Ye kin pit them oan when ye get tae Lorne School.'

'Not'n yer life! D'ye think ah'm frightened tae show ma colours?'

'That's jist whit's wrang wi ye. Yer never *done* showin yer colours! Look whit happened last year. Nearly in a fight before ye goat tae the coarner!'

'Look, wumman, this is a Protestant country. A Protestant queen shall reign.' He rapped on the table. 'That's whit it says. An if a Marshal in the Ludge canny walk the streets in is ain regalia, ah'll fuckin chuck it. Ah mean wu've goat tae show these people! Ah mean whit wid *he* say?'

He gestured towards the picture of King William III which hung on the wall – sword pointing forward, his white stallion bearing him across Boyne Water. In a million rooms like this he was hung in just that pose, doomed to be forever crossing the Boyne. This particular ikon had been bought one drunken afternoon at the Barrows and borne home reverently and miraculously intact through the teatime crowds. Its frame was a single sheet of glass, bound around with royal blue tape. Fastened on to one corner was a Rangers rosette which bore a card declaring NO SURRENDER.

'An you're asking me tae kerry this wrapped up like a fish supper!'

'Ach well,' she said, shoving the parcel across the table. 'Please yersel. But don't blame me if ye get yer daft heid stoved in.'

Billy grinned at the picture on the wall. Underneath it, on the mantelpiece, was the remains of what had been a remarkable piece of sculpture. One night in the licensed grocer's, Billy had stolen a white plastic horse about ten inches high, part of an advertising display for whisky. On to its back had been fitted a Plasticine model of King William, modelled by Peter, a young draughtsman who was in Billy's Lodge.

But one night Billy had come home drunk and knocked it over, squashing the figure and breaking one of the front legs from the horse. So there it sat. A lumpy Billy on a three-legged horse.

He picked up the splintered leg and was wondering if it could be glued back in place when there was a knock at the door.

'That'll be wee Robert,' he said, putting the leg back on the mantelpiece.

'Ah'll get it,' said Lottie.

Robert came in. He was actually about average height but he just looked small beside Billy. He and Billy had been friends since they were young men. They were both welders, and as well as working together, they belonged to the same Lodge. Robert was not wearing his sash. Under his arm he carried a brown paper parcel which looked remarkably like a fish supper.

'Is that yer sash?' asked Billy.

'Aye. Ach the wife thought it wid be safer like, y'know.'

'Well ah'm glad some'dy's goat some sense!' said Lottie.

'Ach!'

Billy buttoned his jacket and put on his sash, gloves and cuffs.

'Great day orra same!' said Robert. He was used to being caught between them like this and he knew it would pass.

'It is that,' said Billy. He picked up his baton.

'Right!' he said.

'Ye better take this,' said Lottie, handing him his plastic raincoat.

'O ye of little faith, eh!' He laughed, a little self-conscious at setting his tongue to a quote, but he took the coat nevertheless.

'Noo mind an watch yersels!'

Lottie watched from the window as they walked along the

street and out of sight. At least this year they'd got that far without any trouble.

As they rounded the corner, in step, Billy turned to Robert.

'Ah'm tellin ye Robert,' he said. 'God's a Protestant!'

●

EMERGING into the sunlight from the subway at Cessnock, they could hear some of the bands warming up. Stuttered rolls and paradiddles on the side drums, deep throb of the bass, pipes droning, snatches of tunes on the flutes.

'Dis yer heart good tae hear it, eh!' Billy slapped Robert on the back.

Robert carefully unwrapped his sash and put it on, then defiantly screwed up the paper into a ball and threw it into the gutter.

'At's the stuff!'

Billy caught the strains of 'The Bright Orange and Blue' and started to whistle it as he marched along.

'Ther's the bright orange an blue for ye right enough,' said Robert, gesturing towards the assembly of the faithful.

So much colour, on uniforms, sashes and banners. The bright orange and blue, the purple and the red, the silver and the gold, and even (God forgive them!) the green.

The marchers were already forming into ranks. It must be later than they'd thought. They hurried up to where their Lodge was assembled and took their positions, Billy at the side, Robert up behind the front rank, carrying one of the cords which trailed from the poles of their banner. Purple and orange silk, King William III, Loyal and True. Derry, Aughrim, Inneskillin, Boyne. These were the four battles fought by William in Ireland, their magic names an incantation, used now as rallying cries in the everlasting battle against popery.

They were near the front of the procession and their Lodge was one of the first to move off, a flute band from Belfast just in front of them.

Preparatory drumroll. 'The Green Grassy Slopes.' Sun glinting on the polished metal parts of instruments and the numerals on sashes and cuffs.

To Billy's right marched Peter, long and thin with a wispy half-grown beard. Billy caught his eye once and looked away quickly. He was still feeling guilty about ruining the Plasticine model that Peter had so carefully made. A little further on, Peter called over to him. 'The band's gaun ther dinger, eh!'

'Aye they ur that. Thull gie it laldy passin the chapel!'

It was as if they were trying to jericho down the chapel walls by sheer volume of sound, with the bass drummer trying to burst his skins. (He was supposed to be paid a bonus if he did, though Billy had never seen it happen.) And the drum major, a tight-trousered shaman in a royal blue jumper, would leap and birl and throw his stick in the air, the rest of the band strutting or swaggering or shuffling behind. The flute band shuffle. Like the name of a dance. It was a definite mode of walking the bandsmen seemed to inherit – shoulders hunched, body swaying from the hips, feet scuffling in short, aggressive steps.

Billy's own walk was a combination of John Wayne and numberless lumbering cinema-screen heavies. He'd always been Big Billy, even as a child. Marching in the Walk was like being part of a liberating army. Triumph. Drums throbbing. Stirring inside. He remembered newsreel films of the Allies marching into Paris. At that time he'd been working in the shipyards and his was a reserved occupation, 'vital to the war effort' which meant he couldn't join up. But he'd marched in imagination through scores of Hollywood films. From the Sands of Iwo Jima to the beachheads of Normandy. But now it was real, and instead of 'The Shores of Tripoli', it was 'The Sash My Father Wore'.

They were passing through Govan now, tenements looming on either side, people waving from windows, children following the parade, shoving their way through the crowds along the pavement.

The only scuffle that Billy saw was when a young man started shouting about civil rights in Ireland, calling the marchers fascists. A small sharp-faced woman started hitting him with a union jack.

Two policemen shoved their way through and led the man away for his own safety as the woman's friends managed to bustle her, still shouting and brandishing her flag, back into the crowd.

'Hate tae see bother like that,' said Peter.

'Ach aye,' said Billy. 'Jist gets everyb'dy a bad name.'

Billy had seen some terrible battles in the past. It would usually start with somebody shouting or throwing something at the marchers. Once somebody had lobbed a bottle from a third-storey window as the Juvenile Walk was passing, and a mob had charged up the stairs, smashed down the door and all but murdered every occupant of the house. Another common cause of trouble was people trying to cross the road during the parade. The only time Billy had ever used his baton was when this had happened as they passed the war memorial in Govan Road, with banners lowered and only a single drumtap sounding. A tall man in overalls had tried to shove his way through, breaking the ranks. Billy had tried to stop him, but he'd broken clear and Billy had clubbed him on the back of the neck, knocking him to the ground. Another Marshal had helped him to pick the man up and bundle him back on to the pavement.

But this year for Billy there was nothing to mar the showing of the colours and he could simply enjoy the whole brash spectacle of it. And out in front the stickman led the dance, to exorcise with flute and drum the demon antichrist bogeyman pope.

They turned at last into Govan Road and the whole procession pulsed and throbbed and flaunted its way along past the shipyards. Down at the river, near the old Elder cinema, buses were waiting to take them to the rally, this year being held in Gourock. Billy and Robert found seats together on the top deck of their bus and Peter sat opposite, across the passage. As the bus moved off there was a roar from downstairs.

'Lik a fuckin Sunday-school trip!' said Robert, and he laughed and waved his hanky out the window.

from Its Colours They Are Fine (Collins 1977)

HAMISH WHYTE
(b.1947)

Born in Giffnock, Renfrewshire, now lives in
Glasgow. A former librarian, he runs Mariscat
Press publishing poetry. He has edited many
anthologies including *Mungo's Tongues:
Glasgow Poems 1630–1990*.

I regard myself as Scottish, albeit a mongrel, as many Scots are: bits
of Scots, English and Irish. I discovered only recently that my
mother's father's family, who I knew were English, came from
Cromer in Norfolk. The Irish in me comes from my mother's
mother's family, originally Plantation Irish I gather. My mother's
grandfather, William John Ballantine, arrived in Scotland with his
wife Sarah Hewitt (a farmer's daughter) probably around the turn
of last century and probably from County Down (I'm told there are
lots of Ballantines in Newcastle). They had hoped to emigrate to
America, but got no further than Glasgow. William John worked as
a railway clerk and died in 1928.

One family story is that his grandmother, Alicia Hamilton (my
mother's name is Alicia), was an heiress in a landowning family,
who eloped with the coachman. Her father cut her off, but on his
deathbed he relented, called her home and said she could have the
contents of a drawer in his room. It was stuffed with money –
which the coachman husband then drank away. My mother
remembers grandfather William John (always the two names)
telling her that on visiting his grandmother she would show him a
riding crop, all that remained of her palmy days.

I have a different version: on his deathbed Alicia's father called her
to him and told her she could have the contents of the drawer. She
opened it, perhaps thinking there was money, but all it contained
was a riding crop.

There's a coda. One Glasgow holiday my great grandfather
Ballantine was in the crowds at St Enoch Station. Hearing an Irish
voice near him he got into conversation with its owner, an old man

who, amazingly, turned out to be the stable boy who had put straw down on the cobbles in the courtyard to muffle the coach wheels as William John's grandmother made her elopement.

The story of 'Lady' Alicia was brought up in family situations if our genteel origins needed emphasised – or mocked. Nothing was made of the Irishness. In fact, I felt more of an affinity with the South, thanks to a teenage love of Wilde, Shaw and Joyce and an Irish girl called Anne (who had a Scottish surname).

In 1965 I went to Glasgow University and fell in love with Anne and Ireland. I took her to Daft Friday and dreamed of stringing a lyre (not harp – we were Classics students) with her golden hair, wrote poems – the usual romantic twaddle. At Christmas she went off to spend the vacation at her uncle's in Tinahely (magical name) and left me her father's watch as memento. Then things changed, the watch was taken back, she fancied someone else and my passion became like all the best passions, unrequited.

She was not only gone, she was Maud Gonne. Yeats was added to the pantheon, I started wearing green instead of blue and drinking only Guinness; my armchair support of Celtic probably dates from around this time as well. She also introduced me to Bob Dylan, so all was not lost.

So – I am proud to have some family – that is, real – connection with Ireland, but it's only part of me and I don't think it colours my work or life overmuch: it's just there, it's a family story, it's a reason, if reason be needed, to take an interest in what goes on across the water. My middle name is Ballantine and I reckon I am the last bearer of the name in the family. I am curious enough to want to make the probablies in the story more definite. Probably. It will mean a search in the Irish records. We'll see.

The only time I visited Ireland it wasn't the North: sailed from the Broomielaw on a Monday evening, woke up in Dublin the next morning. Along with all the romantic notions of Ireland, I have actual (or virtual) memories too, for the poetic reservoir.

from **Virtual Memories**

the morning Mrs Duff decided
to find out who was singing hymns
off-key –
I thought it was me
but it was Muriel Erskine
(whom I took to the Lifeboys party)
sitting at the same desk

•

In the staff room
Bernadette McCann
drinks Irn-Bru
from a bottle
brooding over a book
on Manuel's murders –
four tables down
Mr Fisher
whispers
at the top of his voice
'I thought it was Mills and Boon!'

•

we crossed the Liffey
by Joyce's bridge
and wandered along
the riverside road
stopped at an antique shop
and this old woman came out
and told us not to lean on the window
it might all fall down
and remembered seeing Queen Victoria
and sold me a silver lucifer case
for my girlfriend –
later in a cafe

the waitress asked if we were from the North
no from Glasgow we said
affronted

●

It began askew
the way dreams are meant to be:
we watched the warm-up
from the top of a lamp post
and the goals were at right angles
to each other.
            We finally
made it to the superstadium
(like going to the Bolshoi:
gents in djs taking the tickets)
and flopped into our seats
just as our friend Kevin passed
wearing the green and heading
upfield at speed, a touch of McStay.
I woke up then
but never mind:
my dream made Kevin's come true.

●

Rummaging in the back
of Grandpa's garage
I found this heavy truncheon
of polished wood.
He said it was issued
in the 1880s
to his father who was beadle
at St Andrew's Episcopal
to give the Fenians what-for
if they tried anything.
It looked unbashed.

previously unpublished

THERESA BRESLIN
(b. 1948)

Librarian and writer with special interest in children's literature. Her books have been dramatised for television and radio, and include *Kezzie* and *Whispers in the Graveyard*. Awards include the Carnegie Gold Medal.

Re the Scots-Irish-Catholic whatsit. It always amazes me that people moan on about this. What a brilliant grounding for a writer. The ceremonies, the incense, the colour – from Lenten purple to Easter's dazzling white – the music, the candlelight, Alpha and Omega, and the Gospel according to John, 'In the beginning was the Word. . .'

And those words, Chasuble, Alb, Stole, Tabernacle – whole sentences, the best lines ever – 'Remember man that thou art dust. . .' the downstroke on your forehead of a heavy thumb loaded with ash, and then a crossbar nine feet wide '. . . and into dust thou shalt return' The drama, the litanies, the Latin – every sense thrumming. Add a dash of Celtic culture, a Scots-Irish instinct to flout any authority, and obviously, it's all going to come pouring out in Art, Music, Literature, Drama, Dance etc. . .

I was never severely chastised by a nun, but hey, you can't have it all.

Act of Love

THE TRICK, as Captain John Ainsley had discovered, was in how you placed the bullet. Too close, and the skull exploded, smearing one's uniform with gore and brain tissue. Too far back, and the deed was left incomplete, with the man on the ground gazing up at you with the eyes of a kitten awaiting drowning.

Once, a starlight shell had burst around him as he had made just such a mistake and the soldier he was crouched beside in no-man's-land, an older man, had looked up at him, smiled, and said, 'You'll have to try again, son.'

He had returned from that sortie trembling, rushing to the brandy flask in the support trench, gabbling what had happened. His C.O. had taken him aside and spoken to him firmly, explaining yet again that what he did was for the best.

'Get a grip, man. Those casualties left lingering out there for the rats to eat alive, or hanging on the barbed-wire night after night, would curse you for not doing it.'

'Actually,' replied the C.O., 'I consider it an act of love.'

It rarely happened now that he got the shakes. He had become an expert at dispatching a man with a single bullet, and avoiding a mess to clean up later. He took the identity disc from the dead private's neck, and put his pistol back in the leather holster on his belt. His fingers scarcely trembled, despite the fact that the boy he had just killed could have been no more than fifteen years old. Ten years younger than himself. . . a child. . . whereas he, after four months of this war without sense, was an old man.

He crawled back to the other soldier who might yet live and began to help him drag himself towards their forward trenches. They moved cautiously, yet in the knowledge of the gentleman's agreement regarding collecting casualties and parapet repairs at night. Enemy action was suspended to allow both sides to retrieve their wounded and get them back down the supply roads in the shadow of darkness.

Each week Captain Ainsley wrote home in pages torn from his field diary, but nothing he wrote described what he saw each day. The stench of the dead and dying pervading each place. Their defences, as the line moved forward and they gained two hundred yards, were built on top of the bodies of the German dead. And no doubt when they were driven back three weeks later, he supposed the Boche used the British corpses for the same end. Should he be surprised when his mother sent him packages of mint tea and bath salts, when he needed carbolic soap and dry matches?

Fleas ran everywhere and lice lay in the seams of your clothes. Insolent bluebottles, swollen so large as to be cumbersome in flight, buzzed round your head, and rats, which they were not allowed to shoot, crawled blood-bloated and rabid among the dead. The vile side of nature triumphant and the sweetness crushed. No birdsong, no flowers, nor plants nor perfumed air.

When he first happened upon Private Sam Hinslewood, chatting with his friends and playing softly on his mouth organ, John Ainsley stopped to listen. And then was drawn back, evening after evening to the same company, standing to the rear of the group as Sam read out his letters from home. There was his wife Mary, trying to manage the farm on her own. They had a boy, Adam, rising ten. Sam described the seasons as they fell. The year was on the turn. The shire horses would be put to the plough, Tom and Colt, turning the earth, preparing the land to receive the seed.

The man had a gift. He was a natural born storyteller. The words, as he said them, came alive. One could hear the peewits in the meadow, see the pale golden ears of barley ripen as he spoke.

On one occasion they had noticed him and as the soldiers scrambled to their feet and saluted, Captain Ainsley made a small sign with his hand.

'Compliments need not be paid on active service.'

He recited the words from the staff manual and moved away, strangely embarrassed at having been discovered.

He had spent his evenings reading at first, then drinking more and more, and always, always, compiling the casualty lists. He never mentioned this in his letters home. His parents wrote back in fulsome praise of his rapid promotion to the rank of Captain. The bridge club had been very impressed. He neglected to inform them that the promotion was automatic and depended on the death of one's superior officer.

He made a grim smile when his father had written to say he was now reaping the benefit of the officer training, which he knew he had hated. Captain Ainsley reflected that learning to pass the port to the left did not seem significantly relevant at the moment. It became much more important to know how Sam's boy was progressing. In the daily letters which his wife wrote she described the lad, ruddy and sturdy-legged playing in the fields around their farm. Her love, and the child's, moved amongst them all.

Once, when they had been shifted along the line, they had halted at a crossroads. Under the trees, outside an estaminet, Sam and his friends had gathered. And the Captain with the rest had laughed out loud at one of his stories. All the men had turned to the sound of the stranger amongst them, and he caught Sam's eye, flushed, and walked away quickly. He found that he was not as happy in the company of his fellow officers. Yes, a shared cigarette under the rain cape, tears of rain dripping from the low eaves of the farmhouses. And the anxious drinking together as they discussed home and troops and the British High Command. But it wasn't the same. Under the roar of the guns, the heavy bombardment that now came day after day and the chatter of the machine-gun fire, he knew where he wanted to be, who he needed to be with.

And if it came to it, as it would, when they went over the top, up the short wooden ladder, whistles screaming, he prayed that he would not fail them. In the choking gas and the smoke, eyes streaming as they had done in the smoke in the railway station where she had come to bid him farewell, her eye sliding away, her attention caught by movement beyond him.

'Oh, George, look!' she'd cried. Laying a gloved hand on his father's arm. 'A military band! I do love a brass band!' And she had walked forward to see the parade. His father, for once aware of his sensitivities, said, 'You mustn't mind your mother so much. Women are always taken with such things.'

His father had shaken his hand firmly and he had saluted and boarded the train.

The smoke still drifted; here and there, each evening, as he searched among the bodies. And as he slithered on his belly now in the sucking mud, hoping for one to bring back, he came suddenly upon a huge rat. Rolling to one side to avoid it, he felt the hard metal of a land mine under him.

It exploded with a crash which knocked him senseless and hurled him into the air yards away. When he opened his eyes at last he knew that it was the same night and that he could not even lift his head.

'What's amiss?' Sam's voice spoke in his ear.

'Arms, legs. . . can't move them,' Ainsley said. And his voice, when he heard it filled him with contempt for himself. Pathetic and weak.

Sam tried to assess the damage. His hands, searching across the uniform, touched the caved-in breastbone, felt the shattered limbs. The Captain was in great pain, his jaw clenched lest a sound escape. Sam calculated: twenty minutes or so to drag him the few short yards to the trench, the wait for the stretcher-bearers, to take him to the reserve post, another twenty minutes to the nearest field dressing station, no morphine, no doctor. Hours on the jolting horse-drawn ambulance cart to get him back down the line. It would be at least a day before the Captain got any relief.

'Leave me. Go back.'

'Uhuh,' the older man grunted.

'Let me raise you up here.' He slid his hand under the tunic collar at the back of Ainsley's neck. The Captain whimpered as he touched him.

As Sam's fingers sank into the soft porridge of the remains of John Ainsley's skull, a magnesium flare lit up the sky above and he could see the man's face illuminated in the glow. The Captain's eyes were dull, the light fading. His face tallow-candle yellow.

'Go back,' Ainsley said again. 'I order you to.'

'No, no, man,' Sam soothed him. 'Hush. Hush.'

There was a rattle of fire along the line. Sam cursed. Some silly beggar. There had been word of troop changes on the German side a few days ago. A nervous new recruit must have loosed off a few rounds.

'Hey!' came a shout from his own side. 'Let up, Fritz. We want some shut-eye over here.'

'Sweet dreams, Tommy,' a voice called back. '*Gute Nacht*.'

'Go back,' the Captain whispered to Sam. 'The men need you.'

'You're the officer,' said Sam. 'It's you they need.'

'You give them hope.'

'And you give them courage,' replied Sam. 'They'd follow you to hell.'

'They have. We are in hell.'

There was silence between them. Sam's arm still lay round the other man's neck.

'We'll wait a bit, he said, 'until it's quieter, and then see if we can get back.'

'Tell me about your boy,' whispered the Captain.

'My boy?' Sam repeated.

'The lad, Adam. The farm. . . your wife, Mary. . . the horses . . . your life.'

'Oh,' said Sam. 'It's very ordinary. Hard work. Up at sun-up, work till sundown. But the countryside is beautiful. Mary collects berries, makes jam, it's peaceful. . . so peaceful.'

He stopped, he hesitated. 'This is what you want to hear?'

Captain Ainsley nodded.

So Sam talked on, describing their way of life, the crops, from seeding to harvest, the animals and the flowers in the hedgerows.

'You have the gift of storytelling,' said the Captain. 'I have the very smell of gardenia in my head. It is my mother's favourite perfume. . . I remember she used to come and kiss me each evening after Nanny had tucked me up in bed. She would be dressed in a pretty dress, always such a pretty dress. . . I wanted her to wait to hug me. . .'

He stopped then, recalling the night when he had clung on, sobbing childish sobs, begging her to stay and she had pushed him back against his pillows, complaining he had crushed her frock. At that moment his father had come into the room. They were already late for the theatre, he said. Did she have to kiss the boy still? He was too old now for that. She would make him soft. And his father had blown out the night-light and he was left in the dark.

He looked about him with a start. It was dark now, a strange closing darkness that was advancing towards him. He began to shake as he had done that night.

'Hug me,' he cried. 'For the love of God, comfort me.'

Sam gathered the boy to him and held him close against his chest. And stroked his face and told him more of his son and his farm.

The stars were fading. Sam looked to the sky in the east, louring and ominous with dark cloud. He knew he must move, but he kept talking, although he was aware that the Captain was barely conscious. It seemed to him that the boy was merging with the landscape, grey face, grey bones, becoming as one with the surrounding glutinous mud.

So then Sam, without withdrawing his arm from under his Captain's neck and still speaking quietly as if to gentle a skittish mare, reached with his free hand to slide the muzzle of the pistol into position beside John Ainsley's head.

GERRY LOOSE
(b. 1948)

Born London, has lived in Ireland and since
1983, in Scotland. Translated *Tongues of
Stone: Poems from Ogham* (1998). Currently
Poet in Residence, Glasgow Botanic Gardens.

Odd perspectives – born in London – grown – sprouted in Ireland
like an onion in a sack – aware of exile, of history, of weight of
tradition, of diasporas – of the revelation of

'The *rath* in front of the oak wood' [1]

and of horses & high rise city blocks – modern nations coming to
terms with another millennium; of lyricism

'. . . the warrior from the *side* dropped wholesome herbs and
grasses into Cuchullainn's aching wounds and several sores so that
he began to recover in his sleep without knowing it' [2]

of herb growers inside city boundaries, of addicts dreaming in
remote Atlantic rain-sodden townlands, of the birth and growing
pains of abstraction & the coming home of words built from the
interconnections of weeds, herbs, nightclubs. A Scots/Irish bangra
of fusions which always existed in these islands of factions fitting
like mismatched jigsaw puzzles.

To address nations is dangerous. To address nationalism is more so.
To address national identity is to discover sawdust after the saw has
been at work on the wood. Addressing identity is to find nothing as
graspable as sawdust. I came to Scotland in search of Dal Riada &
found David Bowie on a loop tape in Argos Superstore. I looked
for Columcille & my car broke down on the M8 in snow. The map
intrudes on the territory until landscape asserts itself; like banks of
nettles bursting through the cracked asphalt of railway sidings.

My ears ringing, I began to hear the speech of Scotland & to enjoy
the way it confounds expectations – uttered as it is from many
tongues (Irish being one) Gaelic, Scots, English, Urdu, Hindi.

---

1 Anon; pre 6th century CE Irish
2 *The Táin*; trans Thomas Kinsella; OUP/Dolmen 1969

Coming from is less interesting that being at. Being now & here is to be busy weaving wholesome herbs & tinsel into tartan – to be part of people forming and reforming – images everywhere – dust in the shafts of sun streaming through my 5th floor city window which overlooks the Clyde, Cathkin Braes, the Kilpatrick Hills. Aspects of Dal Riada rattle around my head, as does the *rath* in front of the oak wood; but what I see is the Finnieston crane. What I write is what I see, in fact, in memory & in imagination; where Ireland is a stratum, now below Scotland, now heaved above & beside by metamorphic memory and metaphoric imagination. A fusion of rocks with a new – as yet indecipherable – name written through the centre.

Terra Incognita

where is the clang
of this spade on stone

where is the fruit of the tree
that made this shaft

where is the fire and rod that made
beads of weld on this steel

I stole the soft mist
it was mine always

I stole the air from the wind
it never knew

I stole the heron's gaze
she had fished enough

tell me: what can I take,
what cannot be taken

Discussion on Making All Things Equal

it's no accident I'm walking here stifflegged ankle
deep in the water of the quicksilver estuary which
stretches to every horizon but the one I have my
back to   (my face to the sunrise)

every horizon but the solid dream which I can rap
with my knuckles like a coffin

The solid dream from which I walk away as from a
wrecked car

I walk away from the wrecked car a little stiff

why do I think of a heron walking here?

St George's Cross

sixty feet up now
filling an old honey jar
with ragwort   Senecio jacobaea
and hedge mustard   Sisymbrium officinale
from the dogshit wastelot
smoking a cigarette
glass of wine
Tanglewood on the radio
my inheritance
of weeds delighting
and clouds filling my eyes
old tools well worn
each in its place

The Long Lunch

for Caroline O'Toole (& Frank O'Hara)

after lunch at the Tron
I smoked a cigarette

we moved table for that
& your lips moved just so

when my friends arrived
we moved table but the baby

Caitlin was not let in the bar
we moved table

& your smile moved just so
my friend's baby moved us

as you   that time   listened
then your friend and her

daughter Caitlin showed   by chance
and we moved chairs

I moved table
& smoked a cigarette

the while watching
friends   you

it may be that coincidence
is the trust we put in each other

from coincidence we
make what we will

what we will is a trust
a lunch where all tables

are vacant   reserved   strange
friendships Frank   when you (dead)

talk to me   & Caroline
you hear   & now   I

speak to you both directly
what is taking place here

For Kate on her Birthday

I wake one morning
to the sound of traffic and the cackling of gulls
I have mislaid my seventeenth wedding anniversary
this scene is acted out in three thousand bedrooms this
        morning

we are happened upon
yet small things still retain the power to please
the purchase of a packet of envelopes
the memory of another bedroom window elsewhere

nothing can ever be subtracted
what is not clear is how
with the clouds flying overhead
we avoid the shadows

BRIAN McCABE
(b.1951)

Born in Edinburgh where he still lives.
Novelist, short story writer and poet. Most
recent collection is *Body Parts* (1999).

There were shamrocks on the doilies. On the walls there were
circular, gilt-edged plaques displaying the McCabe tartan: a uniform
green. Irish tartans were that, just different shades of green. I
found this very disappointing, that our tartan could be so dull – it
confirmed for me that we were somehow inferior. Of course, I
wanted a real tartan shirt, one with bright yellow and red checks,
and to wear it while I was riding my bike with an elastoplast on my
forehead in exactly the same place as the smiling boy on the
elastoplast tin had it on his forehead. I think I also wanted his
freckles, if he had freckles. I wanted to be recognised and accepted
as normal, but if anything, the Irish connection made me feel
insecure about this. There were family stories about my father
throwing a priest out of the house and telling him never to darken
our doorway again with his mendacious propaganda. (That must
have been around the time my father was converted to Communism.) My older sisters and brother had gone to a Catholic school,
but I had been sent to the Protestant school. It was all a bit
confusing.

My father came from Cambuslang. My mother came from
Craigmillar. We lived in Bonnyrigg. We were an ordinary, laconic,
repressed Scottish family, with no hint of the Irish blarney, but the
Irish thing was there in our background all the same – before I had
been born, before any of us had been born. Ireland was where we
were from originally – my mother's side of the family as well as my
father's. Sometimes it came to the surface in a tipsy song at
Hogmanay, or in a poem. I don't know if my father got his love of
books from his Irish genes or from the company of his fellow
miners, but he had it, and there were always books in our house.
None of these were by Irish writers as far as I can recall. Some old
books with leather covers I remember: *Poetical Works* by Burns;
The Collected Poems of Byron; The Rubaiyat of Omar Khayyam; Poems

by Shelley; *The Works of E. A. Poe Vol I – Tales*. And there were modern novels in paperback: Upton Sinclair's *The Jungle*; *Lady Chatterley's Lover*; *The Ragged Trousered Philanthropists*; and hidden behind the others, *Fanny Hill*.

The only holiday I remember my parents having was to Dublin. I remember feeling quite upset about them going away. A taxi came to collect them from the scheme of houses we lived in in Bonnyrigg. I described this event in *The Other McCoy*, because although our Irish origin wasn't important to me then, I was aware of it and perhaps it came to play a part when I came to write. Others have pointed out to me that the theme of personal identity seems to recur in my work, *The Other McCoy* being a good example of this: the main character is a compulsive mimic, unsure of his own identity, and his ontological insecurity is partly attributed to the Scottish-Irish confusion in his background. He feels that he is 'an imitation Irishman' – cursed with an Irish name and genealogy, but unable to be Irish.

More recently, Catholicism seems to be cropping up in some of my stories, as if I am trying to reclaim a frame of reference my father threw out of the house with the priest. Although I have never gone to confession, the idea of the confessional interests me, and the role of the priest. I wrote a story recently in which a priest goes to a massage parlour only to be recognised and chastised by the girl who gives him the 'relief' he craves – and he has to seek absolution from her. My intention wasn't to discredit the Catholic church or the priesthood – they manage that quite well by themselves – but to explore the tension between being a man and having the role of the priest. In another story, 'An Invisible Man', a failed priest can't escape the role and goes on being a kind of secular priest in his job as a security guard in a department store. I don't think I am interested in these things now because of the Irish connection, particularly, but there's no doubt that it played a part in my family background and so it may well have had some effect on what I've concerned myself with in my writing.

An Invisible Man

SOMETIMES on dark winter mornings he watched them before the doors were opened: pressing their hands and faces against the glass, a plague of moths wanting in to the light. But you couldn't look at them like that, as an invading swarm. To do the job, you had to get in among them, make yourself invisible. You had to blend in, pretend to be one of them, but you also had to observe them, you had to see the hand slipping the 'Game Boy' into the sleeve. Kids wore such loose clothes nowadays, baggy jeans and jogging tops two sizes too big for them. It was the fashion, but it meant they could hide their plunder easily. You had to watch the well-dressed gentlemen as well – the Crombie and the briefcase could conceal a fortune in luxury items. When it came down to it, you were a spy.

He was in the Food Hall and they were rushing around him. He picked up a wire basket and strolled through the vegetables, doing his best to look interested in a packet of Continental Salad, washed and ready to use. It was easy to stop taking anything in and let the shopping and the shoplifting happen around you, a blur, an organism, an animal called The Public. The Public was all over the shop: poking its nose into everything; trying on the clean new underwear; squirting the testers on its chin, on its wrists, behind its ears; wriggling its fingers into the gloves; squeezing its warm, damp feet into stiff, new shoes; tinkering with the computers; thumbing the avocados.

He was watching a grey-haired lady dressed in a sagging blue raincoat, probably in her sixties, doing exactly that. The clear blue eyes, magnified by thick lenses, looked permanently shocked. A disappointed mouth, darkened by a plum-coloured lipstick, floundered in a tight net of wrinkles. There was something in her movements that was very tense, yet she moved slowly, as if she had been stunned by some very bad news.

She put down the avocados – three of them, packaged in polythene – as if she'd just realised what they were and that she didn't need them. He followed her as she made her way to the express pay-point and took her place in the queue. He stacked his empty basket and waited on the other side of the cash-points, impersonating a bewildered husband waiting for the wife he'd lost sight of. He watched her counting her coins from a small black purse. The transaction seemed to fluster her, as if she might not have enough money to pay for the few things she'd bought. A tin of lentil soup. An individual chicken pie. One solitary tomato. Maybe she did need the avocados – or something else.

The pay-point wasn't the obvious place to catch shoplifters, so they used it. It was like declaring something when you went through customs, in the hope that the real contraband would go unnoticed. Or offering a small sin at confession, hoping that it would distract God from his ferocious omniscience. An amateur tactic. It was easy to catch someone with a conscience, someone who wanted to be caught.

He ambled behind her to the escalator down to Kitchen and Garden. When she came off the escalator, she waited at the bottom, as if not sure where to find what she was looking for. He moved away from her to the saucepans and busied himself opening up a three-tiered vegetable steamer, then he put the lid back on hastily to follow her to the gardening equipment. She moved past the lawn-mowers and the sprinklers until she came to a display of seed packets.

It wasn't often that you had this kind of intuition about somebody and it turned out to be right, but as soon as he saw her looking at the seeds, he was certain she was going to steal them. He moved closer to her, picked up a watering can and weighed it in his hand, as if this was somehow a way of testing it, then he saw her dropping packet after packet into the bag. He followed her to the door and outside, then he put his hand on her shoulder. When she turned round he showed her his i.d. Already she was shaking visibly. Her red-veined cheeks had taken on a hectic colour and tears loomed behind her outraged blue eyes.

'Please,' she said, 'arrest me. Before I do something worse.'

He took her back inside and they made the long journey to the top of the store in silence. For the last leg of it he took her through Fabrics – wondering if they might be taken for a couple, a sad old couple shopping together in silence – and up the back staircase so that he wouldn't have to march her through Admin.

It was depressing to unlock the door of his cubby-hole, switch the light on and see the table barely big enough to hold his kettle and his tea things, the one upright chair, the barred window looking out on a fire-escape and the wall-mounted telephone. He asked her to take the packets of seeds out of her bag and put them on the table. She did so, and the sight of the packets, with their gaudy coloured photographs of flowers, made her clench her hand into a fist.

He told her to take a seat while he called security, but when he turned away from her she let out a thin wail that made him recoil from the phone. She had both her temples between her hands, as if afraid her head might explode. She let out another shrill wail. It ripped out of her like something wild kept prisoner for years. It seemed to make the room shrink around them.

'Now now, no noise please,' he said, like a dentist who'd just drilled into a nerve. He cursed himself inwardly for bringing her here alone – he should have collected a security guard on the way. Now he was on his own with her in the cubby-hole and she was wailing. If the people in Admin heard, it might be open to all sorts of interpretation. His job was under threat as it was, what with the security guards and the new surveillance cameras.

She wailed again – a raw outpouring of anger and loss. Christ, he had to get her out of here. He stooped over her and reached out to take one of her hands away from her head, then he thought better of touching her at all. His hand hovered over her as he spoke:

'Look, you don't seem like a habitual shoplifter –'

She blurted out that she'd never stolen anything in her life before, but it was hard to make out the words because she was sobbing and coughing at the same time, her meagre body shuddering as if an invisible man had taken her by the shoulders and was shaking her violently.

'I'm sure it was just absent-mindedness. You intended to pay for these –' He motioned with a hand to the scattered packets of seeds on the table, but she was having none of it:

'No, I stole them. I don't even like gardening –' The words came out in spurts between her coughs and sobs but there was no stopping her now that she'd started: 'It's overgrown, weeds everywhere. It was him who did it. He was mad about his garden. He spent all his time, morning till night, out in all bloody weathers –'

He let her talk. Her husband had been obsessed with his garden. It had been his way of getting away – from her, from everyone and everything. He'd withdrawn from the world into his flowering shrubs and geraniums. She hardly saw him, and when he'd died all there was left of him was his garden. Now the weeds were taking over. When she'd seen the seed packets, with their pictures of Dahlias and Pansies and Rhododendrons . . . It made a kind of sense. Why had she stolen them rather than pay for them? He should have known better than to ask. He got the whole story of her financial hardship now that she was on her own, including the cost of the funeral. It was an expensive business, dying.

When she'd finished, she fished a small white handkerchief from her coat pocket to wipe the tears from her eyes. It was the way she did this that reminded him of his mother, the way she had to move her glasses out of the way to get the handkerchief to her eyes. He told her to go home. She looked up at him in surprise, then clutched the handles of her bag, realising she should get out while the going was good. When she stood up her blue eyes were alert with curiosity.

'Why are you doing this?'

'I don't know.'

He had made thieves of so many people. But this one

reminded him of his mother. He absolved her with a wave of his hand. Still she made a fuss of thanking him, reaching up to touch his collar. When she'd gone, he noticed the crumpled handkerchief on the floor and bent down to pick it up.

He had stepped into the lift and pressed the button for the ground floor before he realised that the lights weren't working. The doors hissed together and he was alarmed to be shut inside a box of night. He crossed himself without thinking, although he hadn't done so for years. He heard the machinery of the lift working – a slight gasp of the hydraulics he'd never noticed before – then he began to descend slowly through the darkness. He imagined that the lift was his coffin and he was descending into the earth. Then he wondered why they didn't bury people upright, what with cemetery space being at a premium. When his mother had died, hadn't he had to take out a personal loan to cover the funeral and the cost of the plot? As the woman had said, it was an expensive business.

The lift came to a halt, the doors slid apart, but no one was waiting to get in. He looked out at Lingerie. From the crowd of people shambling around the counters rose a line of perfect legs sheathed in stockings and tights, their toes pointing at the roof. Above them the elegant models stood on their plinths, dressed in camisoles and negligees, averting their eyeless faces like disdainful idols.

Some of the creations in there were unbelievable. They were designed to tempt men, so it made sense to put them on the same floor as Menswear. He'd apprehended one man, about his own age, respectable in his choice of casual wear, greying at the sides and balding on top, trying to cram an expensive Gossard scarlet basque into his inside pocket. He'd wanted to buy it – for his wife, he'd said at first, then had admitted later, when he'd got him in the cubby-hole, that it was for his mistress – but he'd felt too embarrassed to take it to a pay-point and hand it over to be wrapped. He'd begged him to let him off – poor man, in his Yves Saint Laurent polo shirt. Maybe not so poor: he'd probably get off with a small fine or an admonishment, and although he was in his fifties, he had a mistress – one who would wear a scarlet basque.

The doors hissed together and he was shut in with the darkness again. She hadn't wanted to be cremated, in case the soul turned out to be located in the Hypothalamus, or some other part of the body. She'd had some funny notions that way. She'd believed in an afterlife, having been brought up a good Catholic, but in her later life – maybe because of him, because he'd turned his back on the priesthood – she'd stopped caring what form the afterlife might take. Heaven or reincarnation – she'd settle for either. In the hospice, she had accepted the services of the priest, the vicar and the visiting humanist, keeping her options open. If there had been a rabbi and a Buddhist coming round, she would have signed up with them too. With more eagerness, maybe, because they would be new to her, and she had always believed in anything she didn't know about, as if the very fact that she hadn't heard of it gave it credence, so complete was her humility.

There was the gasp of the hydraulics as the lift was released and he felt himself sinking again. It all seemed to take much longer in the dark.

He had watched her body shrink into itself like a withering fruit, but she'd gone on smiling, determined to keep up appearances. He remembered the last demented thing she had said to him as she lay there, scandalised by her own condition, about her bedside locker being bugged, about the other patients and their visitors being spies. Then she'd urged him to eat the fruit in the bowl:

'Have a banana, son,' she'd said, then died.

He remembered the moment when the faint pressure of her hand on his had faded away completely, leaving a dead hand there with no touch left in it.

None of it had made any sense to him then, but it did now as he was lowered slowly through the darkness. She'd died in public, in a ward full of strangers. They weren't involved with her death, but they were watching it. She was right – they were spies. And her bedside locker, with its fruit and its flowers and its cards bearing tactfully optimistic messages – in a way it had been bugged.

He hadn't eaten the fruit, but maybe he should have. She had wanted him to, but he'd remembered reading, at the Seminary, about the sin-eaters, the people in ancient times who were hired at funerals to eat beside the corpse and so take upon themselves the sins of the deceased.

If they buried people upright the graves would have to be deeper, of course, but they'd take up less horizontal space, which was what you were paying for, in the end. At the same time, the thought of people being buried in a standing position was ridiculous. It made him think of the dead standing in a queue, waiting to be served. They had chosen, and now they would have to pay the price. Think of the inscriptions: 'He was, and still is, a fine, upstanding citizen.'

He could hear a tannoyed announcement passing from under his feet to above his head – where was he? Surely he'd reach the ground floor soon. Or maybe he'd gone past the ground floor and he was on his way back down to the Food Hall. The motion of the lift began to make him feel queasy, as if he'd lost control of his own movements and was part of the workings of the store. He felt as if he had been eaten and was now being slowly digested by a huge machine.

The lift came to a halt at last, but the doors didn't open. Where was he? Without the illuminated numbers above the door, it was hard to tell. In a dark lift, you could be anywhere. You could be in the confessional, except that there was no one to confess to. All you had was yourself. He felt the sweat trickle from his scalp and took the crumpled handkerchief from his pocket, but instead of dabbing his brow he brought it to his lips. It tasted faintly of salt. Then he felt himself begin to travel upwards through the darkness, like a slow missile launched into the night, or a soul departing the body.

previously unpublished

ANNE MACLEOD
(b. 1951)

Born in Aberfeldy. Anne MacLeod's poetry has been widely published. Her first collection *Standing by Thistles* (1997) was shortlisted for the Saltire First Book of the Year Award. Her second *Just the Caravaggio* was published by Poetry Salzburg in 1999. Her short fiction has been read on BBC Scotland, published in the *Scotsman* and in anthologies from Serpents Tail and HarperCollins.

I have always been immensely proud of my Irish background. My mother came from Magilligan, a tiny village in Ulster. She had to leave home at the age of fourteen to find work when her father's death meant college education was no longer affordable. Instead of going to college she came to war-time Inverness, and worked as a clippie on the Highland buses before she joined the WAF. She met my father, a demobbed naval electrician, when he was rewiring her barracks. Family legend says he wolf-whistled when he saw her stepping from a shower. She was not impressed. He himself had an Irish grandfather. And if my mother was a natural storyteller, my father was too. It was he who fell in love with Scotland when the Hydro schemes drew him north. It was he who loved to sing The Minstrel Boy (loudly, out of tune,) as we bumped in badly sprung cars round as many Highland games as we could find each summer. My mother knew more songs, different legends; but there were things she found too difficult for words. When the late 1960s brought a rash of rebel songs into the pop charts, she was uneasy. It had been hard growing up Catholic in rural Ulster, no work at home for her, or five of her seven brothers and sisters. (The eldest sister died of TB; the youngest stayed to look after the old folk.) Ordinary rural stories these, I know, but compounded by lack of political confidence and a distrust of strangers – distrust masked by an honest and genuinely caring attitude to fellow-humans. My mother lost her Irish accent over the years (except for the y in sky.) She never grew an Inverness one, never dispensed with the rhythms or word patterns of her Irish childhood. She read us poetry, stories. Taught us to count to twenty-nine in Gaelic. Became, before our eyes, characters she'd invented. We grew up with the tenets of her childhood ringing in our ears – be friends with everyone, trust no-one – a free-stater would take the eye out of your head and tell you looked better without it – your blether's near your eye. Her family, Ulster Catholic, was rural, lacking votes; but Ulster for all that. I didn't notice in childhood what is so obvious now; the siege mentality. A Highland Catholic childhood in the fifties and sixties was a different thing from growing up in the central belt. There was no chance of tribal feeling. Catholics were scarce. Religion, schooling, set you apart in primary years; but edges, and there were edges, were rarely articulated. Ecumenical was the coming word. Catholic prayer and liturgy, lyrical even in English, has affected as many Scottish poets, I think, as the King James Bible. (Being Catholic, we went to Mass but rarely read the Bible.) It's different now. The Bible's different. Much less lyrical. What did my background give me? A lyric ear. A singing voice. Love of Celtic myth. Distance. Superstition. A tendency to weep at sentimental stories, and to believe, utterly, that what I read or see is happening; to feel the word, know its weight. I value all of that.

the ballad of Andy Sugar

THIS IS HOW it goes. We're driving home, sweeping up the hill before the wood, when Alma says, 'There's Andy Sugar's house.'

'Who's that?' I ask.

'A boy in my nursery school. That's where he lives,' she nods, self-righteous. 'It's not the witch's house. You said it was the witch's house, but Andy Sugar lives there, so it's not.'

'Oh.'

I'm faintly embarrassed. The pink house looks the part, a sweet effective child-trap, too luscious to be true, with lacy woodwork dripping snow like new-dredged icing.

I hope Alma hasn't told this child I said his house was one where Hansel grew fat in a cage and Gretel learned eventually to cope with the heat in the kitchen. She probably did. I only hope his mother may not hear of it. I haven't met her, don't know the name at all.

We skim the corner swishing wet slush into Andy Sugar's drive. The wood comes next, as always. In snow the wood is beautiful, birches swathed, bending low; even the tiniest twigs shine bright and white and I think how like love a day of snow is: love and snow transform the world, brighten, incapacitate. They never last, but you have to be so careful. Both are dangerous, difficult. You lose control; once in a skid there's nothing you can do.

'Andy Sugar didn't get a present at the party,' Alma says.

'Why not?'

'The teacher didn't have one for him. So I gave him my sweets.'

'That was kind.'

I stop to let a gritter pass. The road ahead is narrow, not much travelled in snow. The path home will be safer following.

'And he ate them all at once, and the teacher said they would make him sick. But he was only hungry. Very, very hungry.'

'Oh?'

We are out of the birch wood now.

'He doesn't have any food in his house.'

'He's teasing you, darling.'

'No. He gives his breakfast to the cat.'

'Interesting boy.'

'He's fat,' says Alma. 'And his hair is black.'

After the wood, the road strikes east across the plateau, thin and very straight. The sky goes on for ever to the south but in the north dense stands of pine imprison it. Those trees must be ready for harvesting any day now.

It won't be much fun travelling this way when they start the felling, huge log lorries thundering up and down, spitting bark. This road is a tense affair at the best of times, single track. We travel it every day, me and Alma.

Alma didn't get her name from the river or the battle but from the singer whose voice smiled. I read somewhere that Alma meant loving, kind; and my Alma is loving and sometimes she's kind, when she's not engaged in battle, though she often is.

Too like her mother, but then she couldn't be like a sibber frien, as my Irish mother would have said. She used the phrase often and often. She died of cancer, lung cancer. Though she didn't drive herself, she made sure I could drive and did not smoke.

Country driving gives you time to remember, time to think. Even narrow roads like this will lead to inescapable conclusions, destinations. Home. And on the way you learn much. You can listen to the radio, a tape. Or Alma.

Weeks pass. A timid grey-green Spring assaults. Light is stretching, bright though we're riding home at five o'clock. We catch a glimpse of Andy Sugar's house, warm and pink.

Alma sighs, 'Can we get a dog?'

'I'm allergic to dogs.'

'A cat?'

'No. Alma. You know I'm allergic to cats.'

'Could we get a camel then? Andy Sugar has a camel. Are you allerject to camels as well?'

'Allergic. Yes, probably. Anything furry. Everything. I'm sorry. Anyway,' I say in a moment of blithe cruelty, 'I bet Andy Sugar doesn't have a camel. You only get camels in zoos.'

Alma sits up now, indignant.

'He does so have camel. He does too. They keep it in that shed behind the house. He comes to nursery on it, and it goes very fast. Andy Sugar told me, but I didn't tell the teacher.'

I like the sound of this Andy Sugar, a boy with bright panache. We pass his corner. Is it imagination, or do I smell camel-dung?

Into the wood.

'Andy Sugar loves animals.'

'That's good.'

I pull into a passing place. A timber lorry thunders by, empty, the central crane loose, swinging crazily. But the birch wood tears the heart less, this mild insipid weather. In the snow it made me cry, not that I cried.

We're crawling up the hill. All through the wood, winter is leaving, leaving. Soon there will be primroses strafing moss and bracken ghosts. Birchfly will be stirring, adders too.

Yesterday I saw a rook with a twig in its beak, nest-building. I should clean the cottage, really clean it, not just dust and hoover; make it sparkle in the white spring light.

'Andy Sugar,' Alma says, 'hasn't got a Daddy.'

'Oh. But he has a Mummy?'

'Yes. She helps him brush the camel. I told him I didn't have a camel. Or a Daddy.'

'You have a Mummy.'

'Andy Sugar knows. I told him.'

We pass the pine wood, dark. No ebb and flow in its fixed shade. A sign, Coldhome; I'm sure it is cold in that dank, thick wood. But would you call your house Coldhome? Uncompromising. You'd never get warm in a name like that.

'It's Andy Sugar's birthday tomorrow. Seven. He'll be seven.'

'You must have that wrong, Alma. If he's in your class, he'll be four, like you.'

'He's seven. He told me.'

'Oh well. Of course, Andy has a camel.'

'That's how he gets to nursery.'

You can't rely on Spring this far north. Driving on the hill, untidy piles of grit still linger, white where the road is dark, but camouflaged in snow. In snow they are hard to find and you are left, engine straining vainly, wheels spinning, ineffectual on packed hard ice.

One day I get stuck in snow at the bottom of my own drive. We have to leave the car, me and Alma, wade through knee-high snow that fades overnight, stranding the car on good black road at the most flamboyant angle.

Alma never mentions Andy on the way to school, perhaps because his house sits snug, set back in birchwood. In the morning Alma focuses on other things, other people. Sometimes she sleeps, I encourage her to sleep.

I'm never at my best before midday; the morning drive does not afford the pleasures of the afternoon. Especially in snow. Once, where the high road swoops to join the traffic from the coast, I slip into a skid, the car swoons round, spins right across the white ridged triangle. I slither east not west, at the mercy of oncoming cars.

'Why did you do that?' Alma says.

'I didn't do it,' I whisper, sick. ' It was nothing to do with me.'

We're lucky. No cars come.

And somehow the car starts easily, my wheels find ready purchase on crisp clean snow.

'When's Rowan coming back?' asks Alma.

'Rowan isn't coming back.'

'Was that Rowan on the phone? When you were shouting?'

'Weren't you asleep?'

'You shouldn't shout. You always tell me not to shout.'

'Don't shout, Alma.'

There are situations you should leave behind and must, like sweet spring snow on mountains. Inherently unstable. This is one of the hardest things.

Alma's voice is low.

'Andy Sugar isn't well.'

'Oh? You didn't say.'

'He's very sick.'

'I'm sorry.'

We're coming to the crossroad. Alma knows this, worries. I thought I'd masked my terror in the skid but she knew; she knew.

'His Mummy's ill as well. She can't take him to the doctor, and his grannie never learned to go a camel.'

I bring the car to a smooth halt, check traffic on the main road before swinging out and over. Alma lets her breath out, weary, too loud and slow for one so small.

She begins to cry.

'What's wrong?' I ask.

'Andy Sugar died,' she says. 'He was so thin. He was only eighteen months. Tell me again, Mum, tell me. I need to tell my teacher: my house, and my phone.'

We go through this every week. She knows the answers off by heart.

'And what's my Daddy called?'

'You don't need a Daddy, darling. You haven't got a Daddy, but you have a Mummy. You'll always have a Mummy.'

'Andy Sugar's Mummy died.'

We park beside the nursery school.

'That's where Andy used to leave his camel.'

She points to a wooden paling.

'He tied it really tight, and we had rides on it sometimes, but never told the teacher.'

'Come on, Alma. You'll be late.'

Driving to work without my small conspirator is much less certain, more confused. Hills lie distant, bright with snow, beautiful as bodies are.

Love begs transfiguration, fades with sudden melt: what's left when snow falls from the tree is wood, which may screen much, or little. Love leaves you in impossible surroundings.

So what do you do?

You live.

You try to learn to be as honest as the failing snow.

You avalanche.

And Andy Sugar's house sits proud, warm against the wood.

'There's Andy Sugar's house.'

'Mum. Did you forget, Andy Sugar's dead? And his Mummy too? She smoked. If you smoke, you die.'

'But what about the camel?'

'Ran away to join the circus.'

'And the dog and cat?'

'Went with him, on his back.'

We trickle through the wood. Alma says, 'Andy Sugar never had a father. Well, only for a short time, a very, very short time. He was thin. His hair was red. He was allerject to the camel.'

'Oh.'

Back home she tumbles from the car, streams across the grass.

'Hey, Mum,' she calls,' Come on, Mum, come and see! A buttercup, lost in the snow.'

But she's wrong. It's not a buttercup.

An aconite sings high and clear of Spring.

GERALD MANGAN
(b.1951)

Born Glasgow, where after university he
worked as a medical illustrator. Now lives in
Paris, mainly as an artist and journalist,
reviewing regularly for the *Times Literary
Supplement* among others.

an extract from **Flitting**

DAD'S father Michael was the only grandparent I knew well,
since his mother died before the war and my mother's parents
were both dead by 1955, when I was four. [. . .] Grandpa had no
visible blood-relatives, apart from his three children, and I didn't
have to grow up very far to perceive a certain vacancy around him,
which still makes the Mangan line a very thin and unsteady trunk
of the family-tree. It's a North-Kerry name by origin, sufficiently
uncommon outside Ireland to require constant spelling-out; and I
took a conscious pride in its rarity even in the infant-class at Holy
Cross Primary, where the neighbouring desks were occupied by
ten-a-penny Sweeneys, Boyles and Maloneys. Catholic Ireland was
our common denominator, obviously, and the knowledge of an
immigrant background contributed to a very early sense of not
quite belonging to the glamorous Scotland of clashing claymores,
which first enchanted me in a comic-strip edition of *Kidnapped*
when I was still learning to read. I can date the feeling from a
church-wedding around the age of four, when I girded my loins in
a kilt for the first and last time, and discovered to my chagrin that
its garish-red Royal Stewart was the only tartan we were entitled
to wear, for lack of our own family-colours. But my Mangan elders
were never a source of that knowledge, which I owed initially to
my mother's Donegal-born mother Rebecca Lynch; and I later
became acutely aware that neither Grandpa nor any of his children

194

had ever identified with Ireland in any respect. None of them ever supported Glasgow Celtic, or any other football team; and our houses were notably devoid of those emblems of emerald pride that festooned the walls of several classmates and Lynch-side cousins. Dad's harmonica-repertoire extended westward as far as 'The Yellow Rose of Texas', but it never included a single Irish tune; and his sense of cultural lineage was so severely limited that he once suggested quite seriously, to my horror around the age of fourteen, that we change our name by deed-poll to something more commonly British, just 'to make life easier' – not least for the irascible postman, who was forever chapping our door with letters addressed to Morgan, Manson, Margin or Manikin.

I must have been about eight years old when I first heard of our famous namesake James Clarence Mangan, the Irish Romantic poet whose lifelong poverty and alcoholism hastened his death in 1849. But the discovery was purely accidental, due to a workmate of Dad's who happened to notice the name in Palgrave's *Golden Treasury*, under the poem 'Dark Rosaleen'; and Dad's reaction to it, when he brought the anthology home and read it aloud to us at the kitchen-table, actually had the effect of a pre-emptive strike against any interest I might have taken in Ireland or poetry at that age. He'd displayed the book with an air of wonder, at seeing our surname in print for the first time; and I can only imagine that his recitation was prompted by our squabbling for possession of it, since it was certainly his first poetry-reading as well as his last. His reluctant, halting monotone could hardly have been less appropriate for a lyric charged with amorous rapture, and a spirit of patriotic self-sacrifice.

> *O my Dark Rosaleen,*
> *Do not sigh, do not weep!*
> *The priests are on the ocean green,*
> *They march along the deep.*
> *There's wine from the royal Pope*
> *Upon the ocean green*

> *And Spanish ale shall give you hope,*
> *My Dark Rosaleen. . . !*

My comprehension never recovered from that baffling first image of an amphibious priesthood, and most of the sense was lost on me; but I could see that Dad was increasingly discomfited by the high-flown sentiments, which seem at first sight to be addressed to a particularly lachrymose and bibulous nun. The apostrophic refrain consists of a string of variant possessives ('O my queen, my life of life. . .'); and he hadn't got more than halfway through it when he succumbed to the urge to puncture the Irishman's grandiloquence with a stab of Scottish bathos. After the third or fourth repetition of 'O my love, O my saint. . .' he muttered 'Oh, my God. . . !' with a weary roll of his eyes, as he snapped the book shut; and the timing of this poker-faced *coup de grâce* was so fetching that my sister and I swiftly adopted the whole routine as a comic turn, in the party-piece repertoire that included Norman Wisdom gags and a tramp-costumed duet of 'We're a Couple of Swells'. We'd elaborate the refrain with hammy gestures of entreaty and despair, to enrich the rug-pulling effect of the punchline, and finish the act by falling literally to the floor, in a swoon of mock-disgust.

The memory of Mangan was preserved by this private joke, which needed explanation in company; but the dog-eared Palgrave had meanwhile been shunted to the bottom of the kitchen bookcase, beneath the Companion Book Club editions of Nevil Shute and Hammond Innes, where it remained for the rest of my childhood. No other volume of poetry entered the house in that time, and I realised only much later that Dad's performance, at an age so impressionable, had given me a lasting conception of Poetry as a species of maudlin blarney, which required to be deflated with a little judicious irony. The lesson was entirely inadvertent, and didn't diminish my voracity as a reader of prose; but I'm quite sure that it helped to deprive me of any further childhood experience of poetry, and helped to confirm Dad's own lifelong indifference to it.

When I visited Dublin for the first time at the age of sixteen, for a cycling-holiday in the Wicklow Hills, I still knew nothing at all about Mangan himself; and I was astounded to learn that his life of deprivation and *delirium tremens* had helped to make him a folk-hero, in the mould of Burns. His eccentric character was still the stuff of vivid local legend, and I was heartened to find that the mere disclosure of my surname could inspire complete strangers to stand me pints of stout in his honour; but I was dismayed by the enduring popularity of 'Dark Rosaleen', which hadn't risen much in my estimation. The most impassioned of these early informants was a poetry-loving dock-inspector at Dublin Harbour, by the name of Patrick Cullen, who picked a theological debate with me as I was waiting to re-embark on the overnight cattle-boat to Glasgow ('You're an agnostic you say: D'you know that's Greek for 'ignorant'?'); and abandoned his supervision of the livestock-loading as soon as I introduced myself. As the cattle on the gangplank clamoured in the background, and the Plimsoll Line sank steadily closer to the water-line, he set up a round in a quayside pub and sang the praises of my supposed 'ancestor', in the special tones of proprietorial affection which the Irish reserve for their favourite martyrs: 'You can keep your Senator Yeats, and all them Protestant nobs! Mangan was a man of the people, a Dubliner bred in the bone. He was a drinkin' man like you or me, and he died of the drink in the end. . .' This sort of encomium made me glow with an unfamiliar sense of family tradition, at an age when the school-magazine was printing sheaves of my own early poems, and I spent every other Saturday soaking in a Clydeside pub full of Irish folksingers. But I had trouble keeping a straight face, when I was regaled with a solemnly sonorous rendition of the same poem I had ridiculed so often as a child. [. . .]

Dad himself never set foot on Irish soil, but he did marry the daughter of an Irishwoman; and it was actually my mother who put up the strongest resistance, when he proposed to divorce us from our name. She argued on practical grounds, from the unpleasant experience of losing her own Lockhart surname at the altar; but she finally admitted to more sentimental motives of pride, and family loyalty. Her mother Becky Lynch was born on the stony shores of Lough Swilly, on a croft near Buncrana that is still occupied by Lynches today; and her migration to Glasgow was sometimes explained by a murky legend of the terror inspired by Black-and-Tans from nearby Derry, who'd burned a house in her parish during a campaign of reprisals. Her cousins were probably affected by some such incident during the Civil War; but I later learned that Becky herself had sailed from Derry with her parents around the age of nine, in the first years of the century, when the family had simply outgrown its land. They'd settled in the Gorbals, with her brother and three sisters, in a tenement-flat much like our own; and she'd already spent most of her life there by 1918, when she married the young Pollokshaws butcher who became Mum's father.

Grandma was buried before I knew she was Irish, or formed any conception of nationality; but I must have been hearing the remnants of an Inishowen brogue when she dandled me in the voluminous lap of her widow's weeds, in the heat of her kitchen-range at Carnwadric, crooning the same *Knick-knack-paddy-wack* she'd sung to her own four children. From my knee-high viewpoint she was hardly more than a huge benign presence, inseparable from the ravishing smell of ham-bone soup and the homely turmoil of weeds in her back-garden, where we wrapped docken-leaves and grass-blades in newspaper to sell as fish-suppers. Her house is forever tinged with the luminous greens of a stained-glass parrot that hung on a chain inside her window, reflecting the leaf-greens of a swing-park across the road; and my image of her is charged with the sort of womb-like warmth that makes such early memories both magical and unreliable. But my sister's twenty-month seniority enabled her to retain the more telling image of Dad cutting Grandma's toenails, at an age when she was too overweight and stiff to perform the operation herself. It would be easier to imagine this task in the hands of Mum or her younger sister Agnes, who looked after Becky till her death. But it seems to have been Dad who clipped and filed her nails regularly, on a footstool in front of the range, when she'd steeped her feet in a basin to relieve her corns; and I can't help seeing it as an almost startling demonstration of love on his part, symptomatic of his nostalgia for the mother he had lost in his teens.

Dad's affection for his mother-in-law was perhaps the closest he ever came to Ireland; and Mum's invocation of her memory was certainly the weightiest argument she could have mustered, in defence of an Irish heritage. She kept a lock of her mother's hair in a velvet jewel-case, a memento I found disturbingly macabre as a child; and she and her sisters identified Becky, with ever-increasing gratitude, as the source of their own age-resistant auburn curls. They all had redhead temperaments, and usually blamed their Lynch blood when they were reproached for their prodigious loquacity ('Shut me up, somebody,' Mum would say, after a breathless ten minute peroration, 'I'm getting worse than my mother'); but her father's cannier Lockhart genes seem to have stabilised the more volatile characteristics they associated with Donegal. Most of Becky's descendants inherited her faith in whisky as a lubricant for the singing-voice, and Mum often broke the ice at my own parties by quoting her mother, as she threw away the cap of a newly-opened bottle ('We won't be needing *that* again tonight. . .'); but I never saw anyone get tearful, incoherent or aggressive at Lockhart get-togethers, where most of the alcohol seemed to burn off in the swelter of conviviality – in throat-stretching choruses of 'Danny Boy' and breakneck conversations, like free-for-all Kerry steeplechases.

Mum's older sister Josie was a natural polemicist who earned a name, and eventually an MBE, as an indefatigable defender of council-tenants' rights. She was Mum's lifelong mentor in matters of social conscience, where her Irish temper was always harnessed to an implacable Scots logic. Mum's indignation would be aroused at least once a day, even in her seventieth and last year, by one of her innumerable *bêtes noires*; and the most virulent edge of her tongue was always reserved for bullies, bigots, hypocrites, bureaucrats and Tories. But she knew how to keep her dander simmering to best effect, when she was fighting her own corner. I never once saw her lose an argument, with Dad or anyone else, by letting it flare out of control; and her anger could usually be dispersed in an instant by a well-aimed wisecrack. Her inflammable laugh made her a magnet for comedians; and the jokes she brought home at night, from her office-job at a local construction firm, were often at the expense of her own expanding girth. ('We've lost a counterweight on the crane, Betsy,' a site foreman said once, in mock alarm. 'Would you mind sitting on the end?') Mum was the actress and mimic, in a family of born storytellers – having first trodden the boards in a church drama-club in wartime, and later worked behind the scenes in the famously radical Unity Theatre in the Gorbals. Acting taught her to handle her everyday presence to dramatic effect, without making her stagey or vainglorious; and my own most heart-rending experience as a spectator was watching her on stage, at the Edinburgh Festival in her sixtieth year, in a role where she'd been wisely encouraged to 'be herself'. She played the bereaved mother of a strike victim, in a play about the Polish shipyard union Solidarity; and she managed to put a lifetime of maternal feeling into it, without a syllable of false pathos.

Mum's clan never gathered without honouring the memory of Becky's boxer-nephew Benny Lynch, the short-lived son of her older brother John, who'd become a martyr-hero of the Glasgow Irish by fighting his way up from the Gorbals to the world flyweight title, and drinking his way back down again. Mum was only eleven when he reached the peak of his meteoric career in 1935, aged twenty-two, as the first Scottish world-champion; and it would be easy to assume that he had flown too high to notice her much. But his Aunt Becky's house had been a home-from-home since his own childhood, when his mother Lizzie ran off with a merchant seaman and left his Dad hugging the bottle for solace; and he figured as Mum's favourite cousin in all the fondest tales of her tomboy-girlhood in Thornliebank, where he climbed trees with the Lockharts and taught them the basics of fisticuffs. Benny was famously open-handed when fortune was smiling, and it was partly due to his largesse that my grandparents owned one of the first private cars in their district before the war, when their butcher-shop was struggling out of the Slump. But they returned all the favours with interest during his disastrous later defeats, when his fairweather friends had all abandoned him. At the time of his sudden premature death in 1946, from pneumonia and alcohol abuse, they were still repaying one of his prewar loans through a notary, and keeping his strength up with a weekly parcel of beef.

The boxing lessons I received from Mum made me a stickler for the Queensberry Rules in the school playground at Batson Street, where I was often elected referee and jacket-holder. My classmates were vaguely aware that I was related to a world champion; but Benny's reputation had shrunk to the confines of oral tradition by that time, and I saw him almost exclusively as a family hero. I had no external evidence of his fame, until I was old enough to meet bar-room historians with prewar memories; and this gave me an early insight into the peculiar hazards of celebrity. The family anecdotes invariably illustrated Benny's modesty, geniality and old-fashioned courtesy; and Mum's generation was unanimously enraged by later mutations of the rags-to-riches legend, in various shoddy stage-plays and hack-spawned shilling-lives, that showed him wallowing legless and foul-mouthed in the 'gutter' where he was supposed to have started out. ('Benny could hold his drink,' Aunt Josie would say. 'And he kept a clean tongue in his head.' She was quoted to this effect by the Glasgow *Daily Record*, after threatening to concuss one of the misinformed playwrights with her handbag in a theatre foyer.) Their last and clearest memories derived from the months before his last spell in hospital, when he still turned up regularly at their mother's Sunday-night piano-ceilidhs, dressed impeccably as ever in his best three-piece navy-blue serge, and finished the night dancing with Grandma to 'Moonlight Serenade'. ('He was always a bonny wee dancer,' my Uncle Bobby told me once. 'That was his secret weapon, in the ring.') The Lockharts had always valued Benny's decency a long way above his pugnacity; and their posthumous defence of him made me realise that the principle of fair-play had been the real point of Mum's coaching. 'The hardest fight that Benny ever had,' she said once, 'was trying to keep his *dignity*.' She regarded that as his most important victory, in the end; and the 'vultures' who fed on the myth were no better than corpse-looters, in her view, when they stripped that last trophy away from him.

The Lockharts claimed to have been Catholic since the time of Robert the Bruce, whose heart was bequeathed in a casket to the first 'Lokhert' for burial in Jerusalem; and Mum unearthed her ancestry herself after her retirement, when she took up genealogy and started learning Gaelic. Her father Robert was the first of eight children born to a Pollokshaws dyer, whose Highland-born grandfather had settled in the district as a weaver in the 1790s; and it wasn't hard to observe that her whole family, despite its Scottish pedigree, had followed a more Irish-Catholic pattern than the Mangans in matters of procreation and cohabitation. Aunt Josie and Uncle Bobby, who'd settled in neighbouring closes of Garturk Street before us, had a total of seven children between them, all born in our tenement since the war; and I learned to talk and walk in the midst of a confusing brood of Lockhart and Livingston cousins, who treated me as a supplementary brother. All nine of us were fed, washed, nappied, smacked, amused or put to bed in each other's houses, whenever it happened to suit our mothers; and it took the departure of the Livingstons to a new housing-scheme, in a back-of-beyond called Castlemilk, to persuade me that the street did not actually belong to the family. Bobby and my eldest cousin both made irreproachably British careers as top-brass officers in the RAF, which sent them to every outpost of the NATO empire; but they both married women of Irish origin, like the Robert they were named after, and sang along to 'Galway Bay' at family reunions. Several of the cousins became grandparents before the age of fifty; and the family enacted a prolific diaspora of its own by sending sisters of three successive generations to New York, where descendants of the Donegal Lynches are now beyond counting.

It strikes me now as fairly remarkable, against that background, that I managed to get through my whole childhood without contracting the mildest sense of tribal loyalty as a Catholic. The shamrock, the Pope and the Glasgow Celtic banner formed a holy trinity of household-icons at the Livingstons', when my closest cousin Tommy played in goal for the Celtic Junior team at Parkhead. But they'd vanished to the outskirts long before I could register that influence, which identified the church so closely with Irish nationalism; and my grandfather's fervent Socialism seems, in any case, to have stamped out all traces of bigotry in his family. Mum was always much less devout than her sister, whose gregarious parish-activism had pulled her reluctantly into the Union of Catholic Mothers; and I was never encouraged to regard Celtic as the figurehead of a distinct community. The street and the school were the first communities I knew, after the family; and Govanhill was in fact blessedly unafflicted by the sort of sectarian demarcations I discovered much later, to my surprise, in districts like the Gorbals and Maryhill. By the age of ten I'd played across every inch of it, and explored a large wedge of the south side beyond it – from Eglinton Toll to Haggs Castle, and the forbidden waste-dumps around the Polmadie shunting-yards. But I was never taunted or bullied as a 'Tim' in any part of it, or saw fellow-Tims gang up on a 'Billy'; and the expressions were not even current in local usage. Despite the proximity of Hampden Park stadium, whose oceanic crowd-roar enabled us to count the goals from our back-close on a Saturday afternoon, I never saw Celtic play Rangers or anyone else; and I managed to reach my teens without even realising that Rangers was an exclusively Protestant team.

from a work in progress

Relics

Trust my mother to hoard them up here,
in the old zinc bath in the attic –
under Dad's regimental snaps,
and the bales of his *Reader's Digest*s.
Jumbled in a collar-box,
in a fankle of child-size rosaries,
are the crimson-wounded crucifix,

and the moulded stookie grotto
some aunt brought back from Lourdes.
The tiny saint's still kneeling
to her vision of the Virgin –
that sliver of luminous paint
that glimmered over my cot,
when the chink in the dark was God
glaring through me every night.

Trust her to keep them here
intact, when her faith had broken
under the weight of marriage –
when my father was her purgatory,
and all these crowns-of-thorns
frowned down on her divorce.
She'd cleared them off the walls
when she showed the priest the door,

but she couldn't dump them out
in a bin-bag with the ashes,
in case the sight might wound
some pious passer-by.

So this is where they've waited
more than half my lifetime,
for my torch-beam to unearth them;

and it's here I pack them up again.
When we've stripped the house
down to its echoes,
and loaded the removal-van,
I close the hatch and leave them
balanced on a rafter,
glowing alone in the dark.

Death of a Romantic
James Clarence Mangan, 1803–49

1
It's always at closing-time I see him:
weaving down the quays from Misery Hill
in his barnstormer cloak and steepled hat,
through a gauntlet of beery catcalls.

They take him for a ham, or a spoiled priest;
but he sees himself falling from higher realms.
In the shopfront-glass where he stops
to gaze at his ghost-white double,

he's a bird too rare to bear a name.
He's an angel turfed out of paradise,
cursing God for the curse on his head;
and the pit gets deeper as he falls.

2
It's drizzle that drips through his gamp,
but he sees a blizzard sweeping over the steppes.
He's out of his depth, and language
is a snow that's turned to slush.

The wind that wails down the Liffey
sounds like the songs he's left behind
like foundlings on foreign doorsteps,
crying for their author. But he's stopped his ears:

all he hears is the famine rumbling
under his cloak, in the cage of his ribs.
The blight is eating him, under the skin.
The blood he coughs is poppy-red.

3
The cloak is partly homespun fustian,
partly his plumage of *noms de plume*.
He flaunts it like a sandwich-board
to proclaim his invisibility;

but it flaps like a crow-black wing
the flock has pecked to shreds.
He who is dressed with sorrows
is falling like a flightless bird –

like a bookworm who's reached too high,
and lost his balance on the topmost rung.
He tumbles all the way through the alphabet,
from Byron down to Zarathustra.

4
Even when the clay has clutched his feet.
he's too entranced by his own despair
to see that waterlogged trench in his path,
where the council's dug up York Street:

that hole in the middle of the century
that swallows his name, and proves
the depth of Ireland's treachery.
All his life, he's rehearsed this death –

where Hell opens up like a rose,
to cloak him in petals of flame.
But the worms coil like the horse-whip
his father wielded in his cups.

DANNY BOYLE
(b. 1948)

First came to prominence as a TV dramatist
with *Leaving* set in his native Greenock.
Subsequent films include *Meat* and *A View from
Harry Clark*. He wrote award-winning scripts
for ITV's *Inspector Morse* and devised and
scripted BBC Scotland's *Hamish MacBeth*.

An extract from the Register Book of Births in the District of
Aghadovey records that Lawrence Mullan was born on the 1st of
October, 1865. His place of birth was Ballygawly, which lies off the
Belfast to Omagh road, and the extract was requested by Law-
rence in connection with the Widows Orphans and Old Age
Contributory Pensions Act 1925. The extract was issued by the
Registrar at Coleraine on the 17th of September 1930, by which
time Lawrence had joined the Irish diaspora and moved to Port
Glasgow.

Lawrence married twice and a son from his first marriage went to
America. His second marriage produced Letitia, Susan, Agnes,
Lawrence junior and Margaret. I knew all of his children except the
son who went to America, and Agnes who died in 1926. I knew
Margaret best of all because she married Duncan Kennedy and they
had a daughter, Helen, who married Daniel Boyle and had me.

On the Boyle side I know of no connection with Ireland, although
the name suggests one. I read somewhere that it was introduced to
the Donegal area by bigwig English colonists and taken as their own
by some local peasants. I suspect that one of those peasants was
my ancestor whose descendants made the same journey as
Lawrence Mullan but preferred Greenock to Port Glasgow.

But none of this affects my writing. When the IRA man replaced
the Red as off-the-peg villain in thrillerdom, I was offered many
books to adapt for television. My refusals had nothing to do with
ancestral origins. They were because of my brain. It couldn't be
shrunk enough to believe in 'ok SAS bloke versus murderous
Paddy,' which always seemed to be the story. Even serious offers

were not without problems. David Beresford's brilliant 'Ten Men Dead' about the Maze hunger strike of 1981 was a serious offer from serious people at Granada Television. The problem was an American co-producer who thought there should be a scene 'up front' where Bobby Sands said to his fellow hunger strikers 'hey guys, I'm going on hunger strike!' Then one of the 'guys' could ask 'Gee, why Bobby, why?' and this way, said the co-producer, the audience would learn what the hunger strike was all about, to wit 'so the guys get to receive mail and wear their own clothes.' I did try to do justice to this great book in a storyline, but was told the co-producer went nuclear when he read it. He wanted to know where the 'love interest' was and why we had to see so many guys starving themselves to death. Needless to say we parted company, but once again it had been my brain that got in the way and not my lineage.

No, Ireland is just another place to me. I've even been there once or twice but it could have been anywhere, really. Yet when Lawrence Mullan and the supposed Boyle made their journeys here they did bring something that has affected my writing. They brought the Catholicism I inherited at birth. Of course, I don't practice any more, but I still feel part of the tribe. This is because Lawrence and the putative Boyle were what is now called 'economic migrants', which means they came here looking for work. Which meant they were perceived as a threat by the indigenous workforce. And because they were seen as a threat they were demonised and their differences maligned. And what was different about Lawrence and the possible Boyle in Protestant Scotland, was that they were Catholic Irish. And these two differences were soon conflated and became one, so that a derogatory reference to an Irish nationalist movement 'Fenian Bastard', really meant 'Catholic Bastard'. And if the indigenous people behaved predictably towards the incomers, the latter's response was equally foreseeable. They circled the wagons and stuck to their own. They fostered their separate institutions and clung even more firmly to their faith in this hostile land.

I still feel part of the tribe because I'm old enough to remember the tail-end of those less than tolerant times. When I was ten my sister had a falling out with another girl in the street. But what began as an argument between children soon escalated into something dark and ugly. I was playing when I heard the raised adult voices, and looking down the street I could see a man shouting into my house. Running through the back greens I was able to avoid the man and get inside. It seemed like all the neighbours in the close were there. They were comforting my mother,who was crying. My father was not yet home from work. From my bedroom window, which looked out onto the street, Lawrence Mullan's daughter, Margaret, then in her fifties and stricken with cancer was engaging the shouting man. He was the uncle of the girl my sister had argued with and he was also very drunk. I was standing right beside my grandmother when he called her a 'dying fenian bastard'. It was only in later years that I came to appreciate the awfulness of that taunt. At the time I was more concerned about my Dan Dare pop-up annual which my grandmother threw out at the man in response to his abuse.

I still feel part of the tribe because I'm also old enough to remember when the answer to the dreaded question 'what school did you go to?' could determine your career prospects, and when, consequently, many of the professions were Catholic-free zones. But my atavism, sorry to say, has also been stimulated by more recent events. Such as when a university chaplain assured me, quite sincerely, that some of his best friends belonged to the 'Church of Rome', or when a medical doctor (from Edinburgh admittedly) told me how the Broomielaw had been jam packed with the 'Catholic Irish' trying to flee the country at the outbreak of war. The doctor had not, it transpired, actually witnessed this act of mass cowardice, but it had been reported to him.

It would be a terrible waste for a writer never to draw upon these experiences, and my chance came when I was commissioned by the BBC to write a drama about the event known as 'Bloody Sunday', when fourteen people on a civil rights march were shot dead by British paratroopers in Londonderry. I decided to tell the story from the point of view of a young paratrooper and the small squad of men he has newly joined in Northern Ireland. All of the incidents depicted in the script, which was never produced, actually happened. I either read about them from contemporary newspaper reports, or was told about them by soldiers who were in the province at the time. One of my fictional Paras was a Scots Protestant named Collison. You may recognise him from some of the above.

extract from **Collison**

[Ext. day.]
[Street. We are watching men erecting huge shutters at the end of the street which is being sealed off from an Orange Parade. Hold on men erecting shutters.]
[Ext. day]
[Same street. The group stand near the 'pig' (armoured personnel carrier). Davis is assigning tasks.]

DAVIS: Mickle. You, Smudge and Betty take the lower end. It should be quiet down there, but you never know. Jonesy. Take Collie and Jimmy up to the barrier. If it gets hairy give us a shout you hear. We'll give you backing.

COLLISON: [Brightly. To Hanks] We get to hear the band.

HANKS: I can't wait.

COLLISON: So come on then.

[We see Collison is carrying a rubber bullet gun.]
[Ext. day]
[Street. Crowds line the pavements to watch an Orange Parade. The scene is bright and colourful. The bandsmen weave about the street as they play their accordians, flutes and drums. At the head of the band a man tosses a staff high in the air and retrieves it skilfully as it falls to earth.]
[Ext. Day]
[Street. Behind the barricade. We are looking at Jones. He is smiling. We see Hanks. He is laughing. The object of their attention is Collison who is weaving about in the manner of the bandsmen.]

COLLISON: [As he weaves.] Give it laldy boys. Da da da da da da dara dada da dara da da da da dara dada da. . .

JONES: [Laughing] Jesus Christ!

HANKS: [Creasing] You're mad! Mad!

[Ext. Day.]
[Shots of marching band.]
[Ext. Day.]
[Street. Collison as before. He's completely gone now.]

COLLISON: [Weaving] It's the twelfth isn't it! We're houfing along Argyle Street! Dara da da da da dara da dada. . . There's two priests waiting to cross the road, only you cannae brek the ranks see. So the polis is haudin them back! Did we give it laldy or what! Dara da da da da dara dada da! Dara da da da da dara da da da! Oh Jesus! You shoulda seen their pape faces. . . dara da da da da ara da da da. . .

[Collison is cut short. Down the street, which is Republican, a window is pushed up and from the house comes blaring, the sound of a record player playing 'The Soldier's Song'. A man in his mid fifties looks from the window.]

MAN: Aweh yan orange bastards yese! Shove yer flutes up yer rotten arses yan orange bastards!

JONES: What the. . .

HANKS: Jesus!

COLLISON: Bastard! Bastardin' pape trash!

[Jones watches Collison]

JONES: Collie!

[Hanks. Bemused. Watches Collison]

JONES: Collie!

[Cut away to: Other end of street. Mickle and co see Collison walking toward the window.]

MICKLE: Where's he going?

[Cut back: To Collison.]
MONTAGE
[The Orange Band playing. The man at the window
shouting. Collison walking towards the man. Hanks,
swithering, watching Jones follow Collison. Jones
mouthing Collison's name. Now the music from the band
and the record player merge into an incoherent cacophony
of noise. Collison confronts the man and they exchange
shouts and insults.]
[We cut to and fro between the two. Then Collison raises
the rubber bullet gun and fires point blank into the man's
face. The man screams and covers his face with his hands.
Blood oozes from between his fingers.]
REACTION SHOTS
[From a stunned Hanks and Jones. Collison, quivering
with rage. The man screaming.]
[Cut to.]
[Ext. Day]
[Street. We see the Orange Band as before.]
[Carry Echo. Ex of music over to.]
[Ext. Day]

LIZ NIVEN
(b.1952)

Born and educated in Glasgow. Currently
writer in residence in Dumfries. She has
written and edited fiction for children
(*A Braw Brew*, 1997) and *The Scots Language:
Its Place in Education* (1998).

Going Back

Ireland. As far back as I can remember, the name was always
around, in the air. Maybe you absorbed it by osmosis. As a child in
fifties Glasgow, it was always around like a relative you'd never met
but knew you'd like when you did. Always around in the letters
that would come: 'Oh, it's from Peggy in Wexford,' my Mum would
say, or 'Mary in Bray's ill again.' And in the music. My dad's
harmonica. Black 78s. *Danny Boy. Galway Bay. Up Went Nelson.*
(complete with bomb sounds!) And, of course, all the priests.

Priests always made reference to Ireland. Even their names were
redolent of shamrocks and greenness, a constant round of
Macnamaras, McDermotts and O'Neills. Even visiting priests would
come from Ireland: at Mass the priest would say, 'I'll be away at
Lourdes/Knock/a retreat/the Celtic away game, and Father . . .'
(we'd hold our breaths) . . . 'O'Connor will stand in for me.'
Confirmed again, all priests were Irish.

And with a maiden name of McGee, ye kent whaur ye came fae.
Gifts came from there too. The small white box filled with shamrock sent each March, the turkey sent at Christmas. How could it
not be a magic place? So from an early age, by subtle means, you
somehow knew that Ireland was important and, somehow, you
were connected with it.

Inextricably linked with this Irishness was religion, like some
equation in a logic exam: 'I know that Ireland is somehow connected with me. I know that Catholicism is connected with Ireland.
I am a Catholic. Therefore . . . I am Irish?' Has this confusion
somehow influenced our disparate affiliations as Scots, and made
its contribution to a national problem of identity, since it concerns
so many of us in this country?

And if, for me as a child in working-class Glasgow, Ireland was a shadowy friend not yet met, Catholicism for me as a teenager became a stalker I couldn't escape from. It wasn't easy – from the first missed Mass on a hill at Tarbet where, as a student working in a hotel for the summer, I watched the clouds over the loch. The dark and grey of a typical Scottish summmer. Waited for the lightning bolt to strike, or a finger point accusingly from the heavens. But there was nothing. So, it could be done after all! You'd had, then, your very own transubstantiation. You no longer just *seemed* to disbelieve: you genuinely didn't.

But the stalker was in place. Watching. That phrase 'Once a Catholic, always a Catholic' struck me as strange. Surely, once you've left, it's over. But it creeps back. Not the desire to believe any more, but that sense of something buried in your psyche — a time capsule of prayer books, rosaries, candles, incense, pretty white dresses and headdresses (such luxury objects when we were usually so poor! So this *must* be important.).

And so the stalker creeps back around Christmas when the candles are lit and the carols are being sung; takes another quick glance when a funeral frog-marches you into a church and the smell of incense penetrates your soul, the new format of the un-Latin Mass merely a variation on an old theme, the singing sounding like a childhood rhyme so rooted in your heart. Or seeing shops with rosaries hanging in the window, and you remember the thrill of opening a present as a child and a new set emerged from a pink shell box, its silver cross sparkling, the beads round and hard in your small unquestioning fingers. These are the legacies. Life-long, I dare say. And I haven't mentioned the deeper sadnesses, the family divisions due to a child not baptised . . . Communion not taken at the family weddings . . . and I won't . . . can't. Not yet.

So, that's my Ireland. Well, my Ireland of the past, for I've been now to the North as well and realise that there are many faces and voices to our cousin country. It is, in fact, much more like Scotland than it seemed to me through childhood eyes, with many of the same tensions and related problems – a Scotch broth of mixed marriages, religions, languages, geographies. Living now in South West Scotland, an Irish jig's distance from Belfast, I've revised my childhood views in many ways.

Having said all that, the background of Irish Catholicism is wonderful grounding for writing poetry, with the sensation of things being other than they seem, of objects taking on a greater significance, like the bread or the wine. Symbols and patterns loom large in Catholicism as in poetry. Also, abandoning religion doesn't mean that it has abandoned you. It 'will be ours till/ the fires all fade,/ the last notes die' ('Background Music'). I always wanted to correct people who used the term 'a lapsed Catholic' because it implied an expectation of return in the future, but maybe it reflects an ongoing mental state. And we are constantly, mentally, going back.

Past Presents

Every March, a tiny cardboard cube would come from Ireland;
So light surely it was empty?
We doubted briefly till the box was opened
And out would spring our shamrock
Fragile, green as Aunty Biddy's Wexford fields,
And still damp.
She sent it always soaked in Holy Water, whispered words
And each of us would wear a little sprig upon a pin,
Against our chest on Patrick's Day,
Like some ash upon our foreheads.

Every December, heavy this time,
A lumpy parcel came in dun coloured paper.
A huge, fresh turkey lay upon our kitchen table.
Six small faces gazed and marvelled at the gift,
Our present from Ireland.
And then we'd ask about our past.
Living long in Glasgow's greying city,
We glimpsed our ancestry, knew where we had come from.
And who wouldn't love a land which sent such gifts?
You wouldn't send a thistle in a box.

At sixteen I went once to Dublin, Wexford, down to Bray,
Past barbed wire fences and soldiers dressed in green
To see the source of all our gifts.
'There's a hitcher at the door, Mum,' cousin Mary said,
And Aunty Biddy, old and frail, stared blankly back at me.

Background Music

Born a Glasgow girl,
I thought my roots lay there
With a glottal stop, no Gaelic lilt;
Rare country trips a treat
For smoky, city bones.
A rural glimpse of Gaelic mists
Were not my bedtime tales,
Though father sang of Ireland
When his mandolin was tuned
Or played harmonica to haunt my dreams.
But of his father's land
I never caught a glimpse of green
And nor did he for many years
Though I began to feel its presence.

Then, entering Ireland this year,
(A fortieth wedding gift from all the family,)
My father's harmonica was removed at Customs
A 'suspicious instrument' indeed.

Once into the South, far from the Troubles
At the Wexford farm of an old aunt,
They gathered round to hear his tale.
Peat fires, hot scone smells mingled
The wind hummed animal sounds.
Suddenly, his aunt rose, black skirts rustling
Knobbled wrist reaching to the rafters
And on a beam lay the ancient Hohner.

Old faces smiled, cousins clapped
My Scottish father played
Till the wind dropped and the fire died
And through them all,
Behind the very fabric of the house,
Sang the music of the years
That link us all.

Once home to Glasgow's South
Harmonica retrieved
We gathered round to hear his gift retold
Gas fire contracting, microwave buzzing
City wind whistling a traffic sound concerto
And second hand we lived the trip
Got back the confiscated roots
That will be ours till
The fires all fade,
The last notes die.

CHRISTOPHER WHYTE
(b. 1952)

Born Glasgow, educated there and
Cambridge. Has been a university teacher in
Rome and Glasgow. Writes poetry in Gaelic
(*Uirsgeul/Myth*, 1991) and novels in English,
most recently *The Cloud Machinery* (2000).

As much as I was able to learn about our family history is preserved
in a blue notebook. I filled its opening pages more than seventeen
years ago, when the principal sources, one particularly forthcoming
aunt on both my father's and my mother's sides, were still alive.
Every family is different, yet some of the figures contained in that
notebook can provide food for thought and even edification.

My mother's grandfather, William Fergusson, was an Orangeman's
son. His father had a business in Newry, my aunt told me, but
William was put out to wetnurse with a Catholic family in a nearby
village, Mayobridge, at the same time paying regular visits to the
local rectory so as to be educated in the Protestant faith. His father
came to see him at weekends in a pony and trap. Aged 14, William
refused to return to Newry. The father was never seen again. His
son got married in the Catholic church at Mayobridge to a certain
Bridget Barry (or Berry, described by my aunt as 'planter people').
He brought his wife over to Scotland, bought land in Blantyre
between the station and the main street, and attended Holy Mass
twice in all his life: once in Mayobridge, and once in Blantyre. His
very Catholic daughter Agnes bore John McCrossan ten children.
Two of my mother's sisters became nuns. One, who was a
Carmelite, I only ever saw through a spiked grille.

John McCrossan's grandmother, Catherine Douglas Hamilton, was
the daughter of an Episcopalian minister. Before marrying, she kept
house for her brother, a doctor. When a child was left on their
doorstep, they conscientiously had it baptised a Catholic, as they
believed this to be the most likely religion of the parents. (I have no
way of gauging the accuracy of this assumption, or whether it was
merely the effect of prejudice.) In time the woman who had found
the baby converted, too.

On my father's side the strands are no less tangled. His maternal grandmother, Ellen McDevitt, left Glenties for Glasgow soon after marrying Michael McAloon, and the move was permanent. They settled in Maryhill, where the right side of the Church of the Immaculate Conception was known as the Donegal side. Girvan Beach, my aunt commented sardonically, was as close to Ireland as poor Ellen got after that. The man her daughter married, however, was a child of Scottish parents. Thomas Whyte's mother, Dottie Mackay, was certainly a Protestant. This did not stop him holding meetings of the very Catholic Knights of St Columba in the back room of the family shop.

So on this evidence, I would find it hard to label myself as being either Catholic or Protestant, of either Irish or Scottish origin. Labelling, indeed, strikes me as a way of wiping people out, of cancelling individuals and encouraging prejudice. When that strangely persistent (in Scotland) label of Irish Catholic is applied to me, I cannot help being puzzled. Would it be possible to prize those two words apart and invent a new label, Scottish Catholic, which did not make it necessary for one to trace one's ancestry back to before the Reformation? The fact that the two words are glued so obstinately together is indicative of a reality I cannot deny, that religious prejudice in central Scotland is a mask for ethnic prejudice. Yet who could conceivably argue that the racial mix of the 19th century populations of Ulster and the Clyde Valley was so distinct as to offer a basis for racism?

There are aspects of this elusive mongrel mix, and of the distaste it arouses in people naive enough to claim less catholic (in the lower case sense) origins, that I cannot help enjoying. One of the last coherent statements that aunt of mine made, before all she could do was gulp down the tub of ice cream my mother had brought and then resume the silent pose of a disgruntled bird, concerned her fellow inmates in the corporation old folk's home: 'The people here,' she whispered, ' they're very *Scottish*, you know.' Both she and my mother were born in Cambuslang. Neither lived for any significant period of time in Ireland. So who is the joke on at this point? In a just and accurate world, the nationality on my mother's passport would be neither Scottish nor British but, quite simply, Glaswegian. In the course of a life of more than eight decades, it has never crossed her mind to abandon the city for any length of time, or rather, the narrowly defined district of it where she lived from the age of 4 onwards.

On the rare occasions when I (still) hear that Calvinism is a core element in Scottish identity, I not only have to stifle a yawn but also stop myself from laughing, reflecting on my own extraction. Though exposed to the distasteful rigours and the thoughtless philistinism of a well-known Glasgow Jesuit school, I cannot regret all the aspects of a Catholic upbringing. Old enough to have regularly attended mass in Latin, I licked my fingertip and leafed through the thin pages of a bilingual missal with fascination. I have loved parallel texts ever since. Visiting Italy for the first time aged 15, religious ritual and church furnishings were unremarkably familiar. Renaissance altarpieces never appeared foreign to me, and I immediately developed a passion for angel spotting which has yet to abandon me.

When this dangerously cosmopolitan and international Catholicism is contrasted with the sturdy virtues of a national reformed church, peculiar only to this country and productive of our rugged Scottish character, all I can do is shrug my shoulders. They expect that I should envy monochrome conformity (as if the Calvinists had ever been able to agree among themselves!) They will be disappointed.

from **An Tràth Duilich**

(1)

Faisg rim ghruaidh
plathadh fann san dorchadas –
dà chois shnuadhmhoir
air an snaigheadh san fhiodh
agus tarrag trompa
le sileadh fala dhith.

Cha ruig mi leas a bhith ag amharc suas.

Is aithne dhomh fhathast an ìomhaigh sin
's i ga aithris 's ga aithris feadh na h-eaglais,

from **The Difficult Time**

(1)

Just by my cheek
a faint glimmer in the darkness –
two shapely feet
carved in wood,
a nail through them,
blood trickling from it.

I don't need to look up.

The image is still familiar to me,
repeated again and again through the church,

drùisealachd neo-cheanalta na Crìosdachd.
Uair is a-rithist, corp fireannaich air a rùsgadh,
glasneulach, na làmhan sracte, is an slios
air fosgladh, gun ach clùd truaghant' a' cleith
cùis na mòr-thàmailt.

Ach 's ann a chunnaic mi san Aithne
rùm an dèidh rùm a dh'fhireannaich dealbhte
an uaibhreachd de chloich
a bha soinneanta, lomnochd, slàn,
a' togail beag air bheag air fad nan linn
an làmhan, a' sìneadh a-mach an gàirdeanan
mar gum b' ann a mhealtainn farsaingeachd
an àile neo-thruaillte mun cuairt orra.

Ach 's fheàrr leis an t-samhla seo an leus a sheachnadh,
siridh e na h-oisnean dubh 's na frògan
air dòigh 's gum bi 'r mac-meanmna
a' cur ri oillt a dhreacha.

(2)

Tha cuid ann a bhios a' moladh
àrd-gnìomhachadh na h-àilleachd:
ach aithnichidh an duaichneachd
a h-euchdan fhèin: *divo Aloysio.*

A Chrìosdaidhean, carson a chaill
bhur n-ealain-se a brìgh?

Cha siud a bha 'na àbhaist dhaibh
an linntean an ath-bheothachaidh
no nuair a shìneadh dealbhadairean
sgannan luachmhor de dh'òr
a-mach air clàr an daraich

sad erotica of Christendom.
Time and again, a male nude,
deathly pale, with torn hands
and open side, and only a miserable
rag hiding the place of greatest shame.

In Athens I saw
room after room of men
carved in proud stone,
serene, naked, whole,
lifting their hands little by little
through the centuries until
their arms stretched out, as if exulting
in the wide, unsullied space around them.

This image would rather keep out of the light,
it looks for corners and niches,
so that our imagination
can add to its horror.

(2)

Some praise masterworks
of beauty: ugliness
will not deny its own
achievements – *divo Aloysio*.

Christians, what
went wrong with your art?

It wasn't like this
at the time of the Renaissance
or before, when painters spread
precious films of gold
over oak panels

mar eunadair a' sìneadh glaoidh
air meanganan, is thigeadh na naoimh
'nan eunlaith ana-mhòir bhoillsgeanta
air spiris orra, an sgiathan a' plathadh
an dràsd 's a-rithist an duirche na h-eaglaise!

Mhath dh'fhaodt' a chionn 's gun do dh'àicheadh leibh
bhur ceangal ris a' phàganachd
a bha 'na fhreumh dar creideamh-se
is a bha comasach a-mhàin
air a chuideachach 's a chumail beò. . .

Is truagh leamsa gun do chrìon
am bruadar dàna sin a bh' agaibh,
bhur fìrinneachd a bhith gun chrìoch,
's nach eil nur n-anmannan an-diugh
ach taighean falamh dubharach,
gaoth fhuar bhur n-eagal a' sguabadh trompa,
bhur neo-thoil a bhith 'g àideachadh
gun do chaill bhur cainnt gach brìgh!

Is neo-fheumail a cheiltinn
am breug-riochdan ealain sgìth –
tha bhur cruaidh-chàs a' nochdadh
an neo-shusbainteachd gach clàir –
tha ceangal aig an ealain ris an fhìrinn
air dòigh 's nach fhaod i bhith 'na bhreugaire.

Mar sin b' fheudar dhaibh
an ealain fhèin a mhasladh
's bhur dia a chur air cathair duaichneachd.

like birdcatchers spreading
glue on branches,
and the saints descended,
great gleaming birds,
and perched on them, their wings
flashing now and again in the dark churches!

Maybe because you denied
your pagan roots, and only
they could keep you alive. . .

I'm sorry that the daring
dream you had has faded,
that your truth isn't everlasting,
that today your souls are merely
empty, lightless houses
the wind of your fear sweeps through,
of your unwillingness to admit
that your words have lost all meaning!

It's useless to try and hide it
in a tired art's lying forms –
your predicament cries out
from the emptiness of each painting –
art is bound to truth
in a way that stops it lying.

And so all you could do
was to reject even art
and set your god on a throne of ugliness.

(1989-90)

from **The House on Rue Jacques**

THE priest glided from one side of the room to the other, as if he were being propelled forward on wheels. When he passed the foot of the bed, he raised his right hand in greeting. There was a diagonal gash across the palm, from the root of the little finger to the base of the thumb. The blood had not quite dried and was still a bright raspberry colour. That was when I decided to write everything down.

Or rather, the decision became clear to me the following morning. What I did there and then was pull the blankets more tightly around me and try to get some sleep. It was so cold in the room I could have seen my breath if it had not been for the darkness. So how was I able to see the priest? Presumably I had been dreaming. It was to be expected that the flat on Rua do Belomonte would be impregnated with Uncle Delfim's presence. He had spent the last eighteen years of his life in it, after his disgrace and definitive removal from the priesthood. Wandering the streets in a dirty cassock and a greasy dog collar while mumbling phrases from his breviary, he would stop in at bar after bar for a glass of red wine and a cigarette, if he could beg one from the customers. For some strange reason he never bought his own. In this way he consumed the meagre pension the family lawyers had assigned him. They were unwilling to let him get his hands on any more of the patrimony until the question of my fate had been settled to their satisfaction. Even so, it was only when Uncle Delfim breathed his last that they went the length of advertising in the press and succeeded, thanks to a series of coincidences, in tracking me down. . .

I was used to hearing the Catholic clergy reviled by my father, at table and in private, from an early age. This coloured my attitude to Uncle Delfim. Disliking him was an act of loyalty. There were, however, other elements in our relationship which disquieted me. I was required to spend a considerable amount of time in his company, so that he could acquaint me with the basic tenets of the Catholic religion, thus counterbalancing the superstitious piety of my grandmother, tinged as it was with dubious and heterodox elements. My father was not enough of a rebel to have me brought up an atheist, though this is what my mother would have preferred. While they did not live in the same house, he was financially dependent on my grandfather, who was therefore granted a say in the upbringing of the boy who bore his name.

Uncle Delfim liked to touch me. And I did not like being touched. Physical contact with him disgusted me. His flesh and skin had the pallid, bloated quality of fish gone past its best which is characteristic of men dedicated, at least nominally, to a life of chastity. Their bodies take on the greasy, opaque quality of the candles burning at the altars where they raise their prayers. Black hair, short and thick, covered the backs of his hands, with dense tufts between the lowest joint and the knuckle of each finger standing out in unpleasant contrast to the whiteness of the flesh. A squadron of ants crawling across stale bread, that is what it made me think of.

Once the doors of my grandfather's study were closed behind us, and my religious instruction had begun, I would catch him looking at me from odd angles while he balanced the catechism in one hand, running the other obsessively up and down his thigh, as if contact with the black material of the cassock excited him. His hand was calmer when resting on me. He would place it on my shoulder, or cup my right cheek in it, so that his thumb fitted into the cavity between my ear and my head. I could feel his palm grow hot and sweaty against my skin. Now and again he gave my ear a tweak, intended to be playful and to underline the point that he was making. At other times he would touch me in the small of my back, taking advantage of the graceful twin arch of the wooden dining chair where I was sitting.

And it was in the dining-room that I managed to put a stop to it. It must have been early springtime. The air was already tepid. We had been eating oranges. Peel was scattered across the table, along with the especially sharp knives we used to cut the fruit, which gleamed in the slanting afternoon light as if in the aftermath of a battle. Everyone except the two of us had gone to sleep, including the maid who served at table and had cleared away the debris of all but the very last course of the meal. Uncle Delfim was explaining something to me I did not fully understand, but which sounded convincing enough to set my heart beating with a thud of alarm. It was disturbing to hear what might be truth coming from those lips. In retrospect I see the purpose of his words, and where they were intended to lead.

He and I, he told me, were two of a kind, exceptional creatures marked out from the rest of the family. This in itself was enough to disturb me, for I took it to mean that I was destined to become a priest like him. No other profession could have filled me with the same repulsion. Given the things my father said about the church, how could I contemplate for a minute entering its ranks? Delfim was sitting on my left, leaning towards me, his right arm encircling my back. He had grasped my hand in his and was moving it repeatedly back and forth to emphasise the points that he was making. The other hand was already on my thigh. It began to slither towards my genitals.

Whether it was the danger that excited me or something different, I cannot say. In any case, my sex was tense inside my short trousers and I was determined that he should not get to touch it. If our position demanded resolution and self-sacrifice, he was saying, it also offered pleasures which are denied ordinary mortals, pleasures which I could taste even at a relatively early age. He was looking towards the window, either from a genuine sense of shame, or because he hoped to deflect my attention from what he was up to. I shook my hand free. Delfim offered no resistance. He probably expected a caress, or else for me to guide him towards his target. Picking up the nearest of the fruit knives, I drew the blade across the palm of the roving hand with all the strength I had, in a quick, transverse movement.

He cried out and leapt to his feet. Blood was pouring from the wound. While he shouted for Ermelinda, the housemaid, to come to his assistance, I carefully removed the drops that had fallen on my bare leg, licking a corner of my linen napkin and rubbing till no trace was left. Then I made my escape into the garden.

I have often wondered how Delfim explained this injury to my parents and my grandparents. I heard nothing more about it and never came into physical contact with him again. Even when bidding farewell to the assembled family at the end of one of his visits, he would wave to me, rather than lowering his cheek for a kiss, as had been his habit. It flatters me to think how much I frightened him.

MAGI GIBSON
(b. 1953)

Magi Gibson has worked with writing and
performance groups in local communities
and in prison. Her poetry collections include
Kicking Back (1994) and *Strange Fish* (1997)

The influence of Irish/Celtic culture is strong in 'What my mother
told me of my birth', and indeed this poem has a lot to do with my
own strange heimweh for the west coast of Ireland. Strange
because my father (conceived in Ulster, born in Scotland in 1910
into an Orange Ulster family), would not have accepted my strong
feelings for Ireland as a whole, despite his own mother being a
McNeilly and therefore most likely from original Irish (pagan/
Catholic) stock.

Being brought up in an Orange west of Scotland town did not
dampen my feelings of Irish ancestry, my fascination with the
forbidden boys from Croy (oh, there has to be a poem there I
haven't yet written!), and the Irish/Celtic influence in my writing
which comes through strongly in my collection, *Wild Women of a
Certain Age*, the title poem of which was conceived on the floor of
a bar in Clifden, Connemara.

What my mother told me of my birth

I was fathered by a grey sea mist that kissed
my mother's breasts and crept into her womb
while she gathered kale down on the shore.

Nine months gone, huge as a whale
she clambered slow and sore
up the steep flank of a mountain of pain
panting loud as Macha.

At the topmost peak, naked as daybreak
she sank down on a bed of jagged scree
and when her waters broke
a waterfall more beautiful
than the Grey Mare's Tail
gushed and tumbled to the blood-red sea.

The sun set and the moon rose high
while she writhed and thrashed,
her mountainous belly heaving
as granite and schist and gneiss once heaved
in the passion of creation.

Two days and two nights she struggled
with the devil's red-hot irons in her heart,
with stallions' hooves pounding at her skull,
with wolves' jaws tearing her apart.

Lightning sparked in thundery skies,
the wind howled like an unhallowed soul,
but always the moon watched over her –
a gentle mother with a fevered child.

Until the pain began to sink
as the sun sinks in the western sea
and a baby with gabbro eyes,
its lips as blue as glacier ice
a caul upon its brow.

Liffey Dreams

Outside our hotel room
the Liffey waters roll, thick as treacle,
dark as the blood of Kerry witches,
black as Cromwell's soul.

It's 2a.m.
a man is screaming
and I can't tell if he's calling out
from pleasure or from pain.

A shout. A crash of glass. Feet running.
A siren wailing, insistent as
a wakeful child, looping out into the dark.

Through all this dreams come –
dreams of a baby, born to a girl
I saw last night, shivering
in O'Connell Street.

Dreams of a baby wrapped in a rag
swimming its way down to the sea
under O'Connell Bridge
in dark Liffey water,
past the thin family frozen in bronze
and the mangy mongrel
whimpering at their heels.

Even with her eyes downcast
even in her misery
and her hunger and her pain
as she treads forever Destitution Road
the thin mother sees
the drowned baby swimming

wide-eyed as a seal pup
and the mizzling rain streams down her face.

It's 8a.m.
propped against cloud pillows
I watch for traffic as it flows
a relentless river of rubber and metal
over O'Connell Bridge.

Grey sky, grey wind, grey rain, grey day
a world of monochrome
and one bright red van.

from Wild Women of a Certain Age (Chapman 2000)

JOHN BURNSIDE
(b. 1955)

Born West Fife, grew up in England. To date he
has produced six collections of poems and two
novels, of which the most recent is *The Mercy
Boys* (1999). *Burning Elvis* (stories) and *The Asylum
Dance* (poems) are published in 2000 by Cape.

On first response to such questions as how my 'Scots-Irish'
upbringing affected me as a writer, I naturally balk. I don't think of
myself as belonging to a specific group: I am Scots by birth, but I
left Scotland at the age of eleven; I am Scots-Irish by blood, but
that mixture was more of a source of conflict than anything else
when I was growing up. My mother was the child of devout
Catholics – one from Ireland, the other Scots; my father didn't
know his parents, but had been brought up in anti-Catholic, (rather
than specifically Protestant) surroundings. Anti-Catholic feeling was
surprisingly strong in the communities in which I grew up, in West
Fife and in Corby, Northants, where my father moved to find work
in the steel mill in 1965. Certainly, I have no distinct memories of
being enriched by a 'Scots-Irish' culture, but this may have more to
do with rejection of the limiting, self-destructive and often bigoted
elements of that culture to which I was exposed as a teenager.

So I did not share my parents' culture. What is a culture, anyway, if
not the things you absorb by osmosis – in my case, American
movies, *American* Soul music, a few poems, some Beethoven and
more American movies. Like most working-class Scots (and Irish)
people of my age, that was it. Everything I wanted was American,
from the black and white nights of Nicholas Ray films to The
Jefferson Airplane. Being a Catholic, I was as Irish as my genuine
Irish classmates: my friends had (mostly) Irish names, for example.
But like them, I was a displaced person: I belonged to a 'home' that
was elsewhere, and somewhere along the way, that elsewhere
became America. On my wall there were two maps: New York
City and the whole of the United States. Like many of my contem-
poraries, I was the willing victim of a cultural imperialism I didn't
care to resist. To this day, I know all the words to most of Dylan's
songs, but the only Irish song I recall is *She Moved Through the Fair*.

This is naive, of course. If I have any identifiable sensibility at all, it is a Celtic one – whatever that actually means. The idea of a personal, male god (with attributes) as identified in my Catholic religious education is absurd to me, (especially the male part – but then that's probably true of most practising Catholics), and I'm probably as beguiled by European culture now as I am by American, (and have, I hope, a more critical awareness of both). Returning to Scotland five years ago, as something of a mongrel, was one of the happiest, richest and most rewarding events of my life, as a writer and as a person – but the Scotland I came back to was a landscape and a climate, and I love it because, for reasons beyond my control, this is where I belong.

The Resurrection

Something is green in the house
of a sudden:
all morning I finger the windows,
revealing the moisture, the heartbeat that rises through
    stone,

and later, in the stillness after Mass,
I guess what it might have been
to discover the tomb:
the empty linen printed with a stain

of presence, like a broken chrysalid,
where something has struggled loose, through
    remembrance and pain,
and the angel, a handsbreadth away,
in the blood-scented shade,
a breathless, impossible being, diverting my gaze
from that which is risen, the living unnameable God.

from The Myth of the Twin (1994)

Angels Eyes

Under the curve of the sickle
a region of speedwell and lime
where birds disappear,

and rainwater sipped from the grass
becoming the song in your mouth
of summers and endings,

where angels arrive through the hedge,
and the dead from your schooldays
are waking through nettles and elms,

or walking away in the corn, and leaving no trace
save the grey of a bruise on your wrist
and the blur in your eyes

where someone reached out from a drowning, a lifetime
        ago,
and held you for minutes, before you could shake yourself
        free.

from The Myth of the Twin (1994)

The Soul Friend

This is the fish-coloured bible,
buried in the garden, under webs
of bone and rain,

the love letter scratched on a desk,
then smoothed away
in waves of sweat and grain,

the taste of hallelujah in the dark
when the prayer for the dead is begun
and the candles burn out on the altar
like daffodils melting,

and this is the form you describe
as witness, like the child you used to be,
standing all day in the playground, measuring frost,
inventing a father from hearsay and fragments of Latin.

from The Myth of the Twin (1994)

Going to Crosshill

We landmarked that road with the silent:
the convent, the school for the deaf,
the lime trees that stood through years
gathering rains, outwearing sleeves of frost,

past where the meadows reached
for a sunrise scarlet and gold
as the flame of the Sacred Heart
on our grandmother's wall.

Remember the morning we stopped
at the holy well,
the dropped coins disappearing in the sand
like fallen souls,

and when we went to kiss her our goodbyes
that weekday evening, in the emptied room,
the silence afterwards that swallowed all
and promised nothing but the dark road home.

from Feast Days (1992)

Dundee

The streets are waiting for a snow
that never falls:
too close to the water,
too muffled in the afterwarmth of jute,
the houses on Roseangle
opt for miraculous frosts
and the feeling of space that comes
in the gleam of day
when you step outside for the milk
or the morning post
and it seems as if a closeness in the mind
had opened and flowered:
the corners sudden and tender, the light immense,
the one who stands here proven after all.

from The Myth of the Twin (1994)

ANNE DONOVAN
(b.1955)

Born Coatbridge, lives in Glasgow. Divides
her work time between teaching and writing.
Best known for her stories in authentic West
of Scotland dialect. Won the Macallan Prize
for 'All That Glisters'.

Irish Connections

Hail glorious St Patrick, dear saint of our isle
On Erin's green valleys bestow a sweet smile
And now thou art high in thy mansions above
– On Erin's green valleys look down in thy love.

The last line was repeated three times, swelling to a rousing
crescendo which gave me a funny feeling in my chest. Was it the
tune that made me sing with such feeling or did the image of a
green island fire the imagination of a wee girl from Coatbridge, a
Lanarkshire town of grey council houses?

I had never been to Ireland yet the idea of it was always there at the
back of my mind. I knew my family had come from there and that
this was something to be proud of. But what did being Irish mean?
The *Irish Weekly*, shamrocks on St Patrick's day, the leprechauns and
shillelaghs which aunties brought back from holiday? My notions of
Ireland as an exotic and wondrous place were confirmed when I met
for the first time a real live Irish person, my great-aunt Minnie.
Round her neck she wore a fox-fur stole, which I wanted desperately
to stroke. Even now I can see its glittery wee eyes and pointy nose.

This interest in Irish culture was further reflected in our choice of
television viewing. Val Doonican (whose sweaters reinforced my
notion that the Irish were a race of people who wore funny
clothes) was a great favourite, while Dave Allen was regarded as
the slightly wild boy of the family, tut-tutted over when he went
too far, but enjoyed because he had an Irish accent and did
sketches about priests. 'He's Irish,' or 'Her mother was Irish, you
know,' were familiar phrases of approval; in those days before the

troubles shocked us into more complex realities, simply being Irish or of Irish descent was enough to make someone interesting.

Was this interest due to Irishness or religion? To some extent it is difficult to separate them since not being a Catholic was as difficult to imagine as not breathing. But there was definitely an Irish dimension to our Catholicism. After all, Italy is a strongly Catholic country yet I don't recall anyone in the family being particularly interested in Sophia Loren, at least not because of her religion.

So what are my Irish connections? I have Irish blood on both sides, but I know more about my mother's parents who were born there. My grandfather came to Scotland at the age of eighteen to work on the railways since the farm could support only the eldest brother. He returned to marry my grandmother three years later and brought her back to Coatbridge where they reared a family of nine, of whom my mother was the youngest. She remembers going to Ireland every year for the summer holidays and staying on the farm with her mother's eldest sister.

I never knew either of my grandparents except through anecdotes and old black and white photos, though, as I grow older, I think of them more frequently, imagining the strange life they must have had; a farm boy and a country girl, living in a crowded tenement, rearing their weans in a dirty, industrial town, going home to Ireland for holidays. Did they miss Erin's green valleys? Did they wish their children could be farmers rather than steel workers? It is easy to romanticise. Possibly they thought they were giving them a better life. Probably they had no time to think about it. Certainly they had no choice, like all the other emigrants of every era.

How does the Irish connection affect me? I am Scottish, born and bred here, but there are many different ways of being Scottish, and mine has to take account of my parents, grandparents and fore-bears, as well as all the other influences on me. The idea that being of Irish descent influences me as a writer at first seems strange since I feel more at home with Scottish than Irish literature. Yet the given, almost un-thought-about parts of my stories, such as the names of characters, are Irish-Scots and Catholic. None of my stories have so far dealt with religion overtly as a theme, but as a matter of course, if there is a funeral, it is a Catholic one and it is assumed that my characters either go or have been brought up to go to mass. Perhaps this is mere laziness on my part but I suppose that my background is so rooted in the fabric of who I am that it is impossible not to write from it, even though I do not often write directly from personal experience.

I suppose I would have to ask where the writing comes from, and the simple answer is that I don't know. The old adage is that writers should write about what they know and many folk seem to think this means writing about yourself. I am always surprised when people ask me whether an incident in a story has happened to me in real life because I rarely write from personal experience, and, like all writers of fiction, if I use a personal experience, it is transformed by the writing process into something quite different, something that might have happened to someone else. Yet, though the writing may bear no relationship to the facts of my life it must, I think, be connected to the truth of who I am. I often use emotions or feelings which I have experienced as a starting point for a story, but the characters and situation may be completely different from my own.

Even more mysterious is the way in which you can write about something you have never experienced but somehow get it right. I wrote a story about a woman who stole a baby from a pram after the death of her own child. The story was inspired by a news item and bore no relation to my own life; in fact at the time I wrote it I had virtually no experience of babies. Various delays meant that it was not actually in print till several years later when my own baby was three months old. When I reread it I was amazed that it did seem to convey some sense of what a mother felt about her child, something I had not personally experienced at the time of writing. How could I have written about something I did not know? Yet such is the magic of the writing process that it taps into areas of which we are not consciously aware.

So is that where the Irishness comes in? Is it simply part of the fabric of the self which cannot be separated out or are there strands which can be unravelled? There is a meditation practice designed to help you to find out who you really are, in which you have to keep asking yourself, *who am I?* Each time you answer you have to discard the answer, peeling away layers of the self as if you were peeling an onionskin (it's enough tae make you greet). I tried it once and among the onionskins were *I am a Scot* and *I am of Irish descent*. I don't intend to discard either of them, even if I could.

A Change of Heart

IT was the ice-cream. That's how ah knew. He's never in his life eaten chocolate ice-cream, never really liked ice-cream at all, maybe take a cone or a wee drop vanilla if it's really hot, but tae see him shovellin rich dark chocolate ice-cream intae his mooth. Ah never said anythin but. After all it's a big operation, he's bound tae be different. The doctor had warned us he'd maybe even be a bit depressed or that.

Then he started gaun tae the park, just sittin, lookin at the floral displays. No that there's any herm in that, but if you'd knew him afore. The only thing he'd spend hours lookin at wis the racin on the TV. To tell the truth it made me nervous. It's nice tae sit and look at flooers for five minutes but efter that ah start wantin tae dae sumpn, go the messages, dae a washin. Ah didnae want tae say anythin for ah wis feart ah'd upset him, so ah went tae the doctor, the young wan wi the fair hair.

—It's aboot Peter, doctor, ah'm worried aboot him.

—I don't think you've any need to worry, Mrs Cameron. Your husband's making very good progress. It'll take a while – after all a heart transplant's a big operation – but by and large we're very pleased with him. Was there anything in particular you were worried about?

—No doctor, it's no that, it's just, well, he's no hissel any mair.

He leaned forward in his seat. His glasses slid doon his nose and he pushed them back.

—You know, after this type of surgery it's quite normal for patients to be depressed or experience mood swings that are totally out of character.

—But it's no that, it's the ice-cream.

—Ice-cream?

—He never ate chocolate ice-cream afore, and he doesny

watch the racin any mair, he sits in the park and when he's sleepin he lies on his left side.

He ran his haun through his hair, pushin it back aff his foreheid.

—When you've been merriet for thirty year you know which side he sleeps on, and he aye slept on the right afore.

—Mrs Cameron, I'm aware you've been under a lot of stress.

—Doctor, whose hert did he get?

—You know that the donor was a young woman who'd been involved in a car crash. I can't tell you any more than that.

—Ah know, but who was she, what was she like? Did she eat chocolate ice-cream?

He cleared his throat and put his haun ower his mooth. Ah knew he wis tryin no tae laugh.

—Look, the heart is just a pump, a big muscle. There's no way that getting someone else's heart could make your husband like or dislike the things they did.

—OK, doctor.

—I think, though, that you're needing a good rest. I'll arrange for Peter to go into respite care for a few days and you go away for a break. Go and visit your daughter. It would do you good.

—Ah'll think aboot it.

—Come back and see me again if you're still worried, but really, everything's fine.

AH STOPPED at the chapel on ma way hame. It's no like me, ah'm no very religious really, but sometimes that cool darkness helps calm me doon. There's an atmosphere in a chapel, some would cry it the presence of God and maybe it is, or maybe it's just that hunners and thoosands of folk have prayed and hoped and sat quiet among the marble and the statues. Ah lit a caunle in fronty the Sacred Hert statue an knelt doon. The tremblin light threw shadows roon the alcove, and the statue stood oot sharp in front. Ah felt as though ah'd never really looked at it properly afore, never seen how strange it wis; Jesus, wan haun raised in blessin, the other pointin at his hert, red and open on his chist. The nuns tellt us it was a symbol of his love for the world. He wore his hert on the ootside because his love was that big it wis for everybody, while ordinary folk had theirs on the inside, for our love wis just human.

It wis all very well that doctor tellin me the hert's just a pump, but that's no how it feels. So ah believed in ma heid whit the doctor said, but ah knew in ma hert that ma Peter wisnae the same man as afore the operation. Ah knew the doctor widnae tell me ony mair, it wis supposed tae be confidential. A young woman who'd died in a car crash. Ah widnae even have known that much, but the nurse let it slip oot. Ah had tae find oot mair aboot her.

THE MITCHELL Library's a beautiful buildin. No a very nice settin since they stuck that motorway right through the fronty it, but the buildin sits grand an dignified, aw lit up at night too. You think you're really gaun somewhere when you walk up they stairs and through the polished widden doors. The big brass haunles have the Glesga coat of airms on them, though the left wan has been rubbed that hard it's nearly flat. Funny that, you'd think the right wan wid be mair worn. Course then ah discover ah should of went in the side entrance and ah had tae deposit ma bag and get a ticket and a crumpled poly bag tae pit ma stuff in, but at last ah fund masel in the Glesga Room, where they keep the newspapers. Ah thought ah'd be lookin through piles of them, but they have them on microfilm noo, so you read them on a screen like a giant TV. Ah cawed the haunle roon an roon, checkin each page. Mair'n likely she'd have died in the area, because they didny like tae move the hert too far. Ah thought it would take ages but ah'd been at it less than twenty minutes afore the words seemed tae jump oot at me fae the *Herald* January 14th.

'Late last night, Fiona Macintosh, 27, a nurse from Greenock, was killed when her car went out of control and crashed. It is believed that the car hit a patch of black ice. No other vehicles were involved and there were no witnesses. Mrs Macintosh is survived by her husband Thomas, 31. She was expecting her first child at the time of the accident.'

Ah sat listenin tae the hum of the machine, starin at the letters on the screen but no longer readin them. The excitement ah'd felt drained away and ah was seized by a creepin cauld. Ah kept seein this lassie, on her way hame fae her work likely, and that moment when she realises her car's oot of control. Ah hope she didnae know, ah hope tae god she wisnae conscious for long, thinkin aboot her wee bairn an the life ebbin oot the two of them.

—Excuse me, are you all right?

The young lassie that showed me how tae find the newspaper stories wis staunin beside the desk.

—You look as if you've had a shock. Are you all right?

—Ah've had a bit of a shock hen, but ah'm OK.

Ma hauns were freezin.

—A wee cup of tea would help, ah think.

—There's a tearoom downstairs, I'll take you down in the lift.

—Thanks, hen.

Sittin at the formica table, ah felt ma hauns warmin in the heat of the cup, tinglin as the numbness wore aff. There ah wis thinkin ah'd find oot mair aboot the lassie, maybe write tae her faimly or even just go tae her hoose and look at it fae the ootside, try tae get some sense of her. It had seemed that important tae know mair aboot her, if she liked gairdens, if she ate ice-cream.

But how could ah dae that noo, efter whit ah'd read. All ah could think aboot wis her man, waitin for her tae come hame, startin tae worry she wis late, mibby lookin oot at the weather, thinkin aboot an accident, but no really believin it, then the polis arrivin at the door and – everythin stops. Just aboot the same time as we're gettin the phone call fae the hospital.

—We think we have found a donor for you.

Nae wonder Peter's no hissel, nae wonder he's quiet and wants tae sit in the park and watch flooers. Sumbdy died and gied him their hert. Ah make ma way oot the library across tae the bridge, high above the motorway where the traffic roars by like a big river. Ah staund in the drizzlin mist, haud tight tae the metal palins, watch cars follow triangles of dirty light.

previously unpublished

HELEN LAMB
(b. 1956)

Poet and short story writer. Her work has
been widely published in anthologies and
magazines and broadcast on BBC Radio 4,
Radio Scotland and RTE. Poetry collection
Strange Fish published by Duende, 1997.

It is difficult to think about my Irish roots in isolation. For like many
Scots, my family origins are mixed, both urban and rural, working
and middle class, Brethren and Presbyterian.

I grew up in West Perthshire with all four grandparents living more
or less on the doorstep. One grandfather was a musician from
Glasgow. The other was local. One gran was Orcadian. She sang,
played the fiddle and the piano. The other was Irish.

As a child, I took it for granted that the important adults in my life
had different ways of living, different ways of worshipping – and
different cadences. Soothing sonorous Perthshire Scots. English
with a pan loaf twang or an Irish lilt. I enjoyed the variety, identified
with them all and felt free to take what I wanted from each.
Language was a flexible tool. To this day, my accent tends to be
variable and I often find myself unconsciously mimicking whoever I
am with.

For various reasons, my Irish maternal grandmother played a major
caretaking role during the early years of my life. She sang *Molly
Mallone* out of tune but her speaking voice was melodic and she
would entertain me for hours with long rambling medleys of
interlinked stories. These tales were always about her family, her
much adored and frequently absent father, eight brothers and
sisters and Elizabeth McCombe, her fearsome fiery midwife
mother. Although my grandmother drew from life, I don't think she
ever let a little thing like the truth get in the way of dramatic effect.
Her stories had heroes and victims and villains and a gypsy potion
and a stolen birthright. So I thought she was just romancing when
she told me her Dutch ancestors came to Britain with King William.

I don't recall the word 'Orange' ever passing her lips and for a long time I believed she must be confused. I thought she meant William the Conqueror and I knew for a fact he was French. I doubt if the Orange Order would have been compatible with my grandmother's Brethren faith but it does seem her roots were Orange and she retained some tribal pride in this.

She was a great one for proverbs and mottoes and pronounced frequently. Words of wisdom, I realise now, though at the time I didn't want to hear them. She had a couple of favourites. Takes two to make a fight. Two wrongs never make a right. She steadfastly refused to take sides in any of my childhood squabbles. I suspect she would say the same thing about the situation in Ireland today. Both sides need to work for peace. Blame will get you nowhere in the search for understanding.

Winter Spell

Let the frost spike my skin
Let the east wind sting

Their cut is true
And you'll never lie
As well as the snow

Let the ice freeze my eyes
Let my kiss be blue

I love this bitterness
Better than you
It is good to be cold

And you'll never lie
As well as the snow.

Three wise oaks

High on the hill above the house
three wise oaks guard my horizon.

They did not see me arrive.
They will not hear or sigh
when I leave.

Every day, I tell the deaf ones
I am sorry but
I do not have the silence
of three hundred years
to steady me.
Besides – I have to shift.
I blame it on my feet.

Every day, I tuck my tongue
behind my teeth, practise
my harmless grin
on the blind ones. See?
How could anyone believe
I would ever cry out
– Timber!

Every day, I take my problem
to the dumb ones
probe the bark's rough braille.
There's an answer
at the tip of my finger.
All I need is the skill
to translate.

They do not care if I learn.

The Deil's Bucket
(Sheriffmuir)

Interminably, the hill wept over it.
The bucket did not spill even one
tear.

The sun sweated
every last drop of moisture
from the muir –

And all the while
the bucket shivered.

Over and over, the rushing white water
plunged in the black
and drowned.

And still the bucket needs
to be filled.

Its cracked lip has been
parched for an aeon.
The thirst is ferocious
– the Deil's ain.

from Thirteen Spells

WILLIAM HERSHAW
(b.1957)

Born Fife, where he lives and works as a
teacher of English and folk musician. Poetry
in English and Scots is collected in *The
Cowdenbeath Man* (1997) which celebrates
the life of Fife mining communities.

My father, Andrew Hershaw, was about the ninth or tenth in a family
of twelve, brought up in the Fife mining village of Kelty in the nineteen
thirties and forties. His father, Auld Wull, was a coal miner. My father's
brother John was killed in an accident at the Lindsay Pit. As a sixteen
year old boy, my grandfather had joined the Scots Guards in the Great
War and later met my Granny, an English nurse from a 'higher' social
background, while recuperating from shrapnel wounds in a hospital
near Epsom. Auld Wull was famed for his dourness.

Auld Wull's faither was an Orangeman from Dublin. He must have
arrived in Scotland around the turn of the century. He was in Ayrshire
and Slamannon before coming to Fife and seems to have followed the
coal industry as it developed across Scotland. He did well for himself
initially and was part owner of a pit before drinking his share away and
ending up having to work in it. He is credited with founding Kelty
Masonic lodge.

My mother, Marie McCormick, was the eldest in a Catholic family of
seven daughters and one son. My maternal grandfather, who was
known as 'Comp' was also a coal miner and the family moved from
the Lanarkshire village of Forth to come to live in Cowdenbeath in
Fife at the end of the Second World War. Comp's grandparents were
Irish and had come to Scotland sometime in the 1880s.

My Mum and Dad were married in St. Bride's Chapel, Cowdenbeath,
in the early 1950s and I was born in 1957. It was the typical Scottish
working class 'mixed marriage'. It must have been difficult, especially
for my father – he had followed the fifties Gers of Willy Waddell and
Geordie Young fame. I remember him telling me how, as a teenager,
he watched and laughed incredulously when the superstitious Kelty
Catholics crossed themselves when they passed the Chapel on the
bus. I think he was subjected to some hassle from his own family

when he got married. My education was in Catholic schools. When I was eleven he bought me a Rangers strip which made me stand out a bit at school.

My father was discouraged from becoming a coal miner and joined the Fire Service. He was promoted and we moved to Motherwell in 1963. Hindsight can be misleading but there was a great sense of changing expectations at this time. Aslan was on the move. I can remember being encouraged to 'stick in' and be the first on either side of the family to go to a university. My childhood memories include Winnie Ewing's victory at nearby Hamilton and Jock Stein and Billy McNeil bringing the European Cup, furled in green and white ribbons, to our primary school. At the age of ten you take such feats for granted. A new priest arrived at St. Luke's in Bellshill, fresh from the Scots College, Rome, called Thomas Winning and he soon had me dragooned into reading the epistle at children's masses, serving as an altar boy and singing in the cathedral choir. I was never comfortable with any of this and I used to try and hide when I spotted the dark figure entering the school.

From an early age I considered myself, instinctively, to be part of a minority culture because I attended a different school from the other kids I played with at the fire station where we lived. I watched Orange parades go past our home with a mixture of fascination and resentment. On the other hand, I always thought of myself as Scottish, unlike many of my class mates who had two Irish parents and who spoke of 'the old country' as their spiritual home. As I grew up I developed a belief that Scotland should become an independent republic. I don't know where this came from as it was never discussed at home. I read a book about Sitting Bull and made a connection. I suppose I was a bright stupid wee boy who read a lot of books and lived in a dreamworld. I have not given up on independence though.

I have a similar background to thousands of Scottish working class people and I pick out and mythologise the bits of it I like and tend to forget the rest. I hate the idea of separate Catholic schools but I can never bring myself to support Rangers, even if they are playing an English team. I have a strong Calvinistic streak although I detest John Knox. I am wary of what I perceive as Celtic New Age bullshit. I am not as secure in my identity as my poems in Scots suggest but I certainly do not feel, even in part, Irish or English. The only thing I am sure of is that if you forget the people who made you and those who made them, you lose your soul.

Miss O'Donnell

Miss O'Donnell
keeps a big black darkie's
heid on her desk.

I dinnae like its iron grin.

Miss McDiarmid

Miss McDiarmid makes
you stand on one leg,
hands behind your head.
When she was a wee lassie
she stole coal off bings
in the General Strike.
Everything we have today
is due to the Labour Party.
Mr Wilson is a good man.
She knew a boy
who swung back on his chair
and was paralysed for life.

What The Darkie Said

Roll up, roll up,
roll up and roll a big broun penny
ower ma thrapple,
then hear the clink o ma Adam's Apple.

Black Babies No. 1

All mornings after prayers
in single file we queue orderly
to sacrifice a leave-piece penny
to the greedy heathen god head,
his gut endless, appetite appalling . . .

A twist o cast-iron lug
and a pink painted metal tongue pokes out.
Place your penny carefully now,
turn again and clunk, swally,
it's gone away to Africa!

Johnny Love

Has ten brithers and sisters,
a crew-cut, a running nose,
a green hame-knitted jersey
wi elbow holes, rips in his shiny breeks
whaur his skinny white legs stick out.
In recompense Mr Wilson
affords him a free denner.

The Loves are devout
wi nae money. However each year
they contrive to gie millions o pounds
o their sweetie money tae the black babies
(sometimes thruppennies or hale tanners even).
When the White Fathers publish the magazine –
there they are, top o the league,
holiest faimily in Scotland.

And though they live in poverty
they sit at God's right hand
and a' hae perfect teeth.

Price Of Salvation

Twa bazooka jocs,
fower sports mixtures,
seevin midget gems
(three black for any other colour),
twa half-penny caramels,
fower black sambos,
a fireman's hose,
a licorice pipe,
a chocolate cigar,
a packet o imitation fags
a penny drink o ginger,
penny caramels, a good chew
up the back o the class,
my favourites being:
strawberry/toffee and egg/cream,
cola cubes, pear drops, soor plooms,
rhubarb rock, sherbet dooks,
lucky bag (tuppence),
bag o stale cakes
fae the back o the bakers',
bubblegum cairds;
Man Fae Uncle or American Civil War,
No. 50, 'Painful Death',
a highly prized asset worth many doublers
or . . .
a corporate act o mercy and a grace top-up.
Heids you win, tails I lose, Two–Face.

Black Babies No. 2

A piece of card
with thirty spaces
for thirty ticks or crosses.
Thirty pieces of copper
names a baby,
baptises a baby in the Faith,
feeds a baby,
buys a baby.

Father Winning

Mither says
He'll go places.
No long back
fae the Scots' College,
fou o new ideas
to shake up St Luke's.
He sometimes comes
tae our hoose
and mither gies him pairs
o faither's black
Fire Brigade socks.

Black Babies No. 3

They run about in the scud a' day
and the sun burns their bums
black as toast.

White Fathers ken better,
stay white and pop out only
to scoop up new recruits.

Black babies
go to Catholic schools
where the burning process
can be reversed.

Flittin

Ma Faither pit out fires
and so after custard and mince
in Cowdenbeath we set out West
for Motherwell
in a black Pickfords lorry
to live above a fire station.
Dad sat wi the driver,
Mum, Roseann and me
squeezed unsafe, illegal and for free,
stowaways among pelmets,
settee, standard lamp and tea chests.
In those days such a journey!
Between Fife and Lanarkshire
was measured in light years.
I sat on a cryo-stasis pouffe
all that Summer as we voyaged,
entombed in stifling darkness
and brilliant pin prick light holes.

When at last the doors were opened
it was late and we were blind as owls.
We were helped, water-legged from our flotsam,
coal-grim fifties Fife astronauts,
splashed down in the middle of the sixties
in the purple haze of a steelworks' sunset.

We had a fish supper for our tea that night.

God Gave Names To All The Animals

Miss O'Donnell has decided:
future black babies will be given the names
of Catholic saints only.
Sadly, my eleventh card is bereft,
barely a cross on it:
Africa will never know

Simpson

Craig   Gemmell

Murdoch   McNeil   Clark

Johnstone   Wallace   Chalmers   Auld   Lennox

Orange Walk

Bowls along the road
in front of the Fire Station.
Thump, rattle, thump
piping flutes, thump
and fluttering purple and orange.
Then they stop beneath our window,
stamp, stamp, stamping down,
determinedly not going anywhere,
marchers frozen in time.

'Why do they stop –
do they know we're in here?'

'Dinnae be daft . . .
come back fae the curtain, son.'

Father Winning Comes Calling

Friday afternoons are for no work
and skives behind raised desk lids.
But at half-past two
Father Winning comes searching
for altar boys and good readers
of Saint Paul's Epistle to the Ephesians
for his new-fangled children's masses.

Sandy haired Mr Dolan,
craggy-faced and kind
lapsed sole man teacher
tips me the wink
at twenty-five past
and I retire to the back cupboard
to write up my poetry project.

It Is Always

Sometime in the sixties in Motherwell
on a raw November night.
In the quiet yard behind
the soot-stained Edwardian Fire Station
the hanging drying hoses
drip on a sixty foot meccano tower
with their heavy brass nozzles snout down.
They are dragons jewelled with rime.
Hobbit shadows, the firemen's bairns
flit in and out of the light
in their inter-denominational play.
Their play dance is circled
by the dim red silent roar
of Ravenscraig and Colvilles
always there and safe and
made by other night-shift dads.

Motherwell Fire Prevention Week

John Mariano's dad had
a well-stocked cafe.
He must have been a Mars Bar millionaire.

Wee John Love had
a family big as The Broons:
enough to make up a football team.

Gerald Donnachie's dad
had a pub. Crisps, beer
and the first colour tele in Wishaw.
I had diesel and the dirt smell of smoke
from returning engines. Dad
was always away on night shift

when Celtic were at home.
Then one day a class trip to my hoose.
I coolly demonstrate a perfect fireman's slide

and disappear from sight
down a pole before organ stop eyes
and admiring jaws.

Benediction

May the ghosts sleep tight
in Motherwell Fire Station,
as meteors bend
ower the braes o the Earth
bless a' us black babies
in our beds the night.

from Black Babies, an autobiographical poem sequence

CHRIS DOLAN
(b.1958)

Born Glasgow, where he lives. Writes fiction
and non-fiction and for film, theatre and
television, as well as supporting writing in
local communities. Won Macallan Prize in
1995. First novel *Ascension Day* (1999).

Turning Turquoise

My family's Irishness was preserved in the aspic of Catholicism.
Pickled and pungent, my childhood religion was deep and devout
and more Papish than anything you'd have found in Ireland. The
dividing line was not between the oul' country and Scotland, but
between Roman and Reformed. Until very recently there was an
involuntary mechanism in my head that kicked in on hearing a
family name for the first time: Fenian or Prod.

Scottish Nationalism was a by-word for anti-Catholicism; the
Liberal Left for abortion and atheism. The whole of politics was
designed for those who didn't already have the one true apostolic
creed that powered us and the likes of us through this world and
onto the next. If there were allies anywhere then they were
other outsiders. My mother remembers moving to a new close in
Glasgow and a neighbour popping down to whisper, 'We should
stick together. Case of the Cohens and the Kellys.'

The outward signs of inward Irishness were not shamrocks or
pictures of De Valera in my house, but holy water fonts, rosary
beads and electric crucifixes. Yet I knew that Ireland was behind
all this somewhere. The priests – easily the most powerful figures
of my youth – were Irish. Our songs were sad emigration
melodies with strange foreign placenames. In my young imagination, Heaven and the Mountains of Mourne were cheek-by-jowl.
Galway Bay a kind of state of grace.

Yet my parents weren't anti-Scotland, the way some of my
friends' folks were. Perhaps it was the immigrant's need to curry
favour with the locals, but we would have passed Tebbit's football
test with flying colours, supporting Scotland avidly, even against

the Republic. My parents loved Glasgow, which was, by and large, their Scotland. But then again, their Glasgow was Irish.

You don't shrug off a childhood like that easily. I reacted badly in my teens, but I've always retained a predilection for big, universal, ideologies. If I'm no longer Catholic, I confess to being Cathoholic. I'm more confident now in my Scottishness and my politics, but the confusion of religion, Celticness, Scotia and Eire – where one begins and the others end – far from diminishing has been *increased* by the fact of my being born here and attaining a deeper knowledge of Scots culture and history. I have real respect for the (relatively) Democratic Intellect of this nation and its Kirk. I now play Strathspeys on the fiddle as badly as ever I played the old Irish reels.

The churches I knew as a boy were Scottish, not Irish. I live every day with profoundly beautiful memories of serving mass on Partick Christmas morns, snow falling on stained glass. I remember vividly assisting the Bishop at a quiet service late on an Autumn evening in old Dunkeld. The Irish priests and nuns of my childhood, far from the ogres they're seen to be now, were gentle, loving, harmonious people. I miss their gentleness; hanker after the old solidarity.

Franny Unparadized is, I think, the only time I have addressed my Catholic upbringing quite so directly. (I've hidden it better elsewhere!) The story brings together, enhanced of course, a couple of true incidents – a childish attempt at occultism and an innocent enough kick at authority. We were more at ease back then with matters spiritual. Ghosts and prayers and rituals were, after all, the stuff of everyday life. The ending depicts my continuing national and theological confusion – I still can't work out if I'm Franny or if I'm Danny.

Despite the schism between the two countries of my youth – which I see embodied in my mind's eye as a viciously grafittied Belfast wall – I'm unable, perhaps unwilling, to make much distinction between them. I see Donegal in Sleat, glimpse Dublin in Glasgow streets. I feel a connection with the sad, twilit spirituality of the Gaeltachdt. Scotland, as we all now know, is a place of oppositions – we Scots Irish just have one more to cope with. Might as well rejoice in the Jekyll and Hyde of upright

Kirkiness, bigotry, myth-making and the Craic. Scots and Irishmen share – in at least 40 shades of turquoise – feelings of loss and inferiority. But the Devout and the Staunch together chink our Tennent's lager in Guinness glasses. In the end, my Ireland *is* Scotland and my Scotland, Ireland. That's a confusion I'm happy – and fated – to live with.

Franny Unparadized

FATHER McKenna hitched up his vestments, skipped down the altar steps and made such a dash for the sacristy that the boys had to break into a run to keep up with him. An undignified sight, but the good Father had explained to the handful of ladies who made up his congregation that Mrs O'Neil was about to give up her soul to the Lord and needed Father McKenna to supply her with the necessary recommendations and papers.

Before he got to the sacristy door Father McKenna was already pulling off his surplice. Inside, he fired instructions at the boys as he let his vestments drop to the floor reminding Danny of Franny's big sister coming in from work on a Friday night and always closing the bathroom door at the vital moment. He reproached himself for a fleeting image of Father McKenna in bra, pants and tights, when in fact the Godly man had his black suit on underneath. Father McKenna told the boys to clear up and entrusted to Danny the tabernacle key. He turned to Franny.

'Remember, you. Do as Daniel says. You're here to learn some responsibility. Here's your chance.'

The minute he was gone, Franny rubbed his hands together and ranged around the room, peering in cupboards and corners. When Franny did this in Danny's house and there was nobody in, it meant trouble.

'Just don't, right?'

Franny looked up, offended. 'Just don't right what?'

'Just don't anything. I'm in charge.' Danny jangled the tabernacle keys. Franny's eyes lit up: 'Know what we could do?' Danny felt the kick in his stomach he always felt when Franny came up with an idea. 'Make a host sandwich.'

Danny thought oh shit. This was worse then he'd expected. Trying on the priest's vestments he'd expected. Lighting the candle tapers to make sparklers he'd expected. Taking a swig from the bottle of unconsecrated wine, even. Franny held out his hands for the keys. Danny clutched them tightly.

'It's cool. I did it at that funeral last month when the Dirty Beast was out blessing the stiff. Give us the keys and I'll show you.'

'No way.'

'Suit yourself. I'll use these.' Franny took the cover off the plate that held the hosts.

'Not those! They're consecrated!'

'I know. Holy jam.'

Franny was a mystery. He was wild at the best of times, but with anything to do with the church he was manic. Franny had his own Liturgy, loosely based on the Divine Office. 'Grant Us Peace' = 'Grampa's piece', 'Hail Holy Queen' = 'Hail Holy Queer', 'Go in Peace' = 'Go an' pish', and, at the end of Mass: 'Thanks be to God' = 'Thank God'.

Franny wasn't the craziest guy in school. He couldn't compete with Jazzy and Wetback and Droon-the-Coolies and the rest of them, who jammed the school annexe door shut with an iron bar when all the teachers were still inside then threw blazing torches in through the windows. Franny, being only a 3rd Year, wasn't invited to take part. He was still saveable, so Father McKenna took him into the altar boys to knock some sense into him. It was the best thing that ever happened to Franny. Here he was the toughest, the wildest, peerless. The church was his patch. Here, Franny ruled.

Franny believed in it all. He believed in God. In the one, holy, apostolic Church. He believed in transubstantiation, and he believed that a confession, sincerely and devoutly undertaken absolved him of his sins and assured him a place in heaven. Danny had his doubts, and confided them in Franny, who was genuinely distressed. The ingenuity and sheer force of Franny's arguments comforted Danny and restored his faith.

'What you do is, you take one of these big stormers the priest keeps for hissel, then one of the wee shitey ones that the ordinary smelly folk get, then another biggie. Hey presto – a host sandwich. Wash it down with a chalice of vino. Breakfast of Champions. Brilliant. You try it.'

'No, I mean, I don't really believe it's the body and blood and all that, but –'

'*You* don't believe it? It's got bollocks all to do with whether *you* believe it or not.'

Danny looked on, open-mouthed, as Franny drank deeply again from the chalice.

'Saving grace this stuff. You can taste it.'

Franny was lucky. He could be as wicked as he liked, but still secure in the Knowledge of Salvation. This gave his transgressions a kind of innocence. Franny's badness was upfront, out there, for all to see and judge. But what went on *inside* Danny's mind, his sins of thought, were of a wickedness so black that even Franny would be shocked. There was Franny's sister for a start. And then the involuntary images, like Father McKenna in bra and panties. When Franny got hacked off with a teacher he said so to the teacher's face; he was flung out of class and that was that. But Danny, Danny sat quietly and tortured the offending teacher in hideously violent ways in his mind.

'Well if it's all true, you'll go to hell for that. Those hosts were consecrated.'

'So? So? So I'm bless-ed. Nay, twice bless-ed, cause I had some during the Mass and all.'

Franny swallowed the last of his sandwich. The danger was over. Danny put the hosts and the plate and chalice back into the tabernacle, and locked up.

'I think you've got this all screwed up, Franny. I think you've just invented a wee religion of your own. None of this is exactly what you'd call *normal* Catholicism.'

'*Orthodox* Catholicism, butt-head.'

'Orthodox, well. The priest says the Devil moves in mysterious ways –'

'That's God, ya prat.'

'The Devil as well. He can make it *look* as though it's God talking to you, when in fact it's the Devil.'

'Shite. That's shite. If you do all the right stuff – go to confession and mass and all that keech, big Satan can't touch you. You're protected. It's like your guardian angel's the Terminator. Invincible.'

'See? That's what I mean, Franny. The Terminator was evil. Bent on destruction.'

'Not in Terminator Two.'

Franny had all the angles covered. He had worked it out in detail. Danny, stumped, shook his head sadly, as if Franny were missing the whole point.

'I'll prove it to you. I'll call the Devil up.'

'There's no phone in here.'

'Very funny. I'll call him up. Here and now. Then you'll see who's feart from who. He'll get brown trousers for having been called up in the House of God.'

'Don't be stupid,' Danny said, but he was scared. Franny never failed to deliver once he had come up with a plan. But summoning the Devil was surely beyond even Franny's talents.

'It's pish easy.'

Franny tried to look unconcerned. 'What if the Dirty Beast comes back?'

'Only takes a jiffy. Don't worry – like I say, when I call him up and he realises where he is, he'll shoot the craw immediately. If he doesn't, I'll waste him.'

Franny's absolute certainty in these matters was breathtaking. He busied himself around the sacristy, whistling softly like he was getting his football gear together or something, while Danny looked on, stuck fast, at a loss for any argument or action that would stop what was about to happen, happening.

Franny took a candle and placed it in front of the mirror on the huge dressing-table that the priest used for putting on his vestments. He took a bible out of a drawer, placed it next to the candle and rifled through the pages until he found the one he wanted. Then he crossed to the door and switched off the light. The porridge-grey morning was tinted crimson through the stained glass of the sacristy. He lit the candle, which flickered nervously in the half-light, then he turned and explained the procedure calmly to Danny.

'The Devil answers to anything which is the opposite of God, right? So what you do is, you read the Our Father backwards and look in the mirror. At the end, he'll appear in the mirror. Any questions?'

'Can he come out of the mirror?'

'Usually he would. But not here. He wouldn't dare.'

'Does he appear behind you or in front of you in the mirror?'

Franny considered this for a moment. 'I'm not sure. I think he appears instead of you.'

Danny was alarmed. 'But that would mean you *were* the Devil. It would be your own Devil you'd be seeing.'

'Don't talk wet. The Devil's out there. In Hell. In the Abyss. He comes out and roams the world now and then. It's not like he's inside you.'

Danny looked doubtful. Franny consoled him: 'He appears in front of you in the mirror, then. It just looks like he's taken your place but he hasn't. When he appears I'll stick my hand up in the air and wave to you from behind him. Okay?'

Danny wanted to run. But he couldn't. Something inside of him had frozen his legs. The Devil. The Devil within was waiting so he could expose himself in all his vileness to the body that was Danny and the Evil One's vehicle. Franny set himself in front of the mirror, drew a deep breath, was about to start, then as an afterthought he picked up the priest's alb that was lying on the dresser. He kissed it, mumbled a prayer, put the alb round his neck. He checked the first phrase in the Bible, then stretched out his hands, threw his head back, and in a stern voice, chanted:

'*Amen!* Evil from us deliver. . .'

Danny prayed for the priest to come back. He dreaded his reaction but thought it probably preferable to eternal and immediate damnation. He thought of the fire, the screams of pain, his own included, the tangle of bodies writhing in agony, all of them naked, men and women alike, and amongst them Franny's sister, exposed, moaning in the heat of the flames. The vision excited him, and he knew for sure at that moment that the Devil was not being called up out of the Abyss but out from within his own body. He wanted to warn Franny to turn around, to realise that the danger was not in the glass in front of him, but behind him, inside Danny himself. But he couldn't speak.

'Bread daily our day this us give. . .'

Danny kept his eyes fixed on the mirror, trying not to feel the evil harden and grow in his body. In the flicker of the candle he saw himself walking slowly down a dark corridor, past Mr Donald, the Latin teacher, with his eyes gouged out, screaming with terror. He felt his arm swing through the air and turned to see Wetback clutching his face, blood running through his fingers. He saw himself walk past his own mother and father who stepped aside for him, their eyes averted in fear. And at the end of the corridor, Franny's sister stood in her underclothes and held open the bathroom door for him. He stared hard into the centre of the mirror to see what lay beyond that door.

'Heaven in is it as. . .'

Danny tried to pray. Please God. Oh please please please God. I'll never doubt again. Honest to God I won't. I'll be good now. Don't do this. Please please going not to do this.

He managed to pull his eyes away. He looked at Franny, saw he was clutching, white-knuckled, the edge of the dresser. His voice had slowed, faltered slightly. But he carried on.

'Earth on done be will Thy . . . Come Kingdom Thy . . .'

Franny took deep breaths between his words, but kept faithfully looking up into the mirror at the end of each phrase. Danny managed to snap his eyes shut.

'Name Thy be hallowed . . . Heaven in art who . . .'

Silence. Danny squeezed his eyes shut as tight as he could, the waiting was unbearable. Then Franny's voice lost its gravity: 'You right, Danny, wee man? . . . *Here's Johnny!*'

There was a rush of freezing air. A new Presence in the room. Danny put his hands to his face, and felt tears run through his fingers and down his arm. The Presence in the room hurtled around them, bellowing in some wordless, incomprehensible tongue. Danny sensed the thing move away from him towards Franny. He thought he could hear it leap on him, but Franny's voice squealed out defiantly:

'FATHER OUR!'

Then quiet again. The sound of breathing hung in the air, like frozen breath on a cold night. He heard Franny panting quietly, sucking in air sharply from time to time. Danny wondered where he was. On the ground? Bleeding? Dying? Danny's own breath hummed in his ears, the way it does when you're floating with your ears under the water. He realised he was bent double, on his hunkers, his hands glued to his face. He couldn't move. He'd been like this before: after the Coca Cola ride at the Garden Festival. He'd been so afraid and hung on so tight to the bar in front of him, that when it stopped he could neither get up or let go.

And then there was a breathing, low and deep and angered. It seemed to be working up to an awesome howl. It took voice, rumbling in some deep fury, then broke through and filled the room.

'Jesus Mary and Joseph! What kind of a monster are you!'

It was Father McKenna's voice, but who was he talking to? The Beast? Danny couldn't undo himself to look up. He heard the priest tugging and pulling at something, asking God to forgive Franny of his terrible crime. There was no response from Franny. Just the quiet panting and sucking of air. Father McKenna gave up on him and strode over towards Danny. He seemed a long time coming, and Danny's body curled in a little tighter. He felt the priest right next to him. Danny heard his own sobs echoing through the room. When the priest at last put his hands on him, it was a gentle touch, and his voice was conciliatory. 'Come on now, son. Get up. Tell me what happened here.' He pulled Danny out of his crouch, and took his hands away from his face. Danny kept his eyes closed tight. Behind his eyelids he could see the priest: in bra and panties and tights, his face rouged and lips painted. This was his damnation. This is how he would always see Father McKenna from now on. He would see everyone now bleeding, snarling, naked, writhing in pain and fury.

At last his eyes opened. The room was still flickering red and grey, but Father McKenna was his old self, though his expression was tormented in a way Danny had never seen before. 'Tell me what happened, son.' But Danny couldn't stop sobbing. The priest sat him down, patted his shoulder, then his face clenched like a fist as he turned his attention again to Franny.

Franny stood gawping into the mirror. He was as white as a sheet and oblivious to Father McKenna's accusations and the tugging at his arm.

'You vile, soulless creature. Bad enough spitting in the face of Mother Church, but to terrify the living daylights out of a poor child?'

Still Franny stared at the mirror, his eyes vacant, frightened. Danny managed to get up and go to him.

'Franny? What was it? What did you see?'

'Don't ask him!' the priest commanded. 'If he saw anything it would be the blackness of his own tortured little soul.'

Danny put his arm around his friend's shoulder and asked him quietly again. 'What did you see?'

'Nothing.'

'The mirror. . . ?'

'Empty.'

Father McKenna grabbed Franny by the shoulders and pushed

him towards the door. 'Get out of here. Don't ever set foot inside this church again.'

Franny shook him off and walked to the door. Then stopped and turned. For the first time ever Danny saw real malice in his friend's eyes. Franny looked at the priest and sneered. 'Don't worry. I'll not be back. What for?'

Father McKenna put his arm round Danny, and they watched as Franny pulled his flimsy jacket around himself and stepped outside. They heard him mumble as he waded out into the gruel of the evening light: 'There's nothing here.'

Father McKenna spoke softly to Danny. 'Don't worry, Daniel. I know you're innocent.' Danny knew this wasn't true; he knew for certain now that he needed God's and Father McKenna's protection from himself. So he stayed close to the priest and watched his friend scuffing his shoes along the road outside, one more little lost man.

from Poor Angels and other stories
(Polygon 1995)

SUSIE MAGUIRE
(b. 1958)

A writer of fiction, journalist and broadcaster, she has edited three anthologies *Scottish Love Stories* (1995), *Scottish Comic Writing* (1997) and *Something Wicked* (1999). Her own first collection of stories is *The Short Hello* (Polygon, 2000)

Irishness

I grew up a Catholic in Scotland. I don't think I considered my Irish ancestry until I was about 9, when I was sent to a school filled with girls of varied heritage. The family – my parents, older brother and younger sister – had decamped from Edinburgh to Argyllshire, then Perthshire, and were soon to settle in Glasgow for a while, and I clearly remember thinking that I was not 'from' any of these places. At that age, I imagined myself a sort of Celtic Viking nomad, whose destiny was sure to be heroic. (Perhaps there's still time. . .)

My mother's family were Highlanders, and my father's, by way of Belgium, Chile, and Manchester, hailed from Glasgow, and were 1st and 2nd generation Irish Scots. Both sides of the family tree had suffered what they felt to be grievous disenfranchisements, and I was made aware of them. Sometimes I have felt that this early lesson was not constructive; pragmatically, I realise that it takes many, many generations for scars to fade and that pride under oppression is mighty strong.

The romantic legends of Old Ireland are of questionable comfort. *A Genealogical History of the Milesian Families of Ireland* (Heraldic Artists Ltd., Dublin 1968) offers this testimony to my ancestry: 'They possessed the entire of Fermanagh, which was called Maguire's Country, and maintained their independence as lords of Fermanagh down to the reign of James I, when their country was confiscated, like other parts of Ulster.'

Like religion, nationality seems to be most important to us in times of difficulty. Awareness of my Irishness was heightened during the many years of t.v. coverage of the 'troubles' in Northern Ireland, which afforded the Maguire family ample opportunity to practise group swearing. I got sent out of a 5th year Modern History class in a Scottish school for mentioning that the 'Irish Problem' had not started in recent years but went back centuries.

The Irish element in my identity is intangible – a stirring in the blood, a response to the culture, a resonance when I hear a soft Irish voice, a yearning, a melancholic and humorous disposition, a skin tone, an instinctive loathing for Britannia in her official robes. And yet I have been there only once, aged 4. It is unlikely that I would be eligible to hold a green passport, but if I had one, what change would it make to my life? I'm not sure. Perhaps I am Irish enough. Perhaps the expatriate Irish carry their own Ireland with them everywhere, a small flint, a firestick, and only need a little friction to reignite the affinities.

It's Good To Talk

—Would you do it again?

—Yeah, probably. Wouldn't you?

—I'd like to think I wouldn't have to, you know? But then again, if you're asking me would 'I' do it again, if I was the same person in the same circumstances, then obviously, yes, I would, wouldn't I?

—I suppose so. . .

—Of course, that's the same kind of arse-numbing pedantry my wife used to complain about. Sorry.

Michael shrugs away the apology. Patrick offers a cigarette to Michael, but he shakes his head. Michael is eating cashew nuts. He finishes the packet and crumples the foil, and tosses it high into the bare branches of a willow tree. Three small birds take off in alarm. Patrick tut-tuts and resumes.

—I don't think I'd hang myself in the spare room though. I must have caused Margaret a lot of worry about structural damage to the roof timbers. Still, it was quick. Not too messy. And she never liked that room anyway.

Michael shakes his head.

—Well at least she found you in a couple of hours. If I was going to do it again I wouldn't cut myself in the bath, I'd drive myself over a cliff or something. Spare everyone the cleaning, you know?

Patrick picks up a piece of litter from the pathway and puts it in his pocket, nodding.

—Yeah. Sure. Ach, poor Margaret. One of the great cliches, isn't it, my wife doesn't understand me? They way they say it on t.v., some pathetic little sod on his knees in front of a young, beautiful woman, saying his wife doesn't understand him, with his hand up her dress. . . it wasn't like that with me at all, it wasn't about sex. She thought it was. And it wasn't that she didn't understand, she just didn't know what to do. She was always watching me, but sort of distant, like if you saw a wild animal with its head in a snare, trying to wriggle its way out. She'd try getting me to hold still, she'd ask me about the noose, she'd ask if it hurt, all that. Quite prophetic. You know. None of it made any difference. They can't really help you.

Patrick runs his palms across the mark where the rope had bitten into his neck. Unconsciously, Michael traces the scars on the inside of his own forearms, then tucks his hands into his trouser pockets. He sighs, shakes his head.

—I had the same thing with my mother. She was always saying 'Ach you'll be fine, you're a big strong fellow'. Like I was a sort of Superman, muscles made of Prozac, and I'd never suffer at all because of my size. No emotions because you can lift weights. That suited her, to be the only one with feelings.

Their walk has taken them some distance already. Michael leaves the path to sit on a wooden bench. Behind him, the leafless trees are dark against a sky which is growing grey and pink. Patrick lights one cigarette from the stub of another. He sits down beside Michael and they gaze at an expanse of water on which there bobs a flotilla of miserable-looking ducks.

—Did you try talking to anyone? asks Patrick.

—Oh yeah. But there was always something, with my mates they were just going to the pub, or the ex-girlfriend, her new boyfriend was there, or for my mother it was Bingo night. Anyway, you know yourself it's bloody hard to phone up and say you want to top yourself, just like that. Who'd listen?

—I know.

—I called the Samaritans once. The man on the other end, he was young and I started thinking, this is stupid, I know why I'm phoning, I know what's wrong with me, and I don't want this prick trying to talk me out of it, what does he know? It made me angry. And I felt I was doing his head in too, somebody I didn't even know who was trying to be kind, a volunteer, imagine how depressing it must have been for him.

Michael takes a packet of mints out of this pocket, offers them to Patrick. Patrick takes one and pops it into his mouth, as he grinds out his cigarette. Michael continues,

—And another thing I couldn't get out of my head, when I was lying there in the bath, the way people say, 'Oh it's the ones who don't talk about it you really have to watch out for'. . .

—I know, such an excuse for their own failings. . .

—Lack of perception, yeah?

—Stupid bastards. . .

—I mean, damned if you do talk and damned if you don't. What a choice there.

They both laugh. The sky grows darker. At the edge of the pond, a slight figure in jeans and a raincoat throws bread to the ducks, who squabble noisily over the manna. Patrick says,

—Did you leave a note?

—Just the usual, sorry I can't go on, sort of thing. Did you?

—It was too hard, I kept tearing them up. And there's the other thing, the guilt conflict, you know, where you feel bad enough that you can't go on, but you feel equally bad about giving everyone and their bloody dog the perfect excuse to be pissed off at you. Because you know they're not suddenly going to accept it, you know they'll talk about your selfishness and cowardice, and then how the cheque in the post the next week would have made a difference, or how the footie team won that weekend and how happy you'd have been if you'd only known.

—And they'll never ever forgive you. . .

—So you're a complete bastard either way.

—Failure One or Failure Two.

—Exactly ! You can't win.

They both laugh.

—It's odd the way we talk about it, like 'winners' and 'losers', isn't it? Like it was all Las Vegas. D'you think this conversation we're having is at all influenced by the lyrics of Country music, Patrick?

—Or Elvis, maybe. Or Abba. Surely there's been a musical on the subject, that Lloyd Webber man, wasn't there?

—No, I think he's missed one.

—Shame. Mind you, he's no talent for comedy.

—Suicide – The Musical. That's more of a Mel Brooks movie, don't you think?

—Tough job writing the lyrics for it. How do you rhyme overdose or amitryptiline. . .

—Ah ! Something something verbose, something something Abilene?

—There, now, you see, you have a talent. You could have been Tim Rice. . .

—I could have been a contender. . .I coulda been. . .somebody.

Michael laughs at his own Brando parody, which is pretty good. Patrick runs his hands through his hair, stretches his arms, shakes his shoulders and yawns. A breeze riffles the surface of the water.

—Tiring all this fresh air and analysis, isn't it?

—It is. Hindsight is a wonderful thing in small doses.

—Must be supper time by now.

—Big plate of stew and tatties in front of the fire, couple of hours of t.v., warm bath, warm bed, good book. . .

—I wish.

—Do you miss it?

—What – life?

—Mmm.

They look out at the pond where, in the last of the light, they can watch the ducks waddling slowly up the bank into the undergrowth.

—Not much. Not my actual life. Do you?

—Sometimes.

—I don't.

—There were some good bits, surely?

—Oh sure. But they were so long ago. And the good bits were like being a kid and getting a toffee from a stranger – you get suspicious after a while about what the toffee is meant to make you accept.

—All the shite.

—Exactly. Exactly that. There is one thing I regret, though. I'd like to have had a slogan tee-shirt made up to wear when I did it.

—And what would the slogan have been?

—'Nihilism Sucks – It's A Depressives Thing'

—Nice one. That would have sold like hot cakes at Euthanasia conventions. . . always wondered if old people got confused by Exit signs in big buildings. . . did I tell you I had a career in advertising?

—Jesus! Pity we never got together back then, we could have made a fortune and died rich.

—They still wouldn't understand us or forgive us. . .

—No. But they'd be crying all the way to the bank.

Michael gets up. He holds out his hand to Patrick, who takes it and comes to his feet smiling. Behind him, the plaque on the bench reads 'Take Comfort, Weary Traveller'. Patrick swings his arm round Michael's shoulder and they walk slowly up the hill to the gates.

previously unpublished

DANNY McCAHON
(b. 1958)

Born and brought up in Greenock, the setting for
his acclaimed short films *A Small Deposit* and
Danger Doyle's Doo. His scriptwriting credits
include *Taggart* and *Doctors*. A stage version of
Waiting for Gabriel was produced in 1999.

Free Lighters, Free Loaves
and the Goal of my Life

My family history is littered with unlikely unions and contradictions.
Our Irishness is the most unlikely of all.

My grandparents were a strange pairing – James McCahon, a
Protestant born and raised in the palm of Ulster's Red Hand and
Mary Corbett, a Catholic born and baptised in Boston, Massachu-
setts. Unwelcome among the Northern family because of their
marriage and without any family in the South, James and Mary
settled in that most Irish of Scottish towns, Port Glasgow.

My dad wore his Irish roots like a badge of honour. Yet he never
set foot in Ireland. I'm not sure whether he was so secure in his
Irishness that he didn't need to prove it by supping Guinness in a
Donegal pub or whether it was just that, unlike my Greenock
neighbours who boarded buses to Moville, Buncranna and
Letterkenney every Friday, we had no family there to put us up.

His Irishness had nothing to do with location or accent. Irishmen
have accents like John Fitzgerald Kennedy, Shane McGowan or my
father: red-haired, as strong as the concrete he worked with and
never afraid to cry at the sight of children suffering or protest at
the thought of social injustice.

Those neighbours' visits to 'The Free State' took on magical
properties for me. They taught me that Ireland was called 'The
Free State' because you got things for nothing there. Lighters and
loaves to be precise. Mrs McFadyen next door, who was partial to
a drop of whisky and milk, always brought my dad a lighter back
from visits. And during a time of hardship on the Clyde, a curate
from our parish brought back a boot-load of sliced loaves. My mum

thought it unfair that only the Catholic weans on the street should have toast before bedtime and gave half of our loaf to a family across the street. But they didn't want it. The mother said, '*I wouldn't give them the satisfaction of knowing they'd fed me. They kept their lights on during the war.*'

Her notion that Ireland might not be perfect was supported by others in an episode that split opinion on our street in 1969. Mrs McFadyen's son went off to Donegal on one of the weekly bus trips and arrived back in an orange Volkswagen Beetle.

We, the weans, loved this exotic car. They, the grown-ups, thought the ease with which he must have obtained his driving licence across the sea – '*filling in a form at the Post Office and spelling out his name right*' – meant he was unfit to park in the street where their children played football.

A year later I had to chance to judge Ireland for myself. The Boys' Guild was going to play football there and I was selected to play. Selected, that was, with around thirty other boys on the basis that my parents could meet the cost of the trip.

Even this sporting homecoming had its contradiction and confusion. Because, you see, I wasn't going to 'The Free State'. I was going where you had to pay your way. I was going to Belfast. A city described by friends of my dad as both '*The place you get the train to Ireland,*' and '*The real capital of Ireland, because people there have had to fight to hold to their nationality.*'

None of that mattered to me. I was going to the land of Dana and Mary Peters. And magic happened for me on that first visit to Ireland. I scored the opening goal in the opening game of the trip. I took the pass across my body and, without breaking my stride, volleyed the ball over the keeper and into the net. It was a goal that the Best of all Belfast Boys, Georgie, would have been proud of. I had never struck a ball so sweetly before and I have never struck one so well on Scottish soil.

That wasn't the only new experience for me on that trip. The next day I tasted a new fizzy drink. I called it Zup and bought a bottle to take home for my wee brother. I was shattered to find out that every child on my street had also discovered the new drink – 7Up – while I was away scoring the goal of my life. Still, that drink will always be Irish for me and like Irishmen, it is everywhere.

I have been back to Ireland many times but it has never been my home. I am Scottish. I am not Irish. I have never felt British. I am currently inclined towards Europe. The constant influence of a distant place in my growing up and the sense of having to fight for equality and acceptance handed down from immigrant forebears make me look outwards, not inwards, for belonging.

Meeting Gabriel

Act I. Greenock 1999
Scene 8. Kitchen

[Terry is loading dishes into the sink. The Celtic scarf lies on the worktop nearby.]

[The back door opens and an old man with a long moustache and smartly dressed comes in.]

STRANGER: Is it all over?

TERRY: Well, he's buried, but the party's in full swing.

STRANGER: Were you close?

TERRY: I'm his son. Terry.

[Terry and the stranger shake hands.]

TERRY: Would you like a cup of tea?

STRANGER: That would be lovely.

[Terry makes a cup of tea; boils the kettle, tea bags in pot, etc. during their conversation.]

STRANGER: I feel an emptiness.

TERRY: Sorry?

STRANGER: It feels like you miss your father.

TERRY: It does feel empty.

STRANGER: It's good to grieve.

TERRY: I was having my doubts anyway. But this could be the final straw.

STRANGER: Doubts?

TERRY: It's made me question whether there is an afterlife. If he was still there, I wouldn't be feeling this lonely.

STRANGER: One of the great mysteries that one. You'll never know. Until you get there, that is.

TERRY: But I have to believe.

STRANGER: Have to?

TERRY: I couldn't carry on if I didn't believe there was an afterlife.

STRANGER: That sounds a bit drastic.

TERRY: I shouldn't be boring you with my problems. A total stranger.

STRANGER: That's what I do. People say I'm a good listener. Go on. Our worries never seem so bad when we say them out loud.

TERRY: [sarcastically] Do you think not?

STRANGER: What was it you were saying? About not carrying on?

TERRY: I'm a priest. If I don't believe . . . well . . . If I don't believe in life after death I can't be a priest.

[Terry hands the stranger a mug of tea.]

ACT I, Greenock 1999
Scene 10. Kitchen

[The Stranger is walking around the kitchen. He helps himself to a biscuit from a barrel and dunks it in his tea.]

TERRY: I feel I've failed him.

STRANGER: Failed your father?

TERRY: He was big on tradition. Used to tell me these stories about his mother. About how she would scrimp and scrape to put aside money so he could go to watch Celtic every week. Family's all the friends you need, he used to say.

STRANGER: I'm sure you were a good friend to him.

TERRY: All my male cousins are on the other side. And priests don't have. . . Well. So the family name will die with me.

STRANGER: I'm sure he would have been proud of your faith. That's a tradition in itself. Maybe the biggest of the lot. Something he passed on to you.

TERRY: No. We ran out of steam. Towards the end all we ever talked about was football.

STRANGER: It's the same the world over. When fathers and sons have nothing else in common, there's always the ball game.

TERRY: He used to say there was nothing in nationality. Where you were born was just an accident of geography. And he had no real interest in politics. Celtic was what he believed in.

[Terry picks up the scarf.]

TERRY: This. This is my heritage.

ACT II. Lisbon Street 1967

[A Lisbon Street scene. A street café at the exterior of the Hotel Lisboa. A park and a church.]

Scene 1. Exterior Hotel Lisboa, Day

[The white light fades to reveal Terry on stage, holding his Celtic scarf. He looks around, surprised at the scene.]

[He stuffs his Celtic scarf in his pocket.]

[Tom Donnelly, a plaster cast on one leg, and Mick Broadley, wearing a kilt and a 1967-style Celtic top, come out of the hotel and sit at a table with long exotic drinks. Tom has a folded newspaper under his arm.]

[Inside the hotel, a male voice choir is belting out a rousing chorus of Hail, Hail, the Celts are Here.]

[Tom opens his newspaper.]

TOM: That's a bad sign that.

MICK: What?

TOM: Every wan o' them's got a perfect head of hair.

MICK: What's that got to so wi' anythin'?

TOM: You name a decent baldy fitba player.

[Terry heads straight for Tom and Mick with his hand outstretched. Tom shakes it.]

TERRY: Mister Don . . . Tom isn't it, and Mick. Mick Broadley. How are you both?

MICK: Aye, fine pal. But do I know you?

[Terry sits down beside them.]

MICK: Make yourself at home, pal.

TERRY: Did you have a good journey over?

TOM: Once this one managed to get through passport control.

TERRY: Oh aye?

TOM: We've been on the road all night to Dover, right. And we're standing there, desperate to get on the ferry for a bevy. Big Eddie's just about burstin' trying to hold his eight bottles o' Guinness he downed on the bus. An' this one here, Mick. He's arguing with the passport guy. Nationality? he asks. Mick says Irish. The guy waves his passport at him and says, Its says here you were born in Britain. Mick, quick as a flash goes . . .

[Mick takes over the telling of the story.]

MICK So? Jesus was born in a stable, disnae make him a donkey.

[Tom and Mick laugh.]

TERRY: I'm looking for my . . . eh . . . for Gabriel McGeechan. Is he with you?

TOM: Course he is. No show without Punch.

[Mick gestures towards the inside of the hotel.]

MICK: Find the burds, you'll find Gabe.

[Gabe comes out of the hotel with two Portuguese women.]

GABE: Right girls? My old mammy used to say, Gabe, ma boy, never trust a woman that doesn't have at least a bit of Irish in her. You play yer cards right an' you could have a big bit of Irish in ye before the day's out.

unpublished script

Donny O'Rourke
(b.1959)

Born Port Glasgow, Renfrewshire. Poet,
songwriter, film-maker and journalist, also
teaches in Glasgow School of Art. Edited
influential anthology of contemporary
Scottish poetry, *Dream State* (1994).

Ireland. Ire-land; an angry country, blowing up and burning down, a
place no longer mythic or ancestral, but, now, for me at 10, in
1969, an island suddenly all too blisteringly real. My mother had
been brought up in Ballymena, home turf to the bigot Paisley and I
remember her angry, frightened tears as we watched the news on
television. Ulster they called this war zone, although two of that
province's counties were in the South.

The stories we grew up on were specifically about the North,
about Antrim. A wheen of years passed before I learned just how
significant that coast had been. Dalriada spanned the sea in
Columba's time, but Mum's lore was more recent and familial. She
was the very self-conscious product of what, in a quaintly odious
phrase, people used to call a 'mixed marriage'. Mum's dad Frank
Quigg had been a Protestant and although he had 'turned', we had
lots of relatives on the 'other' side. His daughter learned the Our
Father in Gaelic from the nuns but was brought up to think of
herself as British first and Irish a poor second. I would guess she
believed herself to have more in common with the Scots she ended
up amongst, than the folks across the border back home.

She never voiced what I have heard from other Northern Catholics
– a certain snobbish disdain for the Irish foundering in a bog of
ignorance and parochialism down South. An especial viciousness
was reserved for the Papish whelps of turncoats and Mum had
much to forgive and forget. Or more exactly to forgive and
remember, for my younger brother and wee sister and I were
encouraged to counter bigotry with even-handedness and charity:
'never descend to their level, love them, pity them, rise above the
hate, they can't stand that.'

Dad's Ireland was more romantic and remote, though he too had endured his share of prejudice. His grandfather had left Ireland under the pressure of hunger, and perhaps some sort of cloud. We'll never know: working class families have short memories. Anyway, his timing was spot on. The aftermath of famine coincided with the technical innovations that rendered wooden ships obsolete and, having trained as a woodturner, he went on to work as a draughtsman in Port Glasgow alongside his fellow immigrants who were only too willing to do the new jobs requiring new skills that the mostly Protestant and Tory working class aristocracy were too sniffily Luddite to do. Segregation, introduced to prevent hostility between scabs and the established workforce, lasted in one form or another almost as long as the yards themselves.

Mind you, we were the descendants of Princes, Dad always maintained in the face of Mum's brisk scepticism and our flattered relish. (Much later I'd visit our patrimony in moist, green County Leitrim – County Ui ruairc until Queen Elizabeth's victory over our forebear Brian and the enforced change of name). In his lovely, light tenor Dad would sing Tom Moore ballads and parlour songs. 'Rebel' songs he neither sang nor condoned. 'Oirishry', he thought vulgar and reductive. He never laid on the blarney, never played the heartsore exiled Mick. 'Go on away home, Ireland's not full yet' he would have said to anyone who did.

Ugly, stymying discrimination was endemic in his early life in Port Glasgow. But his own father had been so vexed by what he took to be the brutish insularity of Catholic schooling that he had taken Dad out of the system, sending him to the non-denominational Highholm School. Only priestly pressure sent my brother, sister and me back through the segregated system. Dad wouldn't let us support Celtic, and he didn't let me join the school cub pack. The scouts opened me up to all sorts of exciting possibilities and religion was never an issue. But making me support Morton! The man had no scruple!

When Celtic won the European Cup in 1967, our Catholic neigh-bours in the respectable upper working class enclave we inhabited flew the tricolour for a day or two. Both my parents thought this was very bad form. 'There's not a thing Irish about Jock Stein and he won that cup. Those players are Scottish every one. . .' That said (and it was, loudly and often), the school teams I played in sounded a lot more Irish than the ones Jack Charlton fielded:

Callaghan, McGinty, McMahon, Doherty, O'Neill, McKenna, Harrigan, McCann.

Our teachers tended to have names like those ones too, Donegal antecedents mostly. Enormous emphasis was placed on assimilation and achievement. But poor children often get poor marks. Very few members of my primary class went on to Higher Education. The teachers tried and I'm grateful to them (the religious maniacs, sadists and narrow minded philistines excepted). I never heard a bigoted word out of even the ones who were demented with devotion.

I'd say Ireland meant more to me than either of my folks, even though one of them was certifiably Irish. Bigotry got me started: why do these wee boys hate us and call us names? Soon I was paddling my own coracle and (precocious wee prig that I was, Donny the solitaire, the triste) reached an Ireland of my own, a Tir nan Og full of fili, seannachies and bards. It was the 'Troubles' that made me gradually get real, leading me towards Heaney, Planxty and the serious study of Celtic history at university.

I'd have been 13, I suppose, when I first heard that Planxty concert from Belfast, music which did nothing for Mum and Dad but which I recognised as mine at once, tunes and songs I added to the guitar repertoire I was trying out, music that you rarely heard in parlours. The Ireland of Durcan, Muldoon, Paulin, Simmons, Montague and Hewitt was realer to me than the actual place they came from. By the time I got to Ballycastle I was in my twenties. My sister Maureen and Mum and I had a teary, cheery series of jaunts down memory lane.

My brother Stephen made a point of marrying in the Protestant Church and casts a jaundiced eye from the South of England on what he calls, 'the Emerald Isle', reserving for my intellectual and spiritual involvement with Ireland, and our sister's deep affection for things Irish, the kind of scathing scorn one associates with people in what the Americans call 'denial'. What our teasing and joking differences reveal, however, is the extent to which my Irishness is elective, complex, ambivalent – deliberate and deliberated. Too much Guinness-fueled stage or page Irishness can leave a poet green about the gills, and broth-of-a-bhoyery has never been my style. Anyone interested in how I feel about Ireland, though, can read all about it in poem after poem. No-one can live or write without a myth, and Ireland figures complexly and seductively in mine.

On the day the people of Ireland went out to vote for change, the *Independent* ran a photo of a picture postcard Irish church, limewashed and dignified against a rosy sunset out at sea. A symbol of hope. My grandfather Frank Quigg lies in the graveyard of that beautiful wee Protestant church at Ballintoy, in Antrim (Dalriada as was).

Ireland's croneyism and begrudgery appal me almost as much as its new found freedom and confidence inspire me and delight me, sometimes to the point of envy. So how Irish am I? Very. The first people in Scotland to call themselves Scots were very Irish too. Kenneth White's coinage 'Scotic' is one I'm glad of. In a sense, Irishness and Scottishness are the same thing. Well, up to a point. When Scotland plays Ireland I cheer on the boys in blue. Lachry-mose, nostalgic, Celtic-supporting Aran sweatery leaves me cold. But offer me a drink and it's stout I'll ask for.

Conventional religiosity plays less and less of a role in my life; a gentle Columban zen provides the solace my contemplative nature needs. The incense-sweetened misogyny, authoritarian hauteur, and intractable social irrelevance that characterises much contem-porary Catholicism is more and more the gruesome doppelganger of the Calvinism which so long denied Scotland life. My Irishness is much more than Catholicism with a shamrock in its lapel. I have more in common with Wolf Tone, Oscar Wilde, Samuel Beckett, the brothers Yeats and Van Morrison than with any of the maudlin, pious mickeens I've encountered (in America) crying into their green-tinted Paddy's Day pints of Harp.

Scottish, Irish, European (and geographically at least, British), I dream of a Republic of Scotland, a truly Free State, on terms and at peace with itself, its neighbours and the world – and able at last to face up to just how Irish this place and people have always been.

Milk

Your custom often
when the house was still

to brew milky coffee
and reminisce.

Child care experts would have frowned
on my late hours,

and bitter adult drinks
and frothy confidences.

Yet your stories stopped my mewling
and continued as I grew

me tending the fire,
you talking of Ireland,

more real to your first born
than the younger ones who slept.

Those nightcaps, Mother,
were our hushed bond.

And though, for twenty years now,
I've drunk my coffee black,

I'm not weaned yet
of that rich, warm milk.

Primary

Every word I've ever read or written
I owe to you Miss Hughes –
dream colleen and crabbit queen
of primary one

With your round white face
and russet perm you could have modelled
Ireland for The Book of Kells

and green –

           your eyes

                    and swankiest

                              sweaters

green

the lightest

           brightest

                  tightest

                        green

Those first terms were mostly religion
sums and reading but you
grew hyacinths in the dark
curdling in that cupboard also
school milk into cheese.
Our first solid achievement.
Your muslin miracle.

It was 1964; we bought 'Black Babies'
wept and wet ourselves
but were excused –
Pees and Queues for the 'lavatory'

never the toilet
A stickler for proper English
and Catholic self-improvement
praying we'd pass for higher class
you spruced up where we came from
helped us out:
'Port Glasgow' was articulated sternly
and in full
                    'The Port, Daniel O'Rourke
is vulgar
                    teeth and tongue now, Porrtt
Glass go.'
You pulled out all the glottal stops
corrected nearly everything we learned
at home

Miss Hughes, you had magnificent breasts
and I loved you
You turned all our cream to crowdie.

Ballintoy

Frank Quigg rests at Ballintoy
in loamy Protestant soil,
the North is truest here, loyal
to the lie of this land –
its ancient truculence of spume.
And Kintyre marks the spot I find my kin in:
you can see Scotland more clearly than ever it sees itself.
Beyond windy cottages blanched as linen,
in the Church of Ireland cemetery
my grandfather's memory I exhume,
seven years buried before I was born,
dowdy in mourning left on this coastal shelf
Scotland was torn
from.

'Could I carry your wee parcel Miss Delargey?'
that was how it started:
love got up in ribbons that never quite came undone,
though soon it was Annie who carted
the whiskey's burden
'mixed fortunes in a mixed marriage –
can you be surprised?' the Lambeg gossips said.
But there was passion and kindness, mostly Annie stayed.
Certainly my mother's father liked a glass;
but he left her always to early Mass.
And many's the hard word
and harder fist, Frank Quigg got
when drink ventriloquised an answer
to some Ballymena bigot,
until his second war took him away;

and sailing convoys out of Scapa,
he calmed, came to love the sea.

'When I go Annie, lay me down here',
he'd joshed one Sunday up the coast.
And so at Ballintoy he lies,
taken at his word, taken from Ballycastle
to this green place where most,
(in sober willing too), he'd wished his stone to stand,
on this adamantine, snaggle shored Antrim land.
And I see it first of a risen Easter Day
by a sun warm and low as the last orange nightcap
in a bottle of Bushmills:
looking to the land his women went to,
oh how the heart fills
with that older Scottish blood
that corrached Colmcille's sea
to Dalriada.
The Ulster blood that pulses proud in me
pounds pape and planter both
At Ballintoy Frank Quigg lies:
green and blue, the kyle's cold truth.

from The Waistband (Polygon 1997)

GERRY CAMBRIDGE
(b.1959)

Born Morecambe, moved to Scotland early
1970s. Poet, nature photographer and blues
harmonica player. Latest collection 'Nothing
but Heather!' (1999) combines poems and
photographs of Scottish wildlife and
landscape.

From the Irish

Among my earliest memories is one of my mother's expressions of
exasperation: 'Holy Mary, Mother of Jesus!' she would exclaim at
justifiable moments. When she learned that, in my late twenties, I
partook of the occasional dram, alarmed, she said: 'You watch
yourself with that now, son, for it's in you to the bone.'

My mother was born and raised in Maghera, County Derry, not far
from Seamus Heaney's birthplace. When I met Heaney, it was like
meeting an Irish Uncle. My father was born in the Falls Road,
Belfast, in 1921, and raised in Bellshill, where his father, also born
in Belfast, was a miner.

The older I grow the more Irish I feel. Whatever poetry is in me I
take partly from the speech of my mother; whatever wit, partly
from the extravagance of my father; my height I take from a range
of statuesque Irish aunts, all at least six feet tall.

My surname Cambridge is a corruption of the Scots Gaelic
MacAmbrois, formerly MacCambridge. It has nothing to do with the
English university town. At some stage the 'Mac' prefix was
dropped, in Northern Ireland.

As a youngster I spent summer holidays with my Irish cousins in
County Derry. We jumped about in hay barns. We raided orchards.
We tried to catch trout in burns with sticks and buckets. We forked
eels with kitchen forks in the river Moyola, immortalised in
Heaney's earlier poems. I recall the scent of eel slices sizzling in a
frying pan in a house which, when I returned to it in 1998 for a
wedding, seemed tiny. My madeleine is the sweet scent of an old
man's pipe smoke in that house.

I spent most of the first thirteen years of my life in various parts of England before moving to Scotland. I have written of my experiences of sectarianism as the only Catholic at a Protestant school in Ayrshire in the introduction to my book 'Nothing but Heather!' Irish Catholicism, sectarianism apart, had a significant but unquantifiable effect on me. My Catholic education, on account of my usually attending Protestant schools, was patchy. I had only the vaguest idea of what Catholicism was all about – guilt, being wrong, obeisance, and a big secret. When I was eleven my father came in one night saying, 'Rose, Alice is almost gone!' My parents instantly dropped to their knees and forced my two sisters and me to join them to say the rosary, something we seldom did. I was a priggish little fellow. I was embarrassed at seeing grown-ups behave with such a lack of dignity. Years later in Scotland I remember on several Good Fridays gloweringly enduring the extra long service inside St. Mary's Chapel while the sun shone outside. I could summon little interest in what seemed to me Christ's 2,000 year old sufferings. I wanted to be doing nothing more than walk the fields looking for peewits' nests.

Adolescence hatched out all my complexes. I sent away for a bodybuilding course entitled, with absurd optimism, Hercules II. The £12 cost of this I earned by a weekend of hoisting hay bales at local Fairliecrevoch Farm. This added considerably more muscle than the three month course itself which, advocating that I consume enormous amounts of protein, served only to outrage my thrift-minded father and enlarge my girth. Alarmed by the latter, I became near anorexic in reaction. This was buttressed by my pleasing sense of sanctity when I learned that, at a certain stage of self-starvation, my sex-drive almost disappeared. I could then view my female class mates less with alarming lust than with a lofty and pseudo-innocent regard. Sex was a sin, after all. So eating had to be a sin, too, for eating led to sex. And sin, though it was how we were all here in the first place, was indisputably bad. I grew thin as a stick, but felt holy. Catholic images of the sanctity of fasting and abjuration of the body are embedded deep in my psyche.

Sex having become an issue, before I discovered near-starvation as a weapon in my fight against lust, I sublimated as best I could the explosion of hormones by becoming a remarkably erudite ornithologist. I knew the lifestyles and Latin names of hundreds of different species. The names I would recite to myself at stressful moments, like parts of a rosary. *Turdus merula, Phalacrocorax carbo, Aquila chrysaetos, Coccothraustes coccothraustes* I would silently intone in the face of Linda Donaldson's awe-inspiring figure. At school, girls were uniformly (and in uniform or out of it) terrifying, creatures to be both worshipped upon one's knees and creamy sirens whom I sinned with in imagination on a nightly basis, only to repent instantly in an orgy of prayer and blushes.

In early 4th year, we had a sex-education lecture in Irvine Royal. I got through it somehow by catching no one's glance. I emerged from the lecture with tertiary syphilis, a just punishment for a sinful 'doctors and nurses' session at age 10. A trip to Irvine Library's medical section confirmed my diagnosis. The disease was fittingly terrible. What I thought of as my lean muscular body and its strength, of which I was so proud, would be corrupted relentlessly. I would be in a wheelchair by the time I was seventeen, and die horribly soon after. I lay in bed at night and imagined hosts of spirochaetes consuming my backbone. I began to understand the meaning of 'possession'. Every morning before school I risked the martyrdom of being spotted by my Protestant schoolpals and spent a half hour praying fervently in a deserted St. Mary's. On one occasion there I was presented with a bird book by a priest. The same priest was recently involved in allegations, going back two decades, of molesting young boys.

Finally, I confessed my fears to a local GP, a Dr. Burns.

'Did you penetrate?' he asked.

'Penetrate what?' I said, bewildered.

'There really is nothing to worry about,' he said chuckling, after a few more such penetrating questions. 'It's all in your mind.' He fixed me with his best serious look and said, 'Forget about it.' I went away, reassured for at least five minutes.

The following week, my obsession in full flood, I insisted he send me to a specialist at what were then known as 'Special Clinics'. He was reluctant to do so, asserting that they were for people with genuine problems, but finally relented.

'What's this?' my mother said, brandishing the brown envelope with its red hospital frank. She had opened it in panic. 'What's a special clinic?'

'I've no idea. Maybe that's just something sent to selected people every few years or so,' I said, with a Catholic's sense of being chosen. 'I'll go and see.'

The day of my appointment at Heathfield Hospital was tremendously wet. I arrived at the reception drookit, and stood in a puddle of water as the receptionist asked, alarmingly, for my 'next of kin'. Outside the consulting room when I reached it a nurse was explaining to a man that he had probably infected his wife with a nasty disease. I was 15. My sexual experience could have been written on the back of a postage stamp. I felt the nurses looking at me, and imagined them later shaking their heads at the promiscuity of the young.

Dr Schofield was a reassuring, cigar-smoking white-haired man who listened with proper gravity to my fears, examined scrupulously my cold-wrinkled member, and took a blood sample. 'You are a very responsible young man,' he told me, generously interpreting terror as responsibility. 'After all,' he went on, with what must have been irony, 'we wouldn't want you infecting half the young women in Ayrshire – though I don't think there's anything for you to worry about, health-wise. Phone me next week.'

'What was all that about?' my mother asked later.
'Oh, a lot of nonsense,' I said, with some justification.

When I phoned a week later, I was told the test was 'fine'. 'That is,' said Dr Schofield for extra clarity, 'There's nothing wrong with you.'
'Thank you Dr Schofield!'
'No, thank *you*.'

I felt absolved, and as pure as after confession, and went off and played out of sheer relief a blinding game of football with schoolpals, after sitting a morning 'O' level.

I have lived in Scotland almost all of my life. I still think of the landscape of Ayrshire around Irvine as the first place I had roots. I love Scotland's magnificent austerity, its natural history, literary pub culture, the extravagance and cynicism of the speech which watermarks my own. I feel less of an exile here than I would feel probably anywhere else, even in Ireland. Pressed, though, about whether I consider myself more Irish or Scottish, I would have to say Irish, and Catholic Irish, for good or ill, as my mother would say, 'to the bone'.

Duck Shooters

Out on the Overtoun Road in the autumn night,
Night of slow showers and the moon a blur,
Immense, calm, prospective night, my thoughts
On you I've hurt, and her; a shower
Stops, and the night world drips, and a veil now
Of cloud drags clear of the constant Plough
Over the dark farmhouse; look, it glints complete,
And star-patterns sparkle about the sky. At Warwickdale
The two duck shooters give me a lift;
I'm in a suddenly different world in the car's back seat,
And the two dark simple heads are framed
On the headlit road beyond. And all is warm
And comfortable, like a deep lulling dream,
Out of the threat of shower and storm;
They were shooting, they say, at Fairliecrevoch, and
Got nine duck – *three mallard, aye, six teal.*
Three mallard, and six teal!
I think of the spirits of air and dark
In the bags, their feathers superbly marked:
Bottle-green heads, cream eye-flashed, emerald specula,
And the wings that counties flowed below: three mallard,
                and six teal,
The eldritch, pristine real
In a jumble as if they were merely asleep
With their eyes now closed, in the bags!

Ye winchin yet? a voice asks. *Oh, on and off,*
I say. *I've just come now from a stormy session.*
Dinny let it get ye beat, says a different voice
An existence away; *ye'll no get oany stranger piece*
O chemistry than a wumman. It's thirty years experience
Ah speak fae. They drop me off at the lane end; again

Sudden wide starlit sky, and above black trees,
The cloud-surrounded full and brilliant moon,
Bore down on by a cloud; the end of words.
And the door of the car
Slams, and tail-lights like red eyes it drives
Diminishing off down the empty road
Certainly, with men and guns, and dark-bagged birds.

Blood Root

There was a single table, in that
archipelago of tables, which was free –
and it had to be next to yours.
As soon as I noticed you, the old
conspiracy of walls moved in,
the blood sprang to my cheeks, the hot
tributaries overflowed
their banks of *may* and *should* and *not*
and flooded my face's land. Though gone
the time of my long loneliness, the rare
intimacies of our eyes, the Christmas card
unanswered that, drunk, I gave you
with its poem – haverings on the moon –
and your every frank appraisal
of my thighs in blood-warm summer
as I passed, still I was afraid
that you would see me there, afraid
of my face's cursed barometer.
You had your back to me, its rind
of white nylon sweater showed the straps
of your bra and the small sweet knobble
where they joined for the unfastening

and the blossoming of roses in our mouths,
the absolute liberties of skin
on skin. Your left hand with its carmined nails
guided again and again the cigarette
up to your lips, and your left leg, crossed,
came perilously near to revealing
the dazzling tops of your patterned stockings.
Had you then turned and looked at me,
would you have seen the blood I need
to be rid of, that sings to be drunk
and gone? In the dark
and beckoning forest of that gaze,
my happiness at half-
measures, half-solutions,
and all the ordered syllables of light I built are lost.

from Mr Burns for Supper (1996)

Crab Spider in Grass

In the minor infinities of green
the green crab spider won't be seen
by whatever will form its prey.
     Ignorant of place or date,
as it were dead it rests in wait
for what may venture, soon or late,
     near, on this Easter day.
Mere yards away the people pass
on the chapel's path; and do not know
what rite is planned here, as they go
in this stoneless church of grass.

from 'Nothing but Heather!' (Luath 1999)

Solstice

The morning I should have heard R.S. Thomas
Reading his poems in a hot far room.
I woke here in silence to primrose rays
Moment by moment shock-freshly arriving
To steam-wisped kettle and page in the gloom:
Cells of light, a pristine praise.

Spruce were viridian, out on the blue-black,
The world a bright hall, sparse-furnished, austere;
Leaping and lively the cat came in from the myriad ways
Through the bare-treed woods and the fields outspread
And shone in the universe, local here:
Cells of light, a pristine praise.

I lifted a teaspoon, and that had a meaning,
As the voice intoned in a distant place
For the forest of faces, the fortunate phrase:
I wrote on the page from the west to the east
As entered here from the sun in space
Cells of light, a pristine praise.

from The Shell House (Scottish Cultural Press 1995)

DES DILLON
(b. 1960)

Born Coatbridge. Poet, novelist and
scriptwriter for film and television. *Me & Ma
Gal* (1995) was his first in a series of vivid
fictions of West of Scotland life. Latest novel
The Return of the Busby Babes (2000).

Irish with a Scottish Accent

My experience as a Catholic writer in Scotland has been painful. I
got serious in 1981 – getting the odd poem published. My prose
was getting nowhere. In 1987 I wrote *Me & Ma Gal* – a novel
steeped in Catholic imagery and symbolism. I felt it was a strong
piece of work. Yet it lay breaking my heart in a drawer for eight
years.

I sent sections to publishers and literary magazines in Scotland.
Rejected every time – some with advice on how to write properly.
I continued peeking through the letter box of Scottish Literature. If
I'd've known it would be eight years before the door opened I'd've
jumped in the canal.

Me & Ma Gal is physically rooted nine miles east of Glasgow but its
spirit is two hundred miles from Scotland. It was eventually
published in 1995 – thanks to the foresight of Derek Rodger of
Argyll Publishing. The novel was critically acclaimed – compared
with Mark Twain, Alain Fournier, Jack Kerouac and Joyce:

*Not since Ulysses or the work of Alain Fournier have I come across
such a satisfying evocation of a single day, of childhood, of friendship,
community and the world. . .*

When I read that – years of rejection were washed away. When the
emotion subsided I got to thinking – I'd never read *Ulysses*. But I did
come from the biggest Irish community in Scotland. A place where
stream of consciousness is replaced by streams of blarney. A town
more Irish than Ireland. While Ireland has moved on Coatbridge has
clung onto ancient and terrifying aspects of Irish culture. *Toichfaidh ar
la* – it says on walls right round the town. But their day won't come –
Ireland has passed them by – embracing change.

I had to ask myself why *Me & Ma Gal* was so comprehensively rejected. Did anti-Catholicism permeate even the literary establishment? Perhaps on a subconscious level? I don't think so. It was something much more subtle than that – and perhaps – in the long run – more damaging to Scotland. Elitism.

How easy it is to denigrate a feisty verve-driven narrative because it doesn't obey the rules of what makes *good literature*. Paradoxically – how difficult it is to write the same narrative. My prose is as thought-out and calculated as poetry.

How can you measure sentences like – *I'll tell you this but I don't want you think there's anything funny about me but it's true.* Scottish Literature's pre-occupation with 'fine writing' is far removed from the flamboyant volksgeist of Irish culture.

My work was rejected because of its language – not its content. All the Chapels and Wakes and Funerals and Communions and Priests and Hail Marys and pairs of rosary beads didn't affect the literary editors – except that they might not empathise with that world. The literary editors did not know what to do with the natural verve of the language. Having not seen anything like it before – they have to reject it. They have no other option using narrow academic criteria – which is always backwards looking and conservative.

Any new art or literature will – and should – pay no heed to the 'Giants' of the past – they are usually Giants because they paid no heed. Aye – I learned my craft from them – but took my stories and language from the people of Coatbridge. I write for them in a representation of their language. I call it Geo-linguistic – language from a point on the globe – and – from a distance – one point's as good as the next – unless it is devalued by others. Parochialized? I'll say two words – Huckleberry Finn.

The language in Coatbridge is Irish English with a Scottish accent. The immigrants adopted a quite proper English which is still in use. In Easterhouse they say *Doon the Shoaps* – in the Brig – it's *Down the Shops* – and cross the border – and I mean the border – into Airdrie and we're going *Doon the Shoaps* again. Check out the word *oul* – for old – you'll only hear it in Port Glasgow – Coatbridge or the Garngad. I could go on but . . .

Take a typical Coatbridge sentence – *He's coming in at six o clock*

the night and he's going to kill you so he is ma Da. I believe – and
there's a PhD in this for somebody – that a culture's sentences are
a microcosm of its storytelling tradition. Much the same as DNA
contains the knowledge of what it is to be you. It's no fluke that
what's held to the end of this sentence is its subject. Coatbridge
storytellers are top class – and their innate knowledge of structure
is so great you'll never be bored – you'll never be puzzled – you'll
be listening at the end of the day. And you'll come back for more.
Coatbridge has no bookshop. You might wonder why. I don't.

Jimmy Brogan

JIMMY Brogan was mesmerised by somethin else an all. It was
the time his feelins were all separatin. Fragmentin. He told me
all about it. What brung it about was a tune. Well two tunes really.
Or mibbi three. I can't remember right what he sayed. But lookin
back now it's easy to see that was the start – the very beginnin of
his troubles.

Rule Britannia. That's what it was. The tune. They were doin
Singin Together an this week the song was Rule Britannia. It was:
John John John the grey goose is gone an the fox is off to his den oh, last
week.

Jimmy Brogan liked that. An he liked Rule Britannia an all.
The whole class's singin away like true patriots.

> *Rule Britannia*
> *Britannia rule the waves.*
> *Britons never never ne-ver shall*
>   *be*
>   *slaves.*

He sung it. He drummed it out on the desk but Miss Boswell

never bothered. He could drum away to his heart's content far as she was concerned. An she was usin her pencil as a baton. The whole class was singin. Jimmy Brogan says he felt tears in his eyes. It was good to be British. Rulin the waves an all that. Lettin no cunt mess. Don't fuck wi the Brits. Union Jack ya bass.

At playtime Donny O'Hare sayed that was a lot of pish what the teacher sayed cos we're Scottish. Jimmy Brogan an him sung Scotland The Brave. When we all went back in it was wi a totally different attitude. Totally different. Donny O'Hare an Jimmy Brogan sang it to the teacher. She thought it was good. Got them to sing it in front of the class. It was great to be Scottish. Fuckin brilliant!

The next Sunday he's been at mass Jimmy Brogan. An it was:

Hail glorious Saint Patrick
Dear saint of our isle
On us thy poor children
Bestow a great smile
And now thou art throned
In thy mansions above
On Erin's green valleys
On Erin's green valleys . . .

Then on to the Granny's. An in his Granny's wi her Irish accent the schism came to him. He couldn't name it a name in them days. He could only see it for what it was all them years later in The Ward. But that was the exact time his head started to go wrong. Right there in his Granny's. That was when he knew. It was one word that done it. OUR. That was the word. Goin through an through him. *Our Isle*. That's what they all sung at Mass. He thought bein Scottish was all Hail Mary's an shillelaghs an John F Kennedy an pictures of the Pope. But that was Irish. An he was Scottish. But he was Irish. Erin is Our Isle. But on the map he's Scottish. But the songs're Irish. All he remembers is lookin at this shamrock covered recipe on the wall IRISH SODA BREAD. It all started spinnin. Next thing he's wakin up in bed wi the doctor there.

•

Jimmy Brogan was watchin the telly years ago. It was any other Sunday. His Da was still wi his Maw. He'd dogged mass an spent the plate money on Curly Wurleys. Three. Sat down the graveyard freezin. It's the second last day of January. He sayed a couple of Hail Mary's about missin mass an watched the clouds. An read what was wrote on the stones. All the names. Harkins. Duffy. Riley. Dillon. Brennan. Cooney. Donnelley. O'Hare. Ryan. Conway. Conlin. Coady. Daley. Regan. Bonar. Doyle. Tolland. Straney. Nalty. Conroy. Foley. Fox. O'Neill. He licked his finger an rubbed some of them an wondered what it'd be like to be dead.

> *John John John the grey goose is gone and the fox is off*
> *to his den oh. . .*

Jimmy Brogan sang through the tombs till it was time to go home. A crow flaps by. Jimmy Brogan wonders if ye really do go somewhere after ye die. Resurrection. He looks about at the stones. Must be some size heaven he's thinkin. An Hell. In the distance he can see the people streamin out of mass an shakin hands. He heads up the road.

It's later on he's watchin Bernie The Bolt. Up a bit. Down a bit. Left a bit. Left left left. Stop stop stop. Fire. Thunk. Ye had to break the thread. An sometimes all the gold coins came out an sometimes they never. He couldn't remember if the coins came out that day or not. But there's somethin he did remember. The News. He sayed that was where he took a wrong turn. That was the day that changed everythin.

So Bernie The Bolt's finished an it's The News. He's on his belly readin a Topper an swingin his feet in the air. An things're good cos there's half a Curly Wurley planked outside. The news man's rattlin on about fuck knows what.

> A civil rights march in Londonderry turned
> into a shoot-out today when British Para-
> troopers fired on the demonstrators, killing
> thirteen and wounding another seventeen.
> Local politicians have dubbed the tragedy
> Bloody Sunday . . .

Jimmy Brogan's tryin to sneak out the door without his Da noticin.

> . . . and attacked military handling of the
> march and its aftermath, although British
> Army chiefs maintained that the soldiers had
> begun firing in self-defence . . .

—Hanna! Hanna c'mere quick an see this, his Da shouts. In comes
the Maw wipin her hands wi a towel. They're lookin at The News.
Jimmy Brogan peeks back round the door.

> The violence erupted as Republican civil
> rights demonstrators tried to break down a
> roadblock in the city's Bogside area and the
> troops began to open fire, initially with
> rubber bullets but then with live rounds. . .

There's this Priest jumpin about wavin a hanky. It's only shinin in
one eye the telly cos Jimmy Brogan's halfway out the door. He tilts
back so his two eyes can see. The telly sucks his whole body back in.
His Granny was always goin on about Ireland. Belfast Derry Donegal.
    —That's where ye want to go Donegal. Get yerself over there
when ye're big an get a nice Irish lassie, she sayed all the time.
That's where yer Mother was born. Goats an Hawks she came
from. Goats an Hawks Donegal. Jimmy Brogan laughed every time.
    —What in the name of Jesus're ye laughin at? That boy's
touched so he is. Touched, she'd go. But he'd be on the floor wi all
this mad stuff goin through his head.

—Hello there ma name's Jimmy Brogan an I'm visitin these parts. Ye couldn't tell a fella how to get to Goats an Hawks could ye now? he went doin his Granny. Then he'd do some mad Donegaly.

—Sure no I couldn't be tellin ye that – I'm from Pigs an Monkeys meself. Never heard of that place you're talkin about now. What would it be called now? Dogs an Cats?

—No ya tattie howkin cunt. It's where ma Graaaaaaaany's from. It's Goats an Hawks.

But he's not laughin here. Not on Bloody Sunday. He's gettin sucked into the telly. It's the Paras.

Over a hundred rioters hurled stones and missiles at the soldiers. Eye witness reports said the first shot was in fact fired by a Loyalist Gunman . . .

They're shootin every cunt. Probably cunts from Goats an Hawks an all. Weans. Priests. Oul Wimmin wi bags like yer Maw. But it's the Priest that gets etched into Jimmy Brogan. He's bent over wavin a black bit of cloth out at the front. Bent over like he's dodgin bricks goin over his head. But it's not bricks. It's bullets. That's how he's bent over. An there's four guys behind him. An they're just ordinary guys like what worked in Dundyvan. Or drank in Mackenzie's. Ordinary fellahs. This one's got a tie on an he's quite neat. Like he must have an office job. He's got the body by the ankles. Grabbin it by the trousers. An a wee guy like Garden Bobby down the lane. Exactly like him. Wee an baldy. He's lookin up an his arm's comin under the body an there's a white hanky in his hand. But even Jimmy Brogan can see the body's dead. They're carryin a dead body. An the wee guy's lookin up at the sky an his face is like he's holdin the body up to God for an explanation.

—What the fuck're ye goin to do about this God? Eh? What the fuck're ye goin to do?

But Psheeew Psheew is all ye can hear an then Jimmy Brogan

knows that fuck all's what God's goin to do. Not a fuckin thing. The next guy's a student. Like John Paul Brennan up the road. He's a student. He's got glasses an a long coat. He's got an arm under the body an another arm over the top grippin the lapel. It's that hand on the lapel that's stoppin the body floppin forwards onto the ground. The body's just a v shape wi the arse near trailin off the ground.

An Psheeew Psheew the bullets're goin. Psheeew Psheew. But there's another man. He looks like he's carryin the body but he's not. He's got a bunnit on an he's lookin at all the blood comin out the head. An his eyes're narrow. An his mouth's open but straight. Ye can tell he's goin to do somethin about it. By fuck he is. Ye can see it in his face. If any cunt's goin to do somethin he's yer man. An Jimmy Brogan wants to be him. The man wi the narrow eyes an the straight lips. The man that wants to do somethin about it.

There's thirteen dead, the Newsman said. And seventeen wounded.

It was The Paras that done it. The Paras. The Brits.

●

This day he sprays IRA on Brolly's wall. Wi a tin of black. He goes across the street an sits on the electric boxes to watch it. See if it's good. Mrs Brolly comes in from the shops. She goes mental. She doesn't think it's good. Not one bit. No sir. She drops her bags an turns this way an that flickin her hair about. Next thing she sees Jimmy Brogan the artist sittin on the electric boxes. She drills the eyes into him. He done a shamrock on Curry's last week. The whole block knows it's him. She looks at the IRA an turns an Black an Deckers him again. Jimmy Brogan looks left an right like he's waitin on some cunt. But no way he's waitin. Brolly's tryin to kill him wi big turnin masonry bits comin out her eyes. Like a cartoon.

But he just sits there swingin his legs an bumpin his Docs off the electric boxes. Brolly's got steam comin out her nostrils like two platinum rods. She picks up the bags an storms off at some speed into her house.

—*There were men from Dublin and from Cork – Fermanah and Tyrone...* he's goin an his rubber heels're doin a good impersonation of a bhodran.

—Dum dum de dum dum dum de dum

Next thing Brolly comes out wi a tin of white paint. Gloss.

—Dum dum de dum dum dum de dum

    Sean South of Garry Owen...

She opens the tin.

—Dum dum de dum dum dum de dum

Brolly starts paintin over the

She's just gettin to the bottom right of the A when the Polis go by. One's starin at Jimmy Brogan but his pal's lookin at Brolly. He slams the brakes on. Jimmy Brogan remembers their Irn Bru jerkin off the windscreen an scooshin everywhere. The cork must've not been on right. It's funny the things some people remember. Specially when ye consider how much ye forget. All they see's this wummin paintin a big white

on the wall.

THUMP

THUMP

The cops get out the car. Brolly struggles like fuck when she's gettin lifted. She's shoutin an pointin at Jimmy Brogan.

—It's him. That wee shite there! I'll be lettin your mother know.

Jimmy Brogan's sittin wi a lolly pop in his mouth.

—Hi Yi Mrs Brolly, he's goin. —Nice paintin.

They stuff her into the car. It's just her fat face an drill bit eyes tryin to bore through the glass to get him. There's wee white circles in the glass Jimmy Brogan says – wee white circles where she's grindin the glass down. An the Polis slappin her on the head tryin to calm her down.

—Bye Bye Mrs Brolly. Enjoy yer trip.

—Dum dum de dum dum dum de dum

Say hello to the Provos. . .
say hello to the brave. . .
say hello to the Provos. . .
an Ireland will be saved. . .

He's singin an dum dum dum go the heels an Mrs Brolly's just a wee shiny square of glass wi a red face. She's a mad paintin disappearin into the infinity of Old Monkland Road.

When she got home that night the

was black again. Jimmy Brogan? Nowhere to be seen.

from The Big Q – a work in progress

313

Rody Gorman
(b. 1960)

Born Dublin, now lives on Skye, teaching at
Gaelic college Sabhal Mòr Ostaig. Writes
poems in both Scots and Irish Gaelic. *Fax and
other poems* (1996) made an impact on both
Gaelic and non-Gaelic readers alike.

I was born in Dublin, Ireland in 1960 and first visited Scotland as a
child on family holidays.

In 1964, our family visited Crossmichael, Kirkcudbrightshire, from
which I remember foxgloves, a golf-course and my sister, not yet
three years old, being startled by an adder and being only slightly
less audible in her truculent ululations than the unfamiliar sound of
a chain-saw from the sawmill in Castle Douglas nearby (where
there was also a boating pond, now I think of it). I happened to visit
Crossmichael again in 1992, from which I sent my mother a
postcard to show how little the place had changed in thirty years.
Nowadays, when I think of the area, it is usually because of its
associations with the poet William Neill.

In 1966 we visited Largs (my recurring memories of which are
Opal Fruits, pancakes and paddle steamers, one of which, *The
Duchess of Hamilton*, my father boarded by jumping from the pier
at Campbeltown, as it had left without him). Two years later, we
stayed outside Oban (I remember being ill on what seemed a
wholly unnecessary voyage from Oban to Tiree and, also, being
woken suddenly by a stag around the caravan in which we stayed in
Gallanach). My father, who belonged to Derryoober in the parish of
Balnakill in County Galway, had visited the Highlands almost
annually from the years after the Second World War/Emergency
(during which time he had been confined at home with tuberculosis, before the introduction of sanitoria).

I visited Scotland again, with my partner, in the 1980s. In 1986, I
attended a short residential course at Sabhal Mòr Ostaig in the Isle
of Skye, to learn Gaelic, to complement my Irish Gaelic which I had
spoken since childhood, but only assimilated properly after leaving
secondary school. I returned to Skye the following year and have

lived there ever since, apart from time spent in Aberdeen (as a student) and in Edinburgh.

I have worked with Scottish Gaelic to a far greater extent than with Irish Gaelic – as a student, librarian, lexicographer, lecturer, translator, editor and poet. Whilst there is a palpable affinity between the two linguistic communities, transcending religious and other minor distinctions, I have rarely experienced a natural mutual intelligibility between speakers of either. Perhaps, the most attractive speaker of both was Calum I. MacLean (1915-1960) who assimilated Irish Gaelic and espoused Roman Catholicism in Ireland after 1939, and whose diaries, kept whilst working in the Hebrides as a collector for the Irish Folklore Commission, I helped to translate. In 1996, I was invited to visit Ireland as a Scottish Gaelic bard, which was both a pleasurably bizarre experience and a sort of historical resonance, when one considers the concourse between poets from the time of Muireadhach Albanach Ó Dálaigh (fl.1220), down through the Ó Muirgheasáin family line who were hereditary bards to the MacLeods to the poetry of William Livingston in the nineteenth century and, more recently still, that of Duncan MacLaren and the dual collections by Meg Bateman, Myles Campbell and Mary Montgomery. In 1998, I was appointed to the position of Writing Fellow at Sabhal Mòr Ostaig, as though I were succeeding to an honorific position after years of diligent training (which is not the case).

I write in Scottish Gaelic more out of force of habit than anything else. I also write in English and Irish Gaelic (a collection *Bealach Garbh* appeared in 1999). The very lack of an ancestral familiarity with either language informs my work to an extent, I believe. My reasons for adopting either language are political only in a very inclusive sense.

Naidheachd

Tha mise bhos an Albainn
Agus thusa 'n Eirinn thall
Is sinn le chèile
A' coimhead air na h-aon naidheachdan
Mar a tha iad air an aithris
Air telebhisean gach duin' againn.

Bu mhath leam leum a-staigh air an sgàilean
Is stad a chur air an fhear-leughaidh
'S a chantail – Feumaidh sinn briseadh
Gus a chur an cèill
Gun d'fhuair sinn fios
Gu bheil gaol aig a leithid seo de dhuine
Air an tè tha seo thall an Eirinn
Agus, nam freagradh ì, gum biodh i fada na comain.

Mo Chuid Aodaich

Bidh mi crochadh mo chuid aodaich
Ri thiormachadh am fianais chàich
A dh'aindeoin na their na nàbaidhean
Feasgar na Sàbaid aig baile,
Rud a tha ann an dòigh ionann
Ri mo ghaol ort a chur an ìre.

News

I'm over here in Scotland
Any you're over there in Ireland
And we're both watching
The same news
As it's read out
On our respective televisions.

I'd like to jump into the screen
And stop the newscaster
And say – We interrupt this broadcast
To make an important announcement
That we have been advised
That such and such a person
Loves this woman over in Ireland
And that if she would respond he would be greatly obliged.

My Clothes

I hang my clothes out to dry
For everyone to see
In spite of what the neighbours say
On the Sabbath at home,
Which in a way is like
Expressing my love for you.

from Fax (Polygon 1996)

Uaine

Gun teagamh,
Dh'iarrainn mo thaic a chur ris
An oidhirp a tha thu cur suas,
Thu fhèin
'S a' bhuidheann gu lèir agaibh,
Gus an àrainneachd dham buin sinn
A ghleidheadh

Ach, aig toiseach gnothaich,
Bidh agam ris a h-uile bad
Dhe do chuid aodaich
A thoirt dhìot, a luaidh,
(Dìreach mar gum b' ann de rùsg na craoibhe)
Gun fhios nach eil a dhath umad
A tha gun a bhith uaine.

Feasgar Nollaige

Chan fhaca mi de mhìorbhail mu Nollaig
Ach na mìltean air mhìltean de rionnagan
A' priobadaich nan cloinn os mo chionn

Ach laigh mi air mo dhruim-dìreach
Gun fhiosda san t-sneachda mum fhàrdaich
'S dh'èirich mi 's dh'fhàg mi lorg

'S nochd ì sa mhadainn nam fhianais
Na h-aingeal air beul an dorais.

Green

Of course,
I would wish to lend my support
To your endeavours,
Yours and those
Of the entire group,
To preserve the environment
Which affects us all

But, first,
I shall have to remove
Every item of your clothing,
Just as one might strip the bark of a tree,
Just in case there's something about your person
Which is not green.

Christmas Afternoon

The only miracle I saw around Christmas time
was thousands and thousands of stars
winking like little children above me

But I lay on the flat of my back
suddenly in the snow by my hovel
and I got up and left a trace

And it appeared to me in the morning
as an angel at the front door.

Soitheach Araidh

Chan eil fhios nach tig an càirdeas
A bh' againn gu crìch ann an da-rìribh
Nuair a thig e air tìr na h-Alba,
Là dhe na làithhean,
Ann an soitheach àraidh
Shìos air cladach air choreigin
A chumas luchd an eòlais
Nan casagan fada geala
'S nam feusagan 's nan glainneachn
A-staigh anns an lann aca
Ri tachas nan ceann
Fad ùine gu math fada.

A Particular Vessel

I'm sure that our relationship
May be considered to have run its course
When it appears on dry land in Scotland
Some fine day
In a particular vessel
Down on some shore or other
Which will keep the scientific bods
With their long white coats
And their beards and glasses
In their laboratory
Scratching their heads
For years to come.

previously unpublished

WILLY MALEY
(b. 1960)

Born Glasgow. Teaches English and Creative
Writing at Glasgow University. Has written
literary criticism, drama and cultural
commentary. With brother John wrote the
play *From the Calton to Catalonia*.

A Billy or a Tim?

—I can't understand you, said Davin. One time I hear you
talk against English literature. Now you talk against the Irish
informers. What with your name and your ideas . . . are you
Irish at all?

—Come with me now to the office of arms and I will show
you the tree of my family, said Stephen.

—Then be one of us, said Davin. Why don't you learn Irish?

(James Joyce *A Portrait of the Artist as a Young Man*)

My name is Willy Maley. I am Professor of English Literature at the
University of Glasgow. I'm a season ticket holder at Celtic Park.
I've a strong interest in Irish history. I think the world of my
country. It's called Scotland. There's only one thing worse than
being a Catholic of Irish origins in Scotland and that's not being
one. Let me explain. My father was born in Glasgow in 1908. His
father, Ned O'Malley, came over from Castlebar in County Mayo at
the turn of the century. Ned, faced with the 'Oh' of anti-Irish
sentiment from prospective employers – 'Oh, Malley, no work for
you' – decided to drop it and his kids became plain 'Maley'.

James – henceforth 'Daddy' – was brought up in Stevenson Street
in the Calton, where he attended St Alphonsus. You'll get some
idea of how much Daddy gives away if I tell you that he informed
me, a couple of years ago, that he had a big brother, a choirboy,
who collapsed and died when he was aged ten or thereabouts. I
asked what he died of and Daddy said: 'Oh, just running. He was
always running'. I haven't looked at the death certificate but I'm
sure it's a little more detailed than that. Anyway, legend has it that
Daddy, being a bright boy at school, was groomed for the priesthood at an early age. (I hadn't realised you needed a special

322

hairstyle.) Daddy's daddy died in 1929, aged fifty-three. We don't even have a picture. All I know is that he had a fifty-inch chest and worked outside in all weathers all his days. (Maybe Daddy fell out with the priests at the time of his daddy's death. I'll have to ask him.)

In 1932, at the age of 24, Daddy, in his infinite wisdom, decided to join the Communist Party and has never looked back, not even on the Spanish Civil War, where he spent six months as a POW after being captured at Jarama in 1937. He's always preferred to talk of the present or the future. As a result of Daddy's politics, Communism has coloured my life much more than Catholicism. We grew up with the collected works of Marx and Lenin, Mao and Stalin. These were our daily bread, our trespasses, that and leafleting for the Communist Party, while Daddy sold *The Morning Star* door-to-door. I always thought that was a nice name for a newspaper, much better than *The Daily Worker*. The Socialist Fellowship was our Friday Mass, but teenage rebellion and the magnetic pull of Mike Yarwood (curse the BBC!) meant that we never graduated to the Young Communist League.

I have a dim memory, perhaps borrowed from Mammy, of us all huddling in the lobby while the priest stood with a foot in the door, seeing our name and so many of us and asking were we turncoats. Daddy told him he couldn't be in Heaven knowing there was one person in Hell. I admire him for that now, but at the time I'd have liked a fuller, family-wide consultation on the subject. I later realised we were living in Hell all along and we just didn't know it.

I once told Fr. Brendan Bradshaw, an Irish historian at Cambridge University with whom I was editing a collection of essays on sixteenth and seventeenth century Irish history, that I was 'Catholic by culture'. He gave me a look that said there was no such thing. Why did I make such an outrageous claim, Proddy dog that I am? Well, I grew up in a large family in an almost exclusively Catholic part of a predominantly Protestant area of Glasgow, supported Celtic FC, went a few times to chapel with my Catholic friends – though this stopped when they threatened to shop me to the priest – and had an unexamined affection for all things Irish. Our neighbours were O'Haras, Fitzpatricks, McHughs, O'Briens, Divers and the like. All good Irish names. I was as near as dammit to being a Catholic, for goodness sake. Only a couple of communions short.

You can't grow up in the West of Scotland with a name like Willy Maley and not be taken – and mistaken – for a Catholic. But I'm not, and never have been, a member of the Catholic Party. I started Possilpark Secondary – where I think there were around 30% Catholic pupils – in 1973, with a big white bag Daddy got me from the Barras that had a green shamrock on it and the legend: 'Glasgow Celtic: Seven Times League Winners'. That bag was forty shades of green by four o'clock on the first day. I took a fairly phlegmatic approach to this, wiped it off when I got home, and never used it again, so that it was as good as new two years later when we were Nine Times League Winners. It's probably worth a few bob now, wherever it is.

I've never, believe it or not, asked Daddy why we weren't sent to the Catholic schools up the road. I'm assuming it was his decision, since he decided everything else. My assumption from childhood was that since Hawthorn Primary and Possilpark Secondary were short walks from our street, and St Theresa's and St Augustine's were long walks or bus journeys, Daddy was simply being his usual pragmatic self. Bussing nine kids to school is a thought for any parent. Of course, Daddy had 'lapsed' – oh what a falling off was there! – but he still had a soft spot for all things Catholic and Irish, except for the church hierarchy. Anyway, that's the way it fell out. He was nearly a priest and we were prods under protest at the local 'non-denominational' schools. I got my bag baptised and the band played on. Years later, when I needed another Higher to get to Uni, I did History at night classes at St Augustine's as an adult returner, and was struck walking down the corridors there for the first time at the social engagement evident in class projects. When I got to Uni though I met many Catholic high achievers who were a little more conservative in outlook. I'd mistaken the scheme experience for the whole show.

Where is my mother – my little 'Mammy' – in all this? Well, she was always bearing up and bearing down. My sisters used to sing a song – I don't know if they made it up or adapted it. It went: 'You'll never learn, learn, learn, I'm sick o' bearin', or was it 'sick o' bairns'? Anyway, Mammy bore the brunt of bringing up the bairns, all nine of us, and a couple that never made it through, while Daddy worked, first on the railway at Cowlairs as a track layer – where he saw the carved heads of the executed navvies Dennis Doolan and Patrick Redding on the bridge at Bishopbriggs – then as a labourer, building houses in Lambhill. Mammy was of solid Protestant stock, and Highland extraction. Her father, William Watt, was a stonemason from Garmouth in the North East, near Elgin. Family folklore says he never saw a Catholic till he was in his twenties. I'm not sure if that means he led a sheltered life.

My sisters gave Mammy the nickname 'Mope-Not', not a compliment but an injunction, while Daddy was 'Did-Not', reflecting his paternal deficiencies. Sure, there were nine pints of milk a day on the table – no fridge – and all the books you could read before they went back to the Book Exchange, but there was overtime and anger too. On one occasion, some time in the late Sixties, we were stranded in Saltcoats with no money and no milk for tea, waiting for Daddy to finish work and come down from Glasgow with fresh supplies. My sisters – five of them, all older than 'the four boys', as we were rather Enid Blytonishly known – started chanting 'Did-Not did not give us enough money! Did-Not did not give us enough money!' Mope-Not was not amused.

When I think of being Irish in Scotland I think of poverty and progressive politics, of communities that had to be close-knit because of the needle they took, the pricks and prejudice they put up with. Yeats was right, too long a sacrifice can make a stone of the heart, but suffering can strengthen the soul too, and clear the head. When you're detached or cynical about Empire and Monarchy and all that's backward in a culture then your perspective is wider and more worldly.

About ten years ago the Scottish socialist historian James D. Young did a profile on me for *The Irish Post*, a very flattering portrait bordering on hagiography. It was entitled 'True to his Origins' and it was embarrassing not just because it was generous to a fault, but because at the time I was just beginning to realise how untrue to my origins I was, indeed how untrue my origins were. Having spent my life, like many Scots of Irish provenance, loathing my country of birth and residence and loving my land of ancient origin, I was becoming a born-again Scot. It had something to do with going to Cambridge for three years, losing my voice, then finding it again.

I was in Galway for a conference on colonialism in the summer of 1995. I had the chance to visit Mayo, egged on by others. There was going to be some great genealogical gathering of O'Malleys. I didn't go. As far as I know Daddy's never been to Ireland in his puff. I've been to the 'ould counthrey' half a dozen times myself, to Dublin, Belfast, Cork and Donegal, but never Mayo. I may go some day, maybe not. The past is another country and there's no going back. In any case, I'm Scottish for the present, though I've always felt ambivalent about my identity. My middle name is Timothy, and when I reached the age where I had to produce ID the bouncers always asked if I was a Billy or a Tim. As a Protestant Celtic supporter christened 'William Timothy' I knew from an early age the problem of being in two minds. I still prefer paradox to doxa, which is why I love literature, especially drama. Art encourages us to look at things from a dozen different angles. To the familiar complaint that I want it both ways, my standard reply is: 'What, are there only two?'

When I look at my work, from academic projects like my PhD on Edmund Spenser and Ireland, to creative work like *Gallowglass* and *The Lions of Lisbon*, I can see that there's an Irish element informing my identity as a writer, governing the choices I make. As for influences, I may do a higher navvying, but I'm sure there's a bit of Ned in me still.

from **Gallowglass**

The Story of the Glasgow-Edinburgh Railway Murder of 1840

[NOTE: On the morning of Friday May 14, 1841, a
crowd of 50,000 gathered at Bishopbriggs Cross,
north of Glasgow, to witness the public hanging of
two Irish railway workers, Dennis Doolan and Patrick
Redding, charged with the murder of an English
ganger on the Glasgow-Edinburgh line. *Gallowglass*
tells the story of the events surrounding their trial and
execution.]

CHORUS: In 1838, the Edinburgh and Glasgow Railway
Company was set up. On 18 February 1842, four years, one and a
half million pounds, and forty-six miles of track later, the line was
complete, and the Second City of the Empire was linked with the
capital. A real red letter day. A wonderful feat of engineering. An
industrial achievement the country could be proud of. But the laying
of the line from Queen Street to Waverley had a high cost in human
terms, and one nation's gain was another's loss. For this great
Scottish railway was built with the sweat and blood of Irish labour.
The Irish potato famine of the hungry forties forced a generation
to leave the shores of the old country to carve out a new life in
Scotland. A sixpence paid their passage.

200,000 came and made their homes in Scotland. They settled
first in Clydeside, which was green as well as red. They left their
mark on bridges, ditches, roads, and railways. They did the dirtiest
jobs for the lowest pay. They rushed in where others feared to
tread, putting their lives on the line for a railway they could not

afford to ride on. They were the vanguard of the industrial revolution in Scotland, but from employers they got contempt, and from fellow workers they drew resentment, and racism.

On 8 December 1840, John Green, an English ganger, was placed in charge of a squad of Irish railwaymen at the Crosshill Cut in Bishopbriggs. His appointment was like putting a taper to a powder keg. Two days later, Green was dead, and the hunt was on for his killers. He was the third ganger to be murdered on the line in three months, and the authorities were hell-bent on a hanging. The men who were executed for his murder were found guilty after a one-day trial by the law, and a six-month trial by elements of the Scottish Press and the Directors of the Railway Company. They were workers. That made them second-class citizens in the eyes of the law. They were Catholics. That was another black mark against them. They were Irish. That was the final nail in their coffins. This story is a reminder of a shameful chapter in Scottish history, and one that's yet to be closed.

Scene 2: No Smoke Without Fire
The Crosshill Cut, Wednesday December 9, 1840

[Doolan, Hickie, and Redding stand together by the rail-way. They are wet and dishevelled. Doolan leans on his shovel, looks up for a moment, and turns to the other men.]

DOOLAN: That's the rain aff, in case yez hadnae noticed.

REDDING: A chance fur a wee smoke.

HICKIE: At long last.

DOOLAN: Wan a life's few pleasures, eh? [He lays down his shovel, puts his hand inside his jacket, produces a pouch, and fingers its contents] Jesus. Me baccy's soaked right through. [Looking at Redding] How about yours, Pat?

REDDING: [Handing his pick to Doolan] Here, hold that. [Doolan takes it and drops it] Now, let's see what we've got here. [He puts his hand down the front of his trousers and produces a sock tied to his belt, from which he pulls a pouch similar to Doolan's. He sticks his fingers into the pouch, then turns to Doolan] Dry as tinder, Den.

DOOLAN: Ah'll take yer word fur it, Pat.

HICKIE: Here, can I have some a that as well?

DOOLAN: You can have some a mine, James.

HICKIE: But yours is soaked through, ye says.

DOOLAN: Ye can blow on it a while. Where's yer initiative, James?

HICKIE: At home with me tobacco.

REDDING: [Flaking tobacco into his hand, then tucking his pouch in] It's yer brains that's soaked through, James.

DOOLAN: No, his brains is dry, Pat. Sure, he keeps them in the same place as your baccy!

HICKIE: [Going in the huff] To hell with the pair a yez. Yez know where ye can stick yer friggin baccy.

REDDING: Come on now, James. There's enough here fur all of us.

DOOLAN: [Pushing in front of Hickie] That's right. Jist form an orderly queue. [Doolan and Hickie knock up their pipes, and wait for Redding to fill them]

REDDING: Any more fur any more? No? Then I'll do me own. [He reaches inside his waistcoat and pulls out a pipe with a long handle].

DOOLAN: [Struggling to light a match against his shovel] Jesus, Pat. Is that thing loaded?

REDDING: Not yet.

HICKIE: Don't be pointing it at me.

REDDING: Ah made it meself. What dae ye think?

DOOLAN: Tell us what it is, and ah'll tell ye what ah think.

REDDING: It's a pipe, for God's sake!

DOOLAN: A pipe, by Christ? The three of us could get a smoke from that. Ye'd better not be lettin Smoker Byrnes see that thing, or he'll be havin it off ye.

REDDING: Tell him I'll make him one fer a shilling.

DOOLAN: Yer a craftsman and a businessman, Patrick Redding. Yer wasted on this railway, ye know that. Men like yourself should be drawin plans, not layin plates.

HICKIE: [Puffing away at an unlit pipe] Aye, ah can jist see him sittin in a fancy office wae all them gentlemen an their wives, an pullin a plan a the railway from the front of his trousers, an all the ladies faintin.

DOOLAN: Why, James. That were very witty.

REDDING: Aye, he's been listenin tae you too long, Den.

DOOLAN: [Staring at Hickie] James, do ye not think ye'd get a better smoke wae that thing lit?

HICKIE: [Noticing for the first time that his pipe is out] Ah wiz waitin fur you tae light me, Den.

DOOLAN: Ah'll light ye alright, James. Ah'll pit a match tae yer arse an point ye at that new ganger, so ah will.

REDDING: [Striking a match against his braces and lighting his pipe] Here, quick Den, afore it goes out! [Doolan takes a light. Redding drops the match. He and Doolan puff away].

HICKIE: Have ye a match fur me, Pat?

REDDING: [Thoughtfully] What about that big woman that's friendly wae Mrs Gray? She'd be more than a match fur ye, James.

HICKIE: Jist gie us a light, an stop yer tricks, eh?

REDDING: [Holding out his pipe] Here, be quick about it, an don't take too much.

HICKIE: [Lights up, and hands Redding back his pipe] Ta.

DOOLAN: [Taking his pipe out and looking at it] This thing's still going, Pat. Ye must've gied me two strands by mistake.

REDDING: Things is tight, Den. Ye know that yerself. Thurz talk of them layin men off for Christmas out at the Moss.

DOOLAN: Aye, an the rest of us'll have tae work twice as hard.

REDDING: Francis Rooney was tellin me that another tunnel had come down out Kirkie way. Poor fellas inside were buried alive. Dug their own friggin graves. Ah'll wager their widows won't get tuppence tae rub together either.

DOOLAN: Ach, we're jis hands tae them, Pat. The Company's killin us tryin tae meet thur contract. There's many a good man has died under the wheels of the iron horse. Progress, they call it. Not for them that's doin the work.

HICKIE: They say yer man the new ganger is no a wan to be crossin. They say he sacked a fella that had seven mouths tae feed.

REDDING: There's always talk against the gangers.

DOOLAN: More than talk.

HICKIE: They say this Green, him bein an Englishman, he loves lordin it over the Irishmen.

DOOLAN: That's what they say, is it?

HICKIE: Wan word from that fella an yer finished on the railway. Seven little wans the fella had an Green smells drink on his breath an gives him his marchin orders. Friggin liberty.

REDDING: The drink is a bad game, true enough.

DOOLAN: If he carries on the way he's doin he'll have no breath left of his own.

HICKIE: He won't have slackers on his line, they're tellin us now. They say he takes a skin off the wages. They say if ye leave him short on the Friday ye'll no be back on the Monday.

DOOLAN: Jesus James! Yer just about peein yer pants there. Has this ganger of yours got horns an hooves an all? Does he fly over the cottage at night an cry – James Hickie, it's you I'm after? – [Pause] Yer afraid of yer own shadow, James, ye know that.

HICKIE: [Embarrassed] I were just tellin ye what the men were sayin.

REDDING: Yer all ears an mouth, James. Ye want to be usin yer eyes more an thinkin fer yerself. [To Doolan] This Green. His bark might be worse than his bite.

DOOLAN: [Turning to Redding] He can go bark at the moon, then. I'll have no dog of an Englishman snappin at my friggin heels.

HICKIE: He wears pistols, ye know. [To Redding] Honest to God, Pat. I seen them with me own eyes. Right fancy wans an all. Pearl-handled. Must've cost the bloody earth. Ah'm tellin ye. [Miming, hands on hips] Walks around like this, he does. Pistols pokin out fer all the world to see. [Redding shakes his head] Ah seen them, Pat.

REDDING: Sure ye did, James.

HICKIE: Ah'm tellin ye.

DOOLAN: James, I don't care if ye saw the Virgin Mary in a bonnet an breeches. Yer puttin us off me pipe.

[. . .]

Scene 14: Shadow of a Hangman
Jail Square, Glasgow, Thursday May 13, 1841

[Lights up centre-stage. Doolan and Redding sit in chains at either end of the bench].

DOOLAN: I never thought it would come to this, Pat. Ye know, sometimes I wake up in the night an think it all must be a dream, then I look up an see the stripes across the face of the moon, an I think to meself, – Why've they put the poor old man in the moon behind bars?

REDDING: That's one way a lookin at it, I suppose.

DOOLAN: Every way ye look at it, it makes no sense. The jailer says they're expecting thousands a folk out at the Cross. Jesus. Ye'd think it was market day or somethin.

REDDING: Death is a popular thing with a crowd, Den. Watching someone else die can give ye a great feelin of superiority.

DOOLAN: There but for the grace a God. . .

REDDING: . . .Somethin like that. They say a public hangin's like a shipwreck. Women an children tae the fore.

DOOLAN: Well, I hope they're not disappointed. I wouldn't like to let anybody down.

REDDING: Ye know, it's strange what you think about when you're waitin to die. I was jis thinkin to mcself how yer born on the end of a rope, afore yer cut from yer mother, like. An now me an you are to die on the end of a rope.

DOOLAN: Only this time there's no midwife standin by with scissors to cut ye free. [Pause] Me mother's at the end of her tether, ye know. An me brother wrote from New York to say he'd take me place on the scaffold. I wrote back askin if he'd mind takin the hangman's place, an bringin a sharp knife an a couple a fast horses with him. [Pause] Me sister's been keepin a vigil outside the jail for a week now. They won't let us talk.

REDDING: Bastards! [Pause] How was James afore he left?

DOOLAN: Quiet. About time too. Ye know, the little bugger had the cheek to ask me to write to his wife an tell her goodbye.

REDDING: An did ye?

DOOLAN: How could I say no? Ye know James. His head is on holiday at the best a times. When they put the pair of us in a cell together up at Bridewell, poor James thought I was goin to do the hangman's work for him. [Pause] I did feel like throttlin him right enough, but he's not the wan to blame. The polis was down hard on him. Roasted him, so they did. He'd have swore against his mother, he said. Ach, it's all water under the brig, now.

REDDING: I hope Australia knocks some sense into him.

DOOLAN: Sure it will. I think this whole bloody business has knocked some sense into him. Shakin like a leaf he was

333

when he heard he'd been spared the noose. Didn't know
whether to laugh or cry. Went into a sort of a fit, he did.
I had to give him a clout to stop him jabberin. Funny
though. I thought it was me that'd get away on a boat.

REDDING: They'll likely have our James buildin a railroad
from Sydney to hell-knows.

DOOLAN: [Clicking his fingers] What do you call them things
that have their little wans in a kind of a sack in front of
them, ye know, with the tail an that? Mind, we saw
one at the Fair?

REDDING: A kangaroo?

DOOLAN: That's it. A kangaroo. Can ye not jis see James
getting carried away by one of them things?

REDDING: He could keep his baccy dry that way.

DOOLAN: An his brains. [Pause] Cold as a crypt in here, ain't
it? [Pause] They spoke hard against us, Pat.

REDDING: The law was behind them, Den. It was the law
that spoke hard against us. The die's cast now. There's
no turnin back the clock.

DOOLAN: Dyin for a smoke, so I am. An to think I gave that
Judas Smoker Byrnes wan of them fancy pipes a yours.
I hope to God the bastard chokes on it.

REDDING: How do they sleep, Den?

DOOLAN: Who?

REDDING: Them that put us here. How do they sleep?

DOOLAN: Like friggin logs, I expect. On feather beds.

REDDING: Selling a man for money. That must weigh heavy
on the conscience.

DOOLAN: Money'll buy ye a new conscience, Pat. Ye know
your trouble? Ye think too well of people, so ye do. Yer
always thinkin things'll be better over the next dyke.

REDDING: Not any more, Den. I've no more hope left in me.
There's no light at the end a this tunnel.

DOOLAN: Father O'Malley told us to light a candle in our
hearts for to take us through the darkness.

REDDING: We could be doin with James's ears now, couldn't we? Mind the way they went all red of a cold morning?
DOOLAN: Here, give me your hand.
REDDING: What for?
DOOLAN: [Turning away] Never mind.
REDDING: No, here. [He reaches across. Doolan grabs his hand. They sit in silence].
REDDING: Dark as hell in here, ain't it?
[Lights out]

by John and Willy Maley, Mayfest 1991

JOHN MALEY
(b.1962)

Born in Glasgow. Has written poetry, drama,
film scripts and short stories. Currently
completing a linked series of stories centred
on a gay bar and its clientele.

My Irish Background

My grandfather, Edward 'Ned' O'Malley, was from County Mayo.
He came to Glasgow at the turn of the century, worked as a
labourer, and died thirty years before I was born. Although I never
knew him, I'm sure something was handed down. So that's the
Irish part of me. I've even been mistaken for a priest a few times.
Mothers of friends have taken me for a priest. I like to think it's
because of my serenity, dignity and quiet grace. But maybe they
just knew a closet queen when they saw one. The Catholic Church
has a peculiar attitude towards homosexuality. Its tolerance now
stretches to a sturdy respect for the modern homosexual, as long
as they are non-practising and kept well away from children.

I can't recall ever being inside a chapel, although I spent a long cold
evening in a church hall when I joined the Boys Brigade (I seem to
remember running up and down the slippy wooden floorboards in
what must have been the junior version of hot pants, this being the
early Seventies – periodically hoisting the Union Jack. I never went
back). Like most Glaswegians of my background and era I was
frequently quizzed about my religion – Catholic or Protestant –
when I strayed more than two yards from our close. You'd lie if
you thought it would save you getting a doing. It's the same with
being gay. It seems so much easier to travel incognito, pass myself
off as John Maley rather than Sean O'Shirtlifter.

Heavenly Father is about intolerance and denial. Homophobia is a
hate crime and perhaps its ugliest paradox is the way it uses hate
and fear against love. It is particularly galling to have the Catholic
Church, which should know the corrosive effects of discrimination
only too well, chasing gays back into the closet. The closet is such a
Catholic space too.

The wee confessional space, just you with your sin and your

secrecy in the dark. I'd like to see a National Coming Out Day
being facilitated by the Catholic Church. I could oversee the
Glasgow one, sitting in the dark with my long black robe, mumbling
majestically, Irish eyes smiling through the grille.

Heavenly Father

THREE days after Father Sheen died, Father Maguire dialled
his telephone number. No-one answered. But he imagined
that Father Sheen had answered, Father Sheen with the thick, dark
hair and the strange blue eyes had answered, and he had told him
that he loved him. He had unburdened his heart to him. 'Please
replace the handset and try again,' a voice had said. How he wished
he had caught him in his arms and told him the truth before it was
too late.

He had gone down to the river, planning to howl headlong
in. He found an old bench, where he could sit alone and look
down at the fast brown river and dream of death. He thought of
the hereafter and his fingers in that dark black hair and the war in
Father Sheen's blue eyes. He thought of one afternoon they had
gone for a walk in the country, on retreat, and had lingered over a
picnic by the burn. Father Sheen had lain back in the golden grass
and closed his eyes, a hand cupping his head. He had thought of
bending over him, touching the dark threat of his beard and kissing
his lips. He had lain back too, resting on an elbow, and studied
Father Sheen's face. How different he had looked with his sad blue
eyes closed, wounded animal eyes. He had gazed on Father Sheen,
oblivious to the burn and the birds and the buzzing. A girl on a
bicycle had gone by, he remembered. Then without warning Father
Sheen had opened his eyes and looked up at him, startled.

It was Mrs O'Hara who had told him about old Mary Daly
giving tongue to the dead. Mrs O'Hara's daughter Bridie had died
of meningitis the year before. Mrs O'Hara had lost two stones and

said there was nothing but dirt or fire at the end of a life, however saintly. She had spat at Father Maguire and wept with fury in his car one morning he had picked her up. She had been out wandering, dark under her eyes and fists in her pockets. Then, one day, she had come to the chapel, ecstatic. Her smile, thought Father Maguire, was devilish, and she held his hands tight and beamed madly as she told him her daughter had spoken to her and sang to her. 'She's alive,' she had gasped, daringly. She said she had gone to Mary Daly's house having heard of her powers from a cousin, who had related a conversation with her long-dead mother. Mrs O'Hara had sat in the back bedroom of Mary Daly's house and waited to see if her daughter would come. Mary Daly took no money and swore whoever called to secrecy, though her activities appeared to be becoming increasingly common knowledge in the neighbourhood. They had sat in silence in the small room, Mary Daly in an old armchair and Mrs O'Hara on an old single bed, which had creaked if she so much as moved a finger. Mary Daly had closed her eyes then opened them again and sang Ave Maria in the voice of her darling Bridie. Her Bridie's voice, who had died at sixteen, from an old woman's mouth, who was a kick in the arse off eighty. Furthermore, Bridie had spoken to her as she had always spoken. It was as if she considered every word carefully beforehand. It was her voice, soft and young, clear and strong, out of Mary Daly's mouth.

Father Maguire didn't know what to say to the poor woman. What she told him was dangerous, ludicrous, nonsense. Yet what a transformation there was in Mrs O'Hara. The darkness was gone now from her eyes and her spirit. She had come to him boldly, in command of herself, and sure of what she had seen and heard. Her Bridie had rose from the grave and sang to her. 'Don't you see?', she asked Father Maguire, impassioned, joyous. 'Don't you see?' He saw clearly the remarkable change in Mrs O'Hara, formerly broken by grief, now seated before him full of zeal regarding her revelation. He wanted to denounce this blasphemy, but recognised that longing to reach out to the dead and hold them alive again in your arms, in your mind's eye. 'No,' he said at last. 'I don't see.'

Mrs O'Hara smiled, unperturbed. 'I came to tell you it was true,' she said. 'The dead live. We are never parted from the ones we love.' Father Maguire was silent. He wondered if his face, his eyes, had betrayed something of his grief and wished Mrs O'Hara would go away. She was clearly delirious. He noticed other changes in her. She was wearing some make-up, her clothes were smarter, her mousy hair, which had drooped down over her thin, desperate face, had been cut and dyed. Perhaps, thought Father Maguire, she had found peace in this delusion. He felt it would be cruel to deny her. 'I heard my daughter's voice,' she said, and pressed her hands once more on his.

That night there was little in the way of sleep for Father Maguire. He wondered what had really brought about the transformation in Mrs O'Hara, and whether she had seen something in his eyes he did not want her to see. He felt vulnerable and exposed. There was a dull ache in his stomach. He kept leaning over and looking at the alarm clock on his bedside cabinet. Time was passing so slowly, it seemed the night was endless. An endless, sleepless night with no respite from his grief. He thought of the brown river and cursed Mrs O'Hara and the old witch Daly. But what had they done but shown him what he knew, what he believed to be true anyway? Beyond death, the dead await us. He thought of Father Sheen again. He remembered late one evening at the retreat, Father Sheen had gone into the bathroom for a shower. He had left the door slightly ajar. From where Father Maguire sat in the lounge he could see a spill of yellow light and hear the water run and Father Sheen whistling. He remembered, too, the thought that had come to him, possessed him. He thought of going down the corridor, into the bathroom, and without a word from either of them, undressing and getting into the shower and into Father Sheen's arms, bathed by the water and the yellow light. He had felt dirty and ashamed then. Now he would fly down that corridor. That door, he decided, was open for a reason, and only his cowardice and denial had closed it. It was gone four in the morning before he finally slept, and he was awake again at six.

Three days later Mrs Hay came to him. She was a frail, brittle widow in her seventies. She was anxious to speak to him. 'It's about Saint Mary,' she said, making eye contact only briefly. She picked at something on her coat sleeve, then took off her headscarf and sat with it in her two hands. 'I mean Mary Daly,' she added. Father Maguire felt afraid. He didn't want to hear more of this. But Mrs Hay raised her head and fixed him with a determined look. 'My husband's been dead ten years,' she said, her voice firm and resolute. 'But I was in Mary Daly's house last night and he spoke to me. She moved her lips and I heard his voice. I asked him questions and he gave me answers. I don't understand, Father. My man's been dead ten years this summer.' She paused, folding and unfolding the scarf. Father Maguire wondered if Mrs Hay had gone to Mary Daly's house at the behest of Mrs O'Hara. He felt angry at the old fool. He wondered if he'd have the whole neighbourhood crowding in on him, swearing to have spoken with the dearly departed. 'You heard his voice?' Father Maguire found himself asking. Mrs Hay nodded solemnly. 'As clearly as I hear yours,' she replied. She was quiet for a few moments. Then she gave out a whimpering noise. Father Maguire saw the fear in her eyes. 'Is it the Devil?' asked Mrs Hay. 'The Devil playin' a trick on me?' He could see tears welling up over her red eyelids. 'No,' said Father Maguire. 'But this is dangerous. Dangerous nonsense.' He told her to stay away from Mary Daly, she was a foolish old woman who was taking advantage of the vulnerable.

Father Maguire was glad when Mrs Hay left. He felt persecuted by these stories about Mary Daly. It seemed she had started something that could veer dangerously out of control. The power of suggestion could not be underestimated. He was still losing sleep, seeing Father Sheen in the yellow light, in the yellow grass. One night he dreamt that he saw Father Sheen open his eyes like he did that morning at the burn, but there was no life in them and he was cold to the touch.

Several weeks passed and the dreams and the grieving and the long nights went on. Then Mrs O'Hara came again to him.

She looked radiant and he knew she was going to tell him something awful. She took his hands in hers, which embarrassed him. She was so happy she burst out laughing. 'She came to me!' she exclaimed, when her laughter had subsided. She was a picture of serenity and looked as young as her lost daughter. 'They can come back to us,' she beamed. 'For one night! My Bridie, she came to me last night and I held her in my arms and we cried. And then all the pain went away. All the pain was gone. Forgive me for ever doubting, Father. It's true. My beautiful daughter, who I thought was stolen from me, she was with me last night. I had no hope and then my daughter came back to me.' Father Maguire felt his heart beating faster. 'It was a miracle,' said Mrs O'Hara. 'Miracles happen.' Father Maguire said nothing, but he knew his face said everything. 'She's a silly old woman,' he heard himself say at last, and immediately felt guilty. But nothing could deflate Mrs O'Hara. Her eyes sparkled and she laughed again. 'Oh Father,' she almost sang, 'My beautiful daughter came to me.'

There was another long night for Father Maguire that night. He was tortured by the stories of these women. He wondered why he was so offended, so angered by them. Did he not believe in an afterlife and the glory to come? Did he think miracles impossible? He got up and made himself tea and sipped at it in the kitchen. He even smiled at himself, doing something as ordinary as this when extraordinary thoughts swirled in his mind. He thought suddenly that he would like to see this Mary Daly in action. He knew Saint Mary only vaguely, by sight. She had lived in the neighbourhood many years. She had been for most of her life a widow, her husband killed in action in World War Two. Father Maguire had heard she was a strange, fey old woman, but these new tales were dangerous and fascinating. He wondered if the bereaved women were hallucinating, or if Mary Daly was just a fly old buzzard who could do vocal impersonations, like the impressionists on TV. She was probably the type of old woman who would scour the obituary columns to see who she had outlasted. It was also feasible that she had known the dead people she was supposedly calling up from the grave. Father Maguire remembered a programme he had seen on TV about an exotic bird who impersonated other birds. He amused himself with the thought of that, Mary Daly mimicking the neighbourhood dead, the sly old bird. The old liar, preying on the grief-stricken. He decided he would see her, the decrepit old charlatan, and denounce her.

Father Maguire followed Mrs O'Hara into the dark close-mouth and round to the left. There was a dark red door with a silver coloured nameplate. M. DALY, read the inscription. There was a glass panel set in the door and this was covered by a white net curtain. There was a light coming from the hall. Mrs O'Hara gave the letterbox three quick, precise raps. They waited silently for what seemed like a full minute. Then footsteps were heard coming down the hall. A chain and then a bolt were undone and the door yawned open to reveal Mary Daly. She appeared smaller than Father Maguire had remembered. She was no taller than five foot and if she was nearly eighty she certainly looked it. She ushered them in, the three of them going into the small back room. There was old worn linoleum on the floor, partly disguised by a large square of blue carpet. There was a single bed, a chest of drawers and one armchair in the room. Mrs O'Hara had told Father Maguire that Mary Daly never actually slept in this room, there was another bedroom across the hall. But this room was where the voices came. It was here that Saint Mary had opened her mouth and Bridie sang Ave Maria so sweetly and Mrs O'Hara wept so hard her face stung with the tears. There were little in the way of civilities offered, no tea, and no chairs for the guests. Mary Daly sat in her old red armchair, diminutive but with a regal air. Father Maguire and Mrs O'Hara sat on the creaky bed. Father Maguire tried in vain to conceal his resentment. He noticed the wallpaper was peeling. The room was lit by an old standard lamp, adding to the effect of dinginess. Mary Daly closed her eyes, opened them again, then began to sing. At least her lips moved, but the voice was certainly that of a young girl. She sang Ave Maria. Mrs O'Hara didn't weep on this occasion, but closed her eyes and smiled.

Father Maguire looked at Mary Daly's mouth. The sound definitely seemed to be coming from her, and how she managed it he couldn't begin to fathom. Her speaking voice had very much reflected her age, a high, wavering voice that suggested only frailty. But the voice she now sang with, strong and young and clear, bore no resemblance to this. When she had finished singing Mrs O'Hara opened her eyes and gave a small sound of approval, a satisfied sigh. 'She came to me,' she said to Mary Daly. Father Maguire looked at the medium's neat, dark grey hair and her small, heavily lined face. He felt he wanted to laugh, it was so ridiculous. 'She came back just like you said, just like I needed.' Mary Daly gave Mrs O'Hara a knowing smile, her dark eyes smiling too. 'I'll wait outside,' said Mrs O'Hara, with a sideways glance at Father Maguire. Seconds later she was in the hall, closing the door behind her. The old woman and the priest faced each other in silence. Father Maguire felt fear then, indescribable fear. Mary Daly closed her eyes then opened them again. Father Maguire looked at the peeling wallpaper behind her. He was trembling. 'I left the door open for you,' she began, except the voice was the low, familiar voice of Father Sheen. 'I left many doors open for you. But I was scared and you were scared. You can go to hell for many things, Maguire. But surely not love. Surely not love.' Father Maguire was too scared and ashamed to look at Mary Daly. He concentrated on the wallpaper. 'That day I lay in the grass I was thinking of you. Then I opened my eyes and saw you and I was as scared as you.' Father Maguire felt a pain first in his nose, and then under his eyes, and knew that tears were springing from them. 'You old liar,' he gasped. He got to his feet. Mary Daly looked up at him. 'Leave the door open,' said the voice of Father Sheen. Father Maguire made a noise as if he had been physically wounded. He walked quickly out of the room, closing the door behind him.

It was impossible for Mary Daly to have known Father Sheen's voice, that lovely low lilt. She had never met him as far as Father Maguire knew. But he knew this, he was sick at heart and susceptible to old shysters like the wizened, blasphemous Mary Daly.

That night Father Maguire left the bathroom door open as he undressed to take a shower. He folded his clothes neatly on the floor and placed a pair of fresh clean pyjamas on the seat of the lavatory pan. He stepped into the shower and pressed the ON button. He adjusted the temperature slightly. He closed his eyes and let the warm water wash over him. When he opened them again, Father Sheen, naked and beautiful, was stepping in beside him.

previously unpublished

from **The Thatcher Years**

IV
The burning burning burning burning middens
smoke me, choke me. Agonies in stony places.
A jessie rattles in a locked closet, done in.
That dream you planted last year in your
heart, has it begun to sprout? Will it bloom
this year? The wisest woman in all of Europe
deals her deadly pack, murderous jokers, open
season. Death on the rock. Bullets and gags.
You! Hypocrite with weird justice, odd peace
smelling of blood, tasting of fear. All profit
and loss, poor ends in the filthy whirlpool.
Suffer us not to mock ourselves with false
hood, a thousand nightmare launches. Lady, ten
Irishmen starved under your cruel iron rule.

from Scream If You Want To Go Faster
(New Writing Scotland 9) (ASLS 1991)

DONAL MCLAUGHLIN
(b.1961)

Born Derry, grew up in West of Scotland.
Studied modern languages in Scotland and
Germany. Short stories published in several
anthologies. Recurring themes: the Troubles,
Catholic experience, encountering other
cultures. Also a translator.

The extent to which I am aware of, or affected by, or reacting
against an Irish background? Christ, I was born there. The North.
Derry – Londonderry – Stroke City: call it what you will. My family
left in 1970 – to emigrate to Scotland. I used to tell folk where I
was born – but that I escaped at the age of nine. At one point, I
thought I wanted to escape from Scotland, too. Now, I don't want
to leave.

I could tell you about losing my accent, and quickly getting a
Scottish one; about learning, and later studying, languages; about, at
some stage, starting always to head abroad, instead of back to
Derry; about ending up being at home in German; about finding my
voice was broken when I wanted to use it to write; about remembering Alfred Andersch's 'Franz Kien' stories, set in Weimar and
Nazi Germany, and inventing 'Liam O'Donnell' to write my own;
about my Da worrying about his family on Bloody Sunday – and the
relief when he heard everyone was safe; about realising that the
child's perspective and the Scottish angle were maybe worth doing;
about deciding to forget foreign-language experiences (for the
moment) and to get those Irish and Scottish voices down, maybe
even in the same stories; about where all that patter, and even the
syntax, can take you; about starting to imagine a whole series of
Liam stories, with the voices – as the years progressed – becoming
less 'Irish' and more 'Scottish'; about some greedy buggers wanting
a novel out of me; about not having the memory for autobiography;
and not having the inclination, anyhow, to write it; about the bits of
me that grew in Germany; about wanting to use that, and my
knowledge of post-war German writing, to write about Scotland

and Ireland; about writing about the seventies being a way of writing about the nineties; about – for a good fifteen years now – reading most of the Scots being published; about my 'insatiable' hunger for readings; about the masses I owe Kelman (I'm not alone) and MacLaverty; Galloway, too; about – through A L Kennedy – discovering Roddy Doyle (*Paddy Clarke*) and Seamus Deane – and beginning to accept more again the Irish in me; about even going back (on business); about translating Stella Rotenberg's Holocaust poems, exile poems, relationship poems; about how Colm Tóibín was wrong to suggest there were no Catholic writers in Scotland; about what 'Catholics' have been known to do to 'the other side' and vice versa; about what 'Catholics' – happy-clappy and lapsed ones, too – have been known to do to 'their own'; about being in James MacMillan's audience; about the thrill of reading someone else with exactly the same background; about echoes of my own experience in work by Asian Scots; about hoping against hope that the peace process would, will, succeed, and my hopes for the literature that might follow; about the legacy, the past, that needs to be 'bewältigt'; about the need for some of that stuff to be written in Scotland; about liking to think we can do it. Suffice to say: when I write, I take stuff like the above for a walk and try to set it echoing.

Have I answered your question?

an allergic reaction to national anthems

NO harm to Lizzy or anyone else, but it wasn't the Queen they waited up for but: it was the late-night horror film. DON'T WATCH ALONE was the name of it, not that there was a hope in hell o' that in the O'Donnells' house – not wi' a houseful of weans lik yon, there wasn't.

The craic them Saturday nights was something else, right enough. They'd all be sitting there, sure, watching it in the dark – wee Orla and Cahal would've been cuddled up against their mother or father or some of the bigger ones – and there wouldn't've been a cheep out of them, not a single one of them – until, that is, every time Dracula was about to bite neck, and their da would free himself from whoever he was sitting beside and creep up behind the settee that was pulled up in front of the fire, and drop his falsers out of his mouth and down the back of some of their necks. Ye want to have heard the screams out of them! Half the suspense would've been wondering which of them their da would go for next; and he would do it to ye even if he'd promised FAITHfully never to do it to ye again. Ciara, say, would be sitting there thinking she was safe, thinking he would keep his promise – she, after all, had been the one to make him a mug of tea – and the next thing she knew his slabbery oul false teeth would be tumbling down the back of her wee frock. Then

THE END

would come up – and it was strange going from that to the photo of Lizzy on her horse and

GOD–

SAVE–

OUR–

They never got past OUR– in the O'Donnell household. It wasn't even as if the Queen got zapped with the remote control, either. Naw, we're talking the days before remote controls here, when you had to get up off your backside, cross the room, and press buttons or turn a dial. Not that the O'Donnell weans let that stop them but:

NO WAY!

No matter how tired they were, sure –

No matter how late it was –

No matter how many o' the wee buggers had dozed off on the floor or the settee, claiming they were resting their eyes and refusing to go to bed –

Even if they were out for the bloody count, for Godsake –

Or if the wee-est ones were past their sleep and grumpy as hell –

I'm not jokin ye: when it came to the band striking up GOD SAVE LIZZY, the whole bloody clan of them would come back to life and race from whatever corner of the livingroom they were in and *descend* upon the poor television set, each desperate to be the one to reach the ON-OFF button first. 'CHRIST SAKE, WEANS!' Bridget would scream out of her as – yet again – holy hell broke loose. She'd visions every time of the TV set coming off the top of the trolley and down on top of one of them. No matter how much she looked at thon husband of hers for support but, he would only laugh – pleased to see he was succeeding in rearing his weans up properly.

In the early days, when the race to turn the Queen off was beginning to be a regular occurrence, one of the Big Ones would normally have beaten the Wee Ones to the button. You could normally have put money on Annette who was as determined and as swift as she was shy and quiet. Liam, the eldest, might've had a good head on him, he was no athlete but, no matter how much it hurt his pride not to win the race.

The same boy – ye have to hand it to him – could certainly produce the odd stroke of genius but. Even his father had to laugh the night the wee bugger sat within easy reach of the plug and –

cool as you like – just whipped the thing out as the rest closed in on the set. Lousy shite: when the others realised what had happened and turned to face him, he'd his head back, laughing, was gloating and goading them: twirling the plug above his head, the bugger was, lik it was Mick Jagger's mike. Another night, – Annette, hoping he wouldn't notice, had already installed wee Orla and Ciara to defend the sockets – he stood up and left the room as the anthem was about to start. To look at him, you'd've thought he wasn't goney compete; that he'd decided the whole bloody thing was beneath him. Turns out he was on his way to the fuse-box under the stairs. The looks on the faces descending on the telly were a picture, apparently.

Rest of them were demanding re-writes of the rule book thon night, so they were. The wee chorus of 'and se-ent them home-ward, to think a-gain' from beneath the stairs was the final bloody straw. 'Daddy, tell Liam he's not allowed to do that, Daddy!' 'Mum, tell Liam that's not fair, Mum!' they chorused. 'Think you're a smart arse, do ye?' was all Annette said when Liam re-appeared, looking pleased with himself.

Aye, Annette and Liam certainly had their moments of glory, no doubt about it. If you study the form over the months and years this carry-on went on but, it was Sean – Bridget and Liam's second boy and the reserve goalkeeper in the school team – who stopped Lizzy in her tracks most. The young fella could be flat out on his back on the mat in front of the fire – and he'd still manage to turn and glide through the air, finger and thumb extended to steal the moment of glory from whichever of his brothers and sisters might have been ahead of the pack this time. 'Bonetti the Cat' or 'Pat Jenkins the Second' his father would call him, laughing as the young fella avoided the trolley and completed his victory roll in the kitchen, returning gulping from a pint glass of water, stopping only to hold it aloft. You had to marvel at the wee bugger's agility; his courage. It's a wonder, in fact, he never got hurt, the way the rest of them crashed down on top of him. Still, it was good practice for the penalty area on Saturday mornings, his father supposed.

Naw, there wasn't oncet, not a single once, the young fella shed a tear, no matter how often or what way the rest of the mahoods landed on him. Naw, if it ended in tears, it was more likely to be one of the Wee Ones, *inconsolable* at not being the one who'd turned the TV off. Sometimes, to pacify them, their mother or father would've had to turn it back on again for wee Cahal or Orla to switch off – and you'd get a snatch of REIGN – O-VER – US before Lizzy was cut off in her prime again. Their mother or father intervening would put an end to the waterworks, alright, normally; you could see deep down, but, that even wee Cahal and Orla, God love them, knew that their mother or father setting it up for them wasn't the same as getting to the set first in the first place.

It didn't help, of course, that one night, Ciara, the wee bitch, spelled it out to Cahal who she was in a huff wi' at the time: 'Don't know what you're looking so happy about, ya wee cry-baby,' she'd sneered. 'Jist cos your daddy turned it back on for you to turn off again doesn't mean you stopped the Queen first. It was still Sean first, *even if* you got to do it, too!' That had started Cahal bubbling again so Ciara got a cuff round the ear, was sent to bed, and was told in no uncertain terms it would be a long bloody buckin time before she'd get staying up long enough to see the Queen again.

IT WAS a different story, of course, when they were listening to Radio Eireann and the Soldier's Song came on. The fact the reception was rotten on their tinny wee tranny was neither here nor there. Their da had picked the thing up for something like 20 new p. at the school jumble-sale, and it stood on the mantlepiece with the aerial fully extended. Big Liam, whoever saw him, would've been footering about all night with it, trying to get decent reception: trying tricks like having the aerial leaning against the clock or touching the mirror. 'Ye wouldn't think it was just across the Irish Sea –' was what he usually said. 'God's my judge: we got better bloody reception the night the Tic played Ujpest Dosza in buckin Hungary!'

Rotten reception or not, the Irish national anthem was allowed to play right through. It was rousing stuff, with bits where you could join in. All you had to do was sing 'God – bless – them!' between the lines sometimes – as if it was a rugby or a football song. Not that Wee Liam, for example, did, but. Not bloody likely! Even at that age, the young fella was allergic, sure. No way could he've listened and, in his own mind, seen, say, footballers lined up, chewing gum and having a good scratch to themselves. Naw, even at that age, visions of raised rifles and men's heads in balaclavas would've got in the way.

The surprising thing is that the young fella can't mind the words no more. What he does mind is his da always getting to his feet in his tea-stained vest: he'd still've had his mug of tea in his left hand and a fag in his right, and he would've pestered the rest of them to get up off their arses, too. 'Show some bloody respect, would yis!' he'd say, tugging at their sleeves. There was something comical, right enough, about their da standing there, saluting the tranny, and trying to drag Liam or Sean up to do the same. Sometimes, but, he'd totally lose his temper and claim they'd a buckin cheek calling themselves Irishmen – or even Celtic supporters! 'The macaroon bars and spearmint chewing-gum – that's all yis bloody go for! That's the only reason yis bloody go. Buckin macaroon bars and spearmint chewing-gum! Don't think I don't know!'

There was hardly a night they were up late, nevertheless, passed, but, without the odd one or two of them joining in – for the final chorus, if nothing else. The Wee Ones didn't know any better, and even they could recognise when the orchestra was coming to the end. The bigger ones would or wouldn't've, depending on the mood they were in. Annette or one of the other girls might've, I suppose, – if only to please their daddy. Certainly, if any of them had got into trouble during the day, it was well-known that joining in – or offering to make him a cup of tea – was a short-cut back into the good books. As for their mother: there was no way on this earth ye would've got Bridget O'Donnell

351

singing. She was totally browned off wi' the whole thing, was past finding it funny, and normally just disappeared into the scullery. Not that it mattered, right enough: sure when it came to the last line, it didn't matter how many were singing: they always took the roof off with that one.

THERE CAME a time, of course, when the older ones would've joined their mother. The fact their father cast it up to her, calling her a traitor and claiming she'd spent too long in England as a wean, wouldn't've stopped them.

Liam was in there, exchanging looks with her, the night the police turned up at the door. It was the night Northern Ireland beat Scotland one-nil in a friendly at Hampden, wi' George Best scoring the only goal. It was their mother's first-ever football match, and her and their father had gone along wi' another couple – from Limavady, originally. Bridget had been so busy talking to the other woman but, she missed the bloody goal. 'Never mind, sure I'll see the replay!' she'd said, as Georgie and the rest of the boyos danced their way back to their own half. Their da had loved telling the weans that one. 'Never mind, sure I'll see the replay!' he kept repeating, tears of laughter flooding out of him.

Anyway, thon was the night the police turned up at the door, and the O'Donnells were still so over the moon at Northern Ireland beating Scotland, you'd've heard them back in Derry. No way were they goney settle for singing the Soldier's Song just once that night: naw, even as it was playing on Radio Eireann, sure, their da looked a single out which had it on the B-side – and he kept the arm back on the record player so as it would play over and over again. Wee Sean – trust him! – was killing himself when he realised, and turned it up full blast, the rascal.

It's not a bit of wonder they didn't hear the bloody police! Liam and his mother wouldn't've heard them, for chrissake, if they hadn't been in the kitchen. Saying that, the two of them weren't even sure it was a knock, so Bridget had asked Wee Liam to go to the door with her. She nearly bloody passed out when she saw the two policemen – managed to say 'Go and get your Daddy, son' before they said anything but. Strange thing was: the police had actually waited for the man of the house. Must've seen the shock written all over the poor woman's face.

It was pandemonium, of course, when Liam opened the livingroom door. He'd to shout 'THE POLICE WANT YE, DA!' twice, for Godsake, before the rest of them began to calm down. His da said, 'What?' and Liam repeated it again. 'They're at the front door wi' Mum,' he said, then marched over to interrupt the record. There was a terrible scratching kinda sound the way he did it; not that his da said anything.

The weans watched in silence as their da pulled his shirt on, quick. He was on the verge of leaving the room, when he stopped to put his tie on after all, and used the mirror above the fireplace to straighten it. Only oncet he was satisfied did he go out to face the music. The poor youngsters could only look at each other, terrified. Finally, wee Orla, God love her, couldn't take it no more and bursted into tears, thinking her mammy and daddy were going to be arrested. Annette had to comfort her.

You could've heard a bloody pin drop. Not a word was spoken as they tried to hear what was happening. All they were able to make out, but, was their daddy using his polite voice to do the apologising and explaining. 'I can assure you two gentlemen it won't happen again,' he said, then a policeman said, 'That's fine then, Sir. Good night then, Sir', and they heard the front door shutting.

Their mother and father came back into the room.

'Bloody buckin bitch next door!' was all their father said.

'May she roast in buckin Hell!' he added, after a minute.

He was raging, crying, nearly, and was still shaking his head as he sat down, so livid was he at what had happened. Ciara, her wee eyes filling up, God love her, was on her way over to fling her arms round him when suddenly he looked up and started giving the woman next door the vicky. Ciara stopped in total shock: she couldn't believe her daddy would do a thing like that. Michael

Duffy had got four of the belt at school, sure, four *sore* ones, for doing that. She looked over at Annette; Annette just shrugged like she was helpless, but.

'One-nil, ye bitch ye,' their da was jeering.

The more he did it, the more the colour was disappearing out of Annette, the quiet one's face. Her daddy was just making things worse by cursing. That was *two* sins on his soul.

There was no stopping him, but. Their mother couldn't do nothing either. The stupid big lump was waving his fingers at the dividing wall, and he just kept doing it – with both hands, too – until his two arms tired.

'Buckin-one-buckin-nil!' he hissed, finally.

Bridget saw her chance.

'That's enough of that, Liam O'Donnell, in front of the weans!' she said.

Their da didn't take her on.

She turned to them instead. 'Right, folks, BED!' she said. 'NOW!'

It was only after the last of them had left to go upstairs, with their mother following after them, that their da noticed the crackle and hiss of Radio Eireann after close-down. He was damned if he was going to stand up but and go over and turn it off.

'Knock that off for me, love, would ye?' he said when Bridget came back down.

previously unpublished

RAYMOND FRIEL
(b.1963)

Born Greenock, Renfrewshire, now works in
Somerset. He co-edited the literary journal
Southfields with the poet Richard Price, with
whom he has also recently published a
collection of poems, *Renfrewshire in Old
Photographs* (2000).

My first blast of Irishness came from a Scottish pulpit: a Derry-born, flint-faced teetotal priest described by Ian Paisley as 'a black-cloaked agent of Rome', who regularly and vividly outlined the sulphurous fate awaiting those who died in a state of mortal sin. Since missing Sunday mass and even an impure thought might be enough to place you in that ontological peril, few among us were unaffected by the hellish vision outlined with such skill and relish. Irish Catholicism: fierce, gothic, penitential.

My grandparents were all born in Ireland, but came over to the west coast of Scotland as children, so my sense of family Irishness was of imagined characters who worked on the tug boats, smoked clay pipes and sang endless, melancholy ballads. It clung on in my name, of course. We'd lost an O' somewhere between Donegal and Cartsburn Street but the remaining syllable was enough to instantly evoke a whole cultural profile when asked for in threatening alleys, or in job applications. Not too long ago that, and what school you went to, was all the bigot-with-fists, or the bigot-in-charge, needed to know. And do we flatter ourselves to assume it's all behind us?

My first sustained contact with the real Irish came in the early 80s when I was a student in the Republic. The day I realised the Irish were different was when some of the students gloated at the battering the Brits were taking in the Falklands. Ireland's advantage. Some of my boyhood friends were on HMS *Sheffield* (Catholic boys but proud to serve their country) so my feelings were much more confused. When the old ghosts had slunk back into hiding, though, I enjoyed the warmth and the ways of these easy-going souls. There should be a health warning, mind: there's a self-destructive and

lawless streak there which will finish you off if your nerve or
metabolism are less than bovine.

Then a bit later my contact with the artistic Irish, primarily the
poets. Heaney. Mahon. Muldoon. At a time when I was looking for
ways to write and things to say, these were the voices that meant
most to me; my mentors.

Out of the Depths

In the cold churches
Of my childhood,
Imagination shoaled
In sonar depths.

Razorbills, perched
On sculpted lecterns,
Preached fire and mortal sin,
Poised to bear down

On any hint of flesh
In the murky deep:
'In bed, join your hands
And think on your death.'

I lay in darkness,
The ocean raising its chorus;
My small hands
Moving shyly . . .

Retreat

Tadhg slid the *Gordons* out of his cassock,
And crystal tumblers, muffled in tissue.
What better libation for Good Friday?

Their talk, in the tingle of gin, drifted
To the intricate pleasures of the flesh,
The secrets of a dappled day in bed . . .

A floorboard creaked outside: scrotum-stapling.
Vigilance
        passed on down the corridor.
Liberality near wept with relief.

A lifetime to the day, on the stroke of three –
One a monsignor, the other widower –
The moment fizzed in their heads like tonic.

Easter Sunday

A mile out of Laugharne our hired Fiesta
Shuddered in perfunctory death-rattle,
Slid backwards into the lay-by, and died
With its bonnet jutting east at rainclouds.

Ratty after a few pints and no lunch,
We traipsed in single file back into town
Clutching plastic bags of remaindered
Biographies and souvenir thimbles . . .

Past the low-slung sitting rooms of King Street –
TVs flickering behind lace curtains;
A police car parked outside Brown's Hotel,
Bleary drinkers blinking into daylight.

In the phone box, static cracked between us.
With the chirp of each unanswered spondee,
I wished us back to a dappled morning
When, in bed, we'd compromised about church,

Saved on the car hire and thumbed a lift,
Wandered over a muddy Sir John's Hill
With the estuary spread out below us;
And a glimpse of the town's little graveyard

Had brought to mind Stanley Spencer's
The Resurrection: Port Glasgow, in which
The dead clamber out of the cold ground
To embrace their loved ones, and give praise.

His Parents' Bed

Pre-nuptial, 'in Rome', she gamefully bunked
On the ground floor with Mary O'Connell –
Great-granny, chain smoker, Irish rebel;
Her room like a souvenir stall at Lourdes.
Post-, she stared at the red glow of the time,
Frozen beside him in immaculate sheets;
While through the mumbling wall, his parents
Pulled out sleeping bags in their makeshift dorm.

Still awake in the small hours, they listened
As the Orange Hall spilled on to the street:
A volley of car doors; 'No Pope of Rome'
Breaking out in raw unison; a fight.
He stirred towards her and apologised;
To find, through duvet, unfamiliar bone.

first published: London Review of Books

ANGELA MCSEVENEY
(b.1964)

Brought up in Ross-shire, Livingston and the
Borders. She attended university in
Edinburgh where she now lives. First
collection of poems *Coming out with it* 1992.
Received Gregory Award in 1993.

I don't feel Irish at all: no stirring of my blood, no pull at my roots
as I think of the old country. I never met my paternal grandfather,
whose migration from Northern Ireland to Lanarkshire at the
beginning of the last century ensured my eventual existence, and
although he's remembered affectionately by some of my older
relatives, I feel no emotional link. Apart from the legacy of my
unusual surname, I don't have any sense of connection to Ireland,
except possibly one other thing.

My grandfather came over to Scotland as a young man and settled
in Shotts where he worked in the coal mines and was a member of
the Orange Lodge. My own father left Lanarkshire in his early
twenties and met my mother while working in the Scottish
Borders. They then spent many years of their married lives in the
Highlands before a few more flits brought them back to the
Borders (an area I don't believe to be known as a seething hotbed
of sectarianism).

My upbringing had no religious input worth mentioning: no
churchgoing, no Sunday School, no bible stories, no prayers at
bedtime, no invoking of the name of the Lord. I wasn't christened
and was greatly taken aback on starting school to discover that
'God' and 'Jesus Christ' were more than just swear words I wasn't
allowed to utter at home. I suppose there was a bit of religious
exposure at school: at all of the four primary schools I attended
there were wee prayers at the beginning and end of the day, grace
before school dinners and a sort of religious service for the entire
school on Friday mornings, with a hymn practice the day before.

By secondary school it had dwindled to one grudgingly attended
service at the end of each term. With the exception of a handful of
Jehovah's Witnesses who were corralled in an empty classroom, the

rest of the school was rounded up and decanted into church, where the majority of the pupils fidgeted, giggled, whispered and acted loutishly for a long-drawn-out hour. Most of us were herded into the Church of Scotland nearest the school, but the Catholic pupils had to trek across town to the only local Roman Catholic church.

And now I will take a deep breath and get to my point: I have a prejudice, an innate, inexplicable knowledge that Protestant equals good, Catholic equals not so good. And for the life of me, if it's not genetic, swilling about in my Northern Irish DNA, I don't know where it comes from. No-one ever sat me down and told me it was so, but from an early age I just *knew*.

If I screw up my memory and think hard I cannot recall a single instance of religious strife at any of my schools and only ever a couple of comments elsewhere, both just as baffling now as they were then. Something along the lines of 'Fancy the procurator fiscal being a left-footer' and 'I'm surprised at her marrying out of her faith'. I'm especially mystified by the latter remark, as I happen to know that the bride in question was a dyed-in-the-wool atheist and hadn't had a faith of any kind to betray since childhood. But there's no escape even in apostasy: you're either a Catholic atheist or a Protestant atheist to some people.

I didn't have a religious upbringing and attended religiously-torpid schools, yet I grew up with this kernel of bigotry nestling inside me. How was it done to me? I'm not proud of it. I wish it hadn't happened; it's a blot on my soul and that's where it hurts and shames the most. I gather we all worship the same God, but I know mine is Protestant and I won't quibble if theirs is Catholic. When I try to rise above it, to leave it all behind me, something struggles and strains in my chest like a done-for butterfly writhing in a net. It's so hard to break free when the drip of indoctrination has gone on so gently, so assiduously all your life that you can't even remember being aware of it. Because I know I can't have been born like this, unless my grandfather's Orange genes did trickle down the generations into me.

And so I do what gays are so often exhorted to do by the church: I acknowledge my prejudices. I struggle against them and I do my best not to express them in any way.

For a number of years I worked on the Royal Mile in Edinburgh near the route of the big Orange walks that take place every summer. One year, out on an errand at lunchtime, I was late back to work as I couldn't get across George IV Bridge for the Orange parade passing by. It was a splendid turnout: wave after wave of flute bands and banners, the best part of the whole event being the two magnificent police horses that brought up the rear. The tourists were going wild, taking photos and filming and I couldn't help but notice that many were Spanish or Italian. I waited in the crowd until the road was clear and I could get back to work. I didn't wave or blow a kiss, though I always do when Gay Pride sashays by.

The Bed and Breakfasts

They beamed into our lives
from nowhere –
one night stands on their Highland holidays.

Such exotica
when a carful arrived from America.

Enthroned in the sitting-room with the piano, best sofa,
the bed and breakfasts relished
fresh-laid eggs, homegrown vegetables.

My infantile craft,
hanging on the garden gate as they drove away,
was usually good for sixpence.

Only once
did anything come back to us
from their faraway imagined countries
– a packet of photos from Holland.

My sisters wear sensible shoes, print dresses.
I'm a toddler with hair curled like wood shavings.

Perhaps those children still smile from a Dutch album:
memories of a twenty years ago holiday?
quaint anthropological studies?

Less than a year later it all changed.
Dad worked in a factory,
we lived in a new town.

Night Shift

I would wake up when I heard Dad
coming in at the front door.

The others slept through his early morning noises:
a toilet flush, one cup of tea boiling.

There seemed no place for him
at home all day Saturday
and most of Sunday.

His skin paled
apart from one weather-beaten patch
at his throat.

'It's no life for a man,' he sometimes grumbled
'this living like a mole.'

During school holidays I made
no noise at home.

Mum went to parents' nights alone.
She was sick of darning where industrial acid
ate away his clothes.

At five o'clock I'd be sent
to waken Dad for tea.

The curtains in my parents' room
were almost always closed.

Janey

My mother had a cousin, Janey.
She was raped when she was seven.
After that she didn't grow.

Relatives remember seeing her always sitting quiet
like a wee doll.

She never spoke to her father and brothers
and crossed to the other side
when they entered the room.

If a man approached her on the pavement
she turned back home.

Ann just had to laugh,
the number of times she was in trouble
for Janey not going to school.

'I've fourteen other bairns to care for.
I cannae be wi her a the time.'

What kind of work was there for a girl like Janey.
No one worried out loud but perhaps
she'd be better in some kind of home.

Janey died suddenly at sixteen
of Spanish flu.

'It's a happy release for her,' diagnosed the doctor
'He should have murdered her too.'

Reviewed

I'm hot with embarrassment
reading this considered paragraph.

Inevitable it has loomed at me
ringed in my mind like obligatory
gym periods at high school.

It's the first time since PE
that I've been called
just my surname;

four grim syllables hurled the length of the pitch
where I floundered in mud,
face like a flushed turnip.

I'm exposed like my legs
as they mottled blue and red
on the hockey field.

A moment drenched in shame
as if I'd missed a catch,
fallen flat.

In the distance Mrs Turner bawls
'McSeveney, run it under a cold tap!'

Gone Wrong

I no longer fear reproaches
from family, teachers, friends.

I remember running amok
screaming till my voice split
but what could I expect?

I wasn't well then.

But in the back of my mind
a child persists.
'Don't blame me,' she says.

Her handwriting is in my old books.
Her teddy is beside my bed.
I have her ponytail in a plastic bag.

I see her robustly ordinary
skipping in a schoolyard.

'It's not my fault,' she claims.
'I read the Famous Five, kept pets,
believed in Santa Claus.'

What are you doing Woman?
I've been a disappointment in you.

from Coming Out With It (Polygon 1992)

ANDREW O'HAGAN
(b.1968)

Born in Glasgow and grew up in Irvine New
Town in Ayrshire. He is on the editorial
board of *London Review of Books* and *Granta*.
The Missing was shortlisted for many awards
and his first novel *Our Fathers* (1999) was
shortlisted for the Booker Prize.

A Wee Reflection on Irishness

Growing up in Ayrshire I often looked over at Arran and thought
about the bigger island beyond it. Ireland was an imaginary place in
our house and in our heads; not only a place for Cuchulain of the
Sea, and Niall of the Nine Hostages, but a place of origins, dark
beers and bitter troubles. We were Catholics in a modern Scotland, and we knew, somehow, that our ancestors had come out of
Ireland, full of hunger perhaps and old talk, and had settled in a
Protestant country, a place only partially hospitable to the likes
of us.

The sound of the Orange band is one of the glooms of my childhood – it was a reminder of old hatreds. And we had hatreds too,
Ibrox and the Queen, and they polluted our sense of who we were
in the world. Yet Ireland remained a foggy place for us; we would
never quite get around to examining what its part was in our
national make-up. There were no novels about being an Irish-
derived Catholic Scot on the west coast, at least none that were
obvious, and that part of life remained under-described, both to
ourselves, and to history.

When I became a writer I wanted to acknowledge this missing part
of our identity. I wanted to find a voice for a kind of experience of
living that I felt hadn't yet made it to the page. It became one of the
central encumbrances and delights of the imagination for me: I'm
still at it.

St Winnin's

M Y first day at St Winnin's RC I recall in slow motion, coloured yellow and brown. It was, and is, more frightening than romantic, and I cried all the way to the school gate. Things had begun to take off with my visit to the high flats at Irvine. I suddenly knew more about the world, and saw our black and white housing estate as a sort of adventure park that opened onto lots of differently coloured and gradually aged surroundings. To get to the school, you had to walk about a mile, through open fields full of cement-mixers and dumpers. Squads of men were laying foundations, putting up walls and prefab units, building Pennyburn's phase two. Starting school was a fantastic ritual: the gear was put on you, your hair was wetted and slicked, and you were stood in the square while neighbours gathered around to point and pinch and stuff coins into the pockets of your new blazer. The blazer, I remember, felt heavy. It had a green and gold badge stitched onto the top pocket, the tie was already knotted, put over your head in one go, and held in place with an elastic loop. The trousers were charcoal and long, and the shoes squeaky. You knew it was the start of something big.

I stood in line at the doors opening onto the playground, turning round every other second, crying, and watching the faces of the mothers biting their nails and waving through the bars of the gate. We were led inside. I'd never smelt a room like it before. The classroom was high windowed and cold, and it had the roving odour of pee and Plasticine. The teacher seemed old, though she was probably only forty-something, and she smelt like a maternity nurse. In other words, she smelt of sick. She warned those of us still sniffling that we'd better stop it right away, and she gave each child a paper doily and felt-tips and told us to colour it in. That was that, and the rest of those first days in Primary One were taken up with colouring-in duty, or standing at a plastic sandpit, or sploshing paint onto slabs of grey card. It became fun, and the room grew familiar. Mrs Nugent's face was all rubbery, and I can very clearly remember it mouthing the word 'apple' over and over. 'Ap-ple.' There were lines around her mouth, they'd stretch and then her lips would bash together every time. 'Ap-ple.' We all said it, and the noise in the room sounded big and crunchy. After saying it for ages, Mrs Nugent shushed us, and pinned a large 'A' above the blackboard. We were learning to read.

Before long, there was a line of letters, the alphabet, right across the blackboard wall, and she handed out books. I feel funny describing it – books would become the most important thing of all. But it didn't feel like it on the day; the one she gave me felt slimy and was hard to understand. It only had a few words on each page, and a very big picture. Mrs Nugent showed all her teeth, and read out the title. '*Dick, Dora, Nip and Fluff.*' The sandpit and the paints were never to be so interesting again. Like the afternoon cartoons and the hairdressing journeys with my mum that were now part of something called the past, these books would suggest a world fuller than suspected. I really admired Dick and Dora, and the way they went to the park and brushed their teeth and lived in a square house out on its own. They gave an idea of a universal community of children; all the same, all here to stay, and to stay for ever the same. There was no darkness and doubt in the world of Dick and Dora, no effort involved in keeping clean, no hurt, no worry or bad weather. The rain was a problem to be solved, usually with an umbrella, and it was generally an excuse for cheerfulness and good character. Dick and Dora knew much more about how to be simple and good in the world than anyone I'd met; they knew everything, and I supposed that was why they were in a book. I already knew, just in the way that you do, that the world – or the world of Pennyburn, at least – wasn't entirely like that. With these little paperbacks, a private world was opening up too, and for years it would play on its own, increasingly removed from the world outside. There would always be Dick and Dora, then Joby, and Black Beauty, and my pal Spadger, to fill the head full of good thoughts, or just thoughts. The noble acts and pure hearts of people in books would be lapped up and loved, but never lived up to. In time we'd read of them, sigh, and go outside, to a place where other influences, other instincts – other knowledge – drove us into fits of childish cruelty and badness never noted in our beloved tomes.

We started praying to Mary at about the same time as we began to read. She wore a blue dress and had roses for shoes. In pictures, she always had her hands up, or clapped together, and she'd be floating in the air. It isn't just any old blue, that sky, it's the sort of blue that stands for goodness and purity and not for Rangers. That is what we'd hear, although not from everybody. Our Lady would do good things for us, if we sent her our prayers and good wishes. We could learn the rosary, and say it for her. She was God's mother and if there was anything we wanted and he was too busy to hear us, we could tell Mary and she'd tell Jesus – who was God's son but was God as well. It wasn't long till our First Holy Communions, then we'd know all about it. Those who taught religion at that school were pretty strict, very bitter, and they always encouraged us to feel that we were very privileged not to be Protestants. We were chosen, and we had the most beautiful churches of all, the most wonderful statues and crosses that we could kneel in front of. We thought we were great, and the classroom was soon full of our drawings of pregnant Mary and sheepish Joseph, trudging, with their grids of teeth, after the brilliant star.

Father MacLaughlin had thick glasses and a weird voice. He was from Ireland and was always yawning and telling us about the Bad Fire. He used the word evil, and talked about grace and sacraments and confession. Yes indeed, the Bad Fire was there for people who couldn't be good, you'd die unloved and unblessed and go to the Bad Fire if you didn't *a*. be good, *b*. not tell lies, *c*. pray, *d*. eat fish on a Friday, *e*. love your mummy and daddy and do what they told you, *f*. go to chapel, *g*. cross yourself morning and night, and bless the Pope, *h*. do something for Lent, *i*. be nice to nuns and not cheek back the priests, *j*. adore the saints, *k*. remember not to drink Holy Water, *l*. make your First Holy Communion in a white dress (girls) or red sash (boys), *m*. get confirmed when you were in primary six, *n*. marry a Catholic, *o*. marry in the chapel, *p*. confess everything, *q*. go to devotions once in a while, *r*. get a priest quickly when you think you are going to die, *s*. ignore the Orange Walk – stay in on the Twelfth, or go to the pictures, *t*. do your full penance after confession; no hurrying it up, *u*. help with church cleaning sometimes, and think about joining the Legion of Mary, *v*. stop touching yourself, *w*. stop doing the Ouija board, and doubting the Immaculate Conception, *x*. lay off the drink, and never smoke fags or start fires, *y*. stop chapping the chapel-house door and running away, and *z*. resist having abortions, or sexual intercourse outside of marriage, or using contraception, or getting divorced without the Pope's say-so. This was Father MacLaughlin's creed: he wanted us all 'to meet one day in heaven' and these were the conditions. We were all pretty fascinated, and wondered what he was talking about, but we promised ourselves never to do it again, and made the sign of the cross. Father MacLaughlin spoke like God, but he didn't look like Him. His eyebrows gathered in the middle of his head, and he made me sure that whatever it was, I was never going to do it ever ever again.

I knew that people could die. I remembered the budgie being called dead, and then, of course, there was the priest before MacLaughlin, Father Burke, who Michael had seen green and dead in his coffin. These stuck in my mind, and I knew that death was terrible, especially if it meant the Bad Fire. But I thought that only animals and old people could die or go away; children were invincible and always around. We could do anything to each other, so long as it wasn't too sore, and nothing would happen. Mrs Wallace was my second teacher, and she taught me how to write things down. She was gruff and kind, with curly red hair. She obviously liked some kids more than others. She would get me to do favours for her, running around and taking messages. She liked me to read for the class, but would often stop me, slap my hand, and say 'off by heart, you're reading it off by heart'. I had no idea what she meant by that, but obviously, now that I think of it, I must have rehearsed the readings and made some of it up as I went along. In 1975, we made our First Holy Communions, and I had my photos taken on top of a furry rug in Saltcoats. We never picked the photos up, but I have the certificate somewhere. We had cakes and a disco round the back of St Winnin's Chapel, in the hall, right after the Mass, and all I kept thinking was Jesus, that bread's chewy – it's the body of Christ.

By that time, they'd built a new Catholic primary for kids from the scheme, and it sat right in the corner of Pennyburn. It was called St Luke's, and we transferred there as the first class. We'd only been there a few weeks when Mrs Wallace died. I heard the new teacher say 'cancer' and I later looked it up. Mrs Wallace was dead of cancer. A group of us from St Luke's went to the funeral Mass, and we all sat singing hymns with the coffin there. I was very confused, but Father MacLaughlin explained it all, and said she was certainly in a better place. Behind the priest, mounted on the wall in front of the altar, was the biggest statue I'd ever seen. It was truly colossal, this thing, at least thirty feet from top to bottom. It was a wooden carving of Jesus on the cross, and it was mesmerizing. His hands were pinned to the wood with giant bolts, blood ran down in thick lines. His feet rested on a wee platform, but were hammered in, with more blood showing. All the limbs looked thin and a bit blue and crooked. Thorns were twined round his head, crushed down, and more blood ran down his forehead. He'd a cloth round his bum, and his eyes were looking up. It looked so sore, and I had loads of questions. But I didn't say anything; I just filed up with everyone else in my row for chewy bread. When I came back, they were singing a new song, and someone had already pulled down the kneeling cushion for us to say our prayers on.

from The Missing (Picador 1995)

Ciara MacLaverty
(b.1968)

Born Belfast, grew up on Islay, where her
father, Bernard MacLaverty, was a teacher of
English. She lives in Glasgow and has had
short stories published in magazines and
anthologies.

Reflection

I was born in Belfast in 1968, but spent only my earliest childhood
there, so my memories of the troubles are vague and fragmented.
It is difficult to know what was real and what's been embellished
through the years, but a few images persist like individual snap
shots: my mother tugging my arm as we ran for a bus after the
echo of gunshot; a man with a blood-soaked green shirt being
stretchered into an ambulance. I can see now, why my parents
chose that time to uproot their young family (I have two younger
sisters and a brother) and move to Scotland.

I remember my excitement at boarding the Larne-Stranraer ferry
(it was the size of ten houses) and having no clue about what to
expect at the other side. Scotland was a different country. I had
never been to a whole other different country before – in my six
year old mind it could have been as different as Disney Land. But it
looked a lot like Ireland except the fields were bigger and there
were more factories and industrialised grey towns. And of course,
there were no bombs or shooting.

We settled first in the village of Ratho near Edinburgh and I made
friends easily enough – but perhaps too eagerly. The story 'Sleep
Over' comes from this time and in it I try to recreate an aspect of
subtle childhood bullying. It's a feeling of being trapped in a
manipulative friendship, something I'm sure a lot of people have
experienced. During that time, there were more overt jibes too,
from boys in the playground who shouted 'thick Irish Paddy' but I
have to confess that (rightly or wrongly) my sense of nationality
then was so abstract and fluid, that I didn't feel the need to take
such stereotyping personally.

I remember winning 'dux' of the class three times in a row and my mother saying proudly 'that'll teach those boys with their thick-Irish-Paddy nonsense.' This kind of logic had never entered my head – that somehow this was a victory, not just for myself, but for all Ireland. Instead I only felt a tingling embarrassment at being singled out and made to collect a dinky 'gold' trophy in front of my classmates.

Another story 'The Babysitters' is also semi autobiographical and stems from the years our family spent on the Isle of Islay. We moved when I was ten and I spent my teenage years there. They were extremely happy years, but they were charged with all the hope and fear and embarrassment that follow teenagers every-where: that heart-thumping desire to always belong and fit in; the scourge of longing and the joy of being accepted.

Years on I am eternally grateful for an easy upbringing and happy school days. I'm not quite sure when I stopped thinking of myself as Irish and started thinking of myself as Scottish – or as now, a mixture of both. I feel lucky to have an affinity with and an affection for both countries. I like having an Irish name, that's rare in Scotland – for years I knew of no other Ciaras. Yet when I go back to Ireland (my parents always call this 'going home'), I feel like part of me belongs. It only takes a day or two for twangs of my Irish accent to sneak back.

Sleep over

'LET'S wave good-bye to your mum,' said Stacey, twisting round in the back seat. Through the windscreen I saw my mum wipe her feet on the door mat, like she was already gone.

'Stacey's so glad you're coming,' said Stacey's mum. 'Her little face lit up when your mum said yes.' I imagined Stacey's head as just a light bulb wearing a pair of pointy glasses, but I didn't laugh. All the other kids in the street call her Specky Egghead, because her second name is Eggleford. I'm allowed to call Stacey's mum Maureen, instead of Mrs Eggleford if I want to, but mostly I don't call her anything. I just say yes and no or please and thank you.

Stacey once told me about the time when her mum used to be a dancer on a cruise ship. There is a framed photo of it on their sideboard. The SS Oriana. 'Isn't she regal?' said Stacey, taking the picture in both hands. It made me think of the Titanic, only without the funnels.

'Looks nice,' I said.

'Oh, those were the days long before Stacey popped out,' said Maureen. 'All singing, all dancing. I could even do the splits in my silvery costume. That was before mummy had a tummy.'

Stacey's mum is always mentioning her tummy even though she wears tight jeans and looks like the main singer from the Nolan Sisters. She has a poster on the inside of her kitchen cupboard that tells her the calories of everything. Me and Stacey have to stand on a chair to get the Wagon Wheels cause Maureen always puts them on the top shelf.

'Ssh don't tell mum,' Stacey says, 'she might throw a wobbly.' I think that Maureen probably notices, cause she throws quite a few wobblies. She says, 'Not now Stacey, can't you see mummy's got things to do?' Mostly it is hoovering but sometimes it is reading magazines. Usually she shouts, 'Look Stacey, mummy's at the end of her tether, Orla will just have to go home and we'll head over to Nana's.'

•

I had never been to Nana's before until Maureen phoned my Mum and asked for me to go with them. Me and Stacey sat on the stairs watching while Maureen dialed the number with a pencil and then crossed her fingers with her big red nails pointing towards the ceiling.

'Hello Mrs Brady? Yes, it's Maureen here. Yes, Stacey's mum, that's right. Oh fine thanks, you know, coping with these two monsters.' Maureen always flicked her hair when she laughed.

'What it is, you see, Stacey was wondering if Orla could come with us to my mother's overnight?'

I was leaning over a bit to try and hear my mum's voice at the end of the phone but it was no good.

'Yes, aha, aha, well, this is it, isn't it?' Maureen was nodding and listening hard.

'Oh, Stacey says Orla is her best friend in the world,' she told my mum.

'She's got her heart set on this sleep over idea. And we mothers can get a bit of peace when they're off playing together. God knows, we deserve it.' I hoped my mum wasn't laughing too.

Maureen put down the phone. 'Okay dokay girls, at least that's one thing sorted.' I tried to make an excuse that I didn't have my pyjamas with me, but Maureen said we could pop round the corner and collect them on the way. I wasn't even able to get out of the car. Stacey said we should both sit in the back so that we could share the McCowan's toffees. My mum just handed me a plastic bag through the window. Stacey offered her a toffee and she said thanks, she'd take one and save it for later. Inside the plastic bag I could see my tartan pyjamas, my toothbrush and two buns wrapped in cling film.

At the traffic lights Maureen was trying to find a station on the radio.

'We want Bay City Rollers,' Stacey shouted, 'Rollers Rollers Rollers.' Maureen stopped it on a woman singing, 'Don't it make my brown eyes blue.' She pulled a tissue from the glove compartment and wiped her nose.

'Mummy's sad cause she had a huge fight with Gavin,' said Stacey out loud. The word Gavin came out funny because of the toffee between her teeth.

'That's right Stacey, you just let Mummy have a wee cry now. Get it out of her system.' Maureen's mascara was all smudgy at the side, like wet spider legs. I started to count the number of cars going the opposite way, but I gave up after 14.

It was only a while ago that I found out that Gavin is not Stacey's dad. I thought if he lived in her house then he must be – even if he goes away on rugby tours sometimes. One time, when he was just back from England, me and Stacey poked around in his Adidas hold-all. We found muddy rugby boots, smelly socks and a nudie magazine.

'Yuck, look at their hairy things.' I said, but Stacey told me that when you grow up you get a hairy one too, and then a drop of blood comes in your knickers.

'Who says?'

'My Mum.'

'Oh naw, I don't want blood in my pants.' Stacey just looked happy that she knew stuff that I didn't.

'It comes to us all,' she said, like she was a teacher or something.

•

When we got to Nana's the sun was poking round the white clouds. She led us through the house and out some glass doors to the back garden.

'They're called French Windows,' said Stacey, 'Nana's got a bungalow, – that's why there are no stairs.' Nana didn't look like the usual type of granny. She was wearing a Chinese dress and her hair was the same as Maureen's, except grey. She had lots of rings, like she might have once been a fortune teller.

'A wee G & T darling?' she said.

'A wee T with extra G is more like it,' said Maureen, flopping on to one of the sun lounger things.

'Hey mum, can me and Orla play in the sprinkler?' shouted Stacey, like she just thought of a great idea.

'Excellent plan,' said Nana. 'Come on and I'll fix you up with some cossies – there should be something that fits.'

Nana pulled open the bottom drawer and waved a dotty bikini top in the air.

'Yeah,' Stacey cheered. 'My old cossy, I thought it was lost.'

'Now, what about you Orla? I'm afraid this is the smallest one I have. Give it a go anyway. It's not like you're entering for Miss World, is it?' Nana's laugh was a bit scratchy. 'Don't worry – no one will spy you in the back garden.'

When I tried it on, it made me look like I had old lady boobs, the way the flowery material was all hard and pointy at the front.

The bum felt droopy like a baby's nappy. Stacey was banging on the bathroom door.

'Hurry up, slow coach.' I came out on to the landing and she giggled. 'Ooh sexy lady,' she said and pinged the bra bit where there was just air inside. She took my wrist as we ran across the swirly carpet, through the French windows and into the garden. The sprinkler was turning slowly like a low helicopter so I just jumped over the little spurts of water, trying not to get the swimsuit wet.

'Nana, can you turn it up? Please, please, pretty please?' Nana got off the sun lounger and walked across the grass in her bare feet. Stacey screamed as the cold water came like a fountain on top of us. I screamed too and I could feel Nana's swimsuit sticking to my skin. It was like cold rain in the middle of summer.

●

Stacey looked funny sitting at the dinner table with wet hair.

'You two look like the puppies that got away,' said Nana, pouring out the salad. 'Woof, woof,' said Stacey, across the table, and put her hands up like kangaroo paws.

'Do you like tomatoes Orla?' Nana had already put some on my plate.

'I think so,' I said, but these ones had a funny sauce over them so I couldn't finish them. I was glad when there was strawberry ice cream for pudding.

'Better not,' said Maureen, patting the top of her jeans.

'It's *deee* – licious,' said Stacey. I nodded my head. 'It's lovely, thank you.'

'Oh go on then, what the heck.' Nana passed her a big bowl and Maureen shook her head and sighed as she sucked it off the spoon.

There were no toys or games at Nana's except the piano. On top of it there were lots of photos in frames. The one of Stacey had an golden oval frame, the same shape as her glasses. Kind of egg shaped. Specky Egghead shaped. Her chin was sticking out in a big happy smile like she'd just swallowed some laughing gas. There was one of Maureen with a cowboy hat and a cigarette but it was a bit fuzzy. Me and Stacey squashed together on the piano stool and she showed me how to play Jingle Bells. I kept forgetting the tune and she took my finger and pressed it on the notes like I was a puppet. I pulled my hand away but she grabbed it back.

'Wait, let's compare nails.' We put our hands side by side on the piano lid. Hers were chubby and bitten and mine were like thin moons.

'Look at *yours*,' she said. 'Cool . . . why don't we try some of mummy's nail varnish?'

'No thanks,' I said. 'I'd rather not if you don't mind.'

Nana said we could sleep in the spare room. It smelt like old library books and there was a silver tinsel Christmas tree on top of the big wardrobe, closed up like an umbrella. When Stacey was in the bathroom I unwrapped the buns and ate them both. I put the papers in my pyjama pocket and hoped they wouldn't fall out between the sheets. Stacey jumped in the bed beside me wearing her Mickey Mouse nightie. It was a big double bed with a mahogany head board like you see in those old black and white films that Maureen watches in the afternoons. I thought it was a bit spooky and I wondered if this could have been the bed that Nana's husband died in.

'Tickling fight, tickling fight,' yelled Stacey, so I used my pillow like a shield.

'Get to sleep girls,' shouted Maureen from the sitting room. Nana came through and pulled the bed covers neat round our feet.

'Now then trouble makers, time for a bit of peace and quiet round here. If you shut your eyes you'll be dreaming in no time.'

'What'll we be dreaming of, Nana?'

'Oh I don't know. What about lazy summer afternoons and strawberry ice cream?' Nana turned off the light and pulled the door over. There was a squeaking noise from under the covers.

'What about big smelly farts?' Stacey's laughing made the whole mattress shake.

•

When I woke up I could see light peeping in from behind the brown curtains. I lay still and listened to Stacey's breathing. It was very quiet so I twisted round and saw her eyes were closed. She looked weird without her glasses on. Like she had a funny moon face, all pale and still. I tried not to make any noise, like I was moving in slow motion. The bedroom door opened easily, but the bathroom door was stiff. I gave it a push and I saw Maureen sitting on the loo. She had no clothes on. She just stared at me like she couldn't remember who I was. I tried to look away quickly but I still saw her hairy bit and her boobs drooping down like the ones in National Geographic, except white. Her belly was bent over and wrinkled and it made me think of the dough in the hot press when my mum makes her milk loaf bread.

' I'm sorry Mrs Eggleton.' On the way back, the sitting room door was open and I saw Gavin lying asleep on the sofa. The cover came up to his belly button and I could see his chest was hairy, to match his furry caterpillar eyebrows. I thought maybe he might have come through the French windows, like a burglar.

When I got back into bed I was burstin' for a pee. I tried not to think about it but I kept remembering my own bathroom with the soft carpet on your bare feet. Maybe if I tried to get back to sleep the feeling would go away. I shut my eyes and I heard the birds tweeping outside. Maybe if I just lay still enough Stacey wouldn't wake up for a while.

previously unpublished